Leckie×Leckie

Scotland's leading educational publishers

MODERN

N4 & 5 MODERN STUDIES COURSE NOTES

Elizabeth Elliott • Jennifer M. Gilruth
Jenny Reynolds

001/16062014

10 9 8 7 6 5 4 3 2 1

ISBN 9780007504954

Published by
Leckie & Leckie Ltd
An imprint of HarperCollins*Publishers*
Westerhill Road, Bishopbriggs, Glasgow, G64 2QT
T: 0844 576 8126   F: 0844 576 8131
leckieandleckie@harpercollins.co.uk   www.leckieandleckie.co.uk

Special thanks to
Louise Robb (copy edit)
Rona Gloag (proofread)
Jouve (layout and illustrations)

Printed in Italy by Lego S.P.A.

A CIP Catalogue record for this book is available from the British Library.

Acknowledgements

We would like to thank the following for permission to reproduce their material:

Images:
Fig 1.5: This file is licensed under the Creative Commons Attribution-Share Alike 3.0 Unported license; Fig 1.7 Brendan Howard/Shutterstock.com; Fig 1.12: AFP/Getty Images; Fig 1.13: AFP/Getty Images; Fig 1.14: AFP/Getty Images; Fig 1.15: This file is licensed under the Creative Commons Attribution 2.0 Generic license; Fig 1.18: AFP/Getty Images; Fig 2.3: This file is licensed under the Creative Commons Attribution-Share Alike 3.0 Unported license; Fig 2.5: AFP/Getty Images; Fig 2.6: AFP/Getty Images; Fig 2.7: AFP/Getty Images; Fig 2.12: This file is licensed under the Creative Commons Attribution-Share Alike 3.0 Unported license; Fig 3.4: AFP/Getty Images; Fig 4.4 AFP/Getty Images; Fig 4.6: AFP/Getty Images; Fig 4.7: AFP/Getty Images; Fig 4.8: AFP/Getty Images; Fig 4.9: AFP/Getty Images; Fig 5.9: AFP/Getty Images; Fig 5.14: AFP/Getty Images; Page 90–91 (Police and EDL): veroxdale/Shutterstock.com; Fig 7.5: UIG via Getty Images; Fig 7.9: Creative Commons Attribution-ShareAlike 2.0 license; Page 132–133: Getty Images; Fig 8.1: fpolat69/Shutterstock.com; Fig 8.4: AFP/Getty; Fig 8.6: Getty Images; Fig 8.7: Getty Images; Fig 8.9: Getty Images; Fig 8.10: Getty Images; Fig 8.11: AFP/Getty Images; Fig 8.12: AFP/Getty Images; Fig 8.13: Getty Images; Fig 9.2: Getty Images News; Fig 9.3: Getty Images News; Fig 9.4: Bloomberg via Getty Images; Fig 9.8: This file is licensed under the Creative Commons Attribution 2.0 Generic license; Fig 9.9: AFP/Getty Images; Fig 10.1: Getty Images; Fig 10.3 AFP/Getty Images; Fig 10.4: Spirit of America/Shutterstock.com; Fig 10.5: AFP/Getty Images; Fig 10.7: Albert H. Teich/Shutterstock.com; Fig 10.8: Northfoto/Shutterstock.com; Fig 10.9: Spirit of America/Shutterstock.com; Fig 11.5: JStone/Shutterstock.com; Fig 11.7: Getty Images; Fig 11.8: Getty Images; Fig 12.2: AFP/Getty Images; Fig 12.5: Getty Images; Fig 12.6: s_bukley/Shutterstock.com; Fig12.10: AFP/Getty Images; Fig 12.12: MidoSemsem/Shutterstock.com; Fig 12.15: fotostory/Shutterstock.com; Fig 13.2: This file is licensed under the Open Government Licence v1.0; Fig 13.5: Boston Globe via Getty Images; Fig 13.7: AFP/Getty Images; Fig 13.8: Getty Images; Fig 14.3 AFP/Getty Images; Fig 15.2: 360b/Shutterstock.com; Fig 15.4: Sadik Gulec/Shutterstock.com; Fig 15.5: Mark III Photonics/Shutterstock.com; Fig 15.10: AFP/Getty Images

All other images from Shutterstock.

Text:
Impact spreads © Scottish Qualifications Authority; P73 Reproduced courtesy of the Scottish Government; P85 Reproduced courtesy of STV; P86 Reproduced courtesy of the Daily Record; P99 Reproduced courtesy of the Scotsman; P103 Reproduced courtesy of STV; P113 Reproduced with permission of Herald & Times Group; P95 Reproduced courtesy of STV; P126 Reproduced courtesy of STV; p127 Reproduced courtesy of the Daily Record; P150 Ukip leader Nigel Farage hits back at 'fascist' hecklers in Edinburgh pub by Andrew Grice © The Independent; P164 Reproduced courtesy of Youth for Human Rights International; P177 Reproduced courtesy of The Institute for the Analysis of Global Security (IAGS); P193 Copyright Guardian News & Media Ltd 2013; P205 © Telegraph Media Group Limited 2012

Whilst every effort has been made to trace the copyright holders, in cases where this has been unsuccessful, or if any have inadvertently been overlooked, the Publishers would gladly receive any information enabling them to rectify any error or omission at the first opportunity.

Introduction

About this book

This book is designed to lead you through you National 4 or National 5 Modern Studies course. The book has been organised to map the course specifications and is packed with examples, explanations, activities and features to deepen your understanding of the topics and help you prepare for the assessment.

At the beginning of each Unit you will find a list of the things you will have learned as part of your broad general education in S1–S3 that you will build upon as you progress through the Modern Studies course. Underneath this you will find the Outcome and Assessment Standards for the Unit; these tell you the different criteria you will have to meet in order to pass the Unit.

In Modern Studies there is a choice in the topics you study for each Unit. This book covers the following topics:

Unit 1: Democracy in the UK and Scotland

Unit 2: Crime and the law in the UK

Unit 3: Terrorism

The final two chapters focus on the Added Value Unit (National 4), Assignment (National 5) and the Unit Assessments, and include lots of useful advice about the skills and techniques you will need.

Features

LEARNING INTENTIONS

This is a list of what you will learn as you work your way through the chapter.

What you will learn in this chapter

- How the political system operates in Scotland and the UK.
- The main rights and responsibilities of citizens in Scotland.

HINT

Hints give you advice and tips to support your learning.

> **Hint**
>
> Constituency MSPs are elected by the FPTP system in exactly the same way as MPs are elected to the House of Commons.

THINK POINT

Think points ask you to consider the implications of what you are learning and help you to develop critical thinking skills.

> **Think point**
>
> What do you think are the advantages and disadvantages of having a direct democracy?

MAKE THE LINK

Make the Link helps you to connect what you are learning to other Units within the course and to other subjects you might be studying. Modern Studies is about what is happening around the world today and you will find that what you learn has links to lots of other subjects like History, Geography, English, Maths, RMPS and many more.

> **Make the Link**
>
> In History you may learn about the factors that led to the Act of Union.

WORD BANK

Words which you might not be sure of are highlighted in the text in red and a definition is given in the Word Bank box; this should help you to become familiar with them and how they are used.

> **Word Bank**
>
> • **Consensus**
> A general agreement, reached by a group as a whole.

ACTIVITY

Activities will get you thinking about what you have learned and help you to practise and develop the skills you will need for your assessment. There are different kinds of activities, including individual research work, paired discussion and class debates.

> **GO! Activity**
>
> **Discuss**
> Discuss with your shoulder partner which government (UK or Scottish) you think sets the age limits associated with certain rights.

QUESTIONS

Questions are included throughout each chapter to test your knowledge and understanding of what you have learned. Many of these questions will also help you to develop and practise the skills you will need for your assessment.

? Questions

1. What is a constitution?
2. Why is the British constitution different?

CASE STUDY

There are lots of interesting case studies in every chapter of this book. Each case study shows you how what you have been learning has an impact on the wider world by telling you about a real organisation, person or event. We have also included lots of newspaper articles so you can see how the topics you are studying are reported by the press in real life. These case studies will give you lots of great examples which you can use as evidence to back-up the points you make as part of your assessment.

> **Anti-social Behaviour, Crime and Policing Bill**
>
> Kenny MacAskill, Cabinet Secretary for Justice, lodged a memorandum in relation to the **Anti-social Behaviour, Crime and Policing Bill** that was introduced in the House of Commons on 9th May 2013.
>
> 'That the Parliament agrees that the relevant provisions of the Anti-social Behaviour, Crime and…

LEARNING CHECKLIST

Each chapter closes with a summary of learning statements showing what you should be able to do when you complete the chapter. You can use the checklist to check that you have a good understanding of the topics covered in the chapter; you can make a note of how confident you feel using the traffic lights so that you know which topics you might need to revisit.

> Now that you have finished the **Introduction to the political system in the UK** chapter, complete a self-evaluation of your knowledge and skills to assess what you have understood. Use the checklist below and its traffic lights to draw up a revision plan to help you improve in the areas you identified as red or amber.
>
> - I can explain what a democracy is. ◯ ◯ ◯
>
> - I can state the main political rights and responsibilities of citizens in Scotland. ◯ ◯ ◯

NATIONAL 5

There are some parts of this book that might be more appropriate for National 5 learners, these sections are shaded as below.

> **N5 Legislative Consent Memorandums**
>
> Legislative Consent Memorandums can be lodged in the Scottish Parliament by the Scottish government, or by any MSP, giving the Westminster Parliament the power to legislate on a devolved matter. Westminster will not pass bills on devolved matters.

Level 3 and 4 experiences and outcomes relevant to this topic

The Democracy in Scotland and the United Kingdom Unit naturally builds upon the knowledge already secured in the third and fourth level experiences and outcomes, and in particular:

❖ I can use my knowledge of current social, political or economic issues to interpret evidence and present an informed view. **SOC 3-15a**

❖ I can understand the arrangements for political decision making at different levels and the factors that shape these arrangements. **SOC 3-18a**

❖ I can debate the reasons why some people participate less than others in the electoral process and can express informed views about the importance of participating in a democracy. **SOC 4-18b**

❖ I can evaluate the role of the media in a democracy, assess its importance in informing and influencing citizens, and explain decisions made by those in power. **SOC 4-17b**

Outcome and Assessment Standards

National 4 *(Democracy in Scotland and the UK)*	National 5 *(Democracy in Scotland and the UK)*
Outcome 1	**Outcome 1**
1 Use a limited range of sources of information to detect and explain bias and exaggeration relating to democracy in the Scottish and United Kingdom political systems by:	**1 Use a range of sources of information to detect and explain exaggeration and selective use of facts relating to democracy in the Scottish and United Kingdom political systems by:**
1.1 Detecting bias or exaggeration using up to two sources of information.	1.1 Detecting exaggeration or selective use of facts using between two and four sources of information.
1.2 Briefly explaining bias or exaggeration using evidence from up to two sources of information.	1.2 Explaining, in detail, exaggeration or selective use of facts using evidence from between two and four sources of information.
Outcome 2	**Outcome 2**
2 Draw on a straightforward knowledge and understanding of democracy in the Scottish and United Kingdom political systems by:	**2 Draw on a detailed knowledge and understanding of democracy in the Scottish and United Kingdom political systems by:**
2.1 Giving straightforward descriptions of the main features of a political issue which draw on a factual knowledge of democracy in Scotland or the United Kingdom.	2.1 Giving detailed descriptions of a political issue which draw on a factual and theoretical knowledge of democracy in Scotland or the United Kingdom.
2.2 Giving straightforward explanations relating to a political issue in Scotland or the United Kingdom.	2.2 Giving detailed explanations relating to a political issue in Scotland or the United Kingdom.

Democracy in Scotland and the United Kingdom

1 Introduction to the political system in the UK

What you will learn in this chapter

- How the political system operates in Scotland and the UK.
- The main rights and responsibilities of citizens in Scotland.
- How the Scottish and UK political systems are structured.
- The relationship between the Scottish and British political systems.
- The ongoing debates regarding the future of Scotland within the United Kingdom constitutional structure.

Figure 1.1: *The road to democracy*

 Think point

What do you think are the advantages and disadvantages of having a direct democracy?

 Think point

Think about why the government sets age limits before people can legally have certain rights.

Democracy

The word 'democracy' has its origins in two Greek terms – demos (people) and kratia (rule by) and translates as 'rule by the people'.

A democracy is where the people have a say in how the country is run. In a direct democracy, the citizens assemble to make decisions for themselves, rather than electing representatives to make decisions on their behalf.

A representative democracy is where citizens within a country elect representatives to make decisions on their behalf. The UK is a representative democracy.

In a democracy, citizens have opportunities to participate in the political process and to influence the decisions that are made in parliament. The success of a democracy depends on the participation of its citizens.

Rights and responsibilities in the UK

We all have rights, things we are entitled to by law, and responsibilities, things we are obliged to carry out.

Within our rights and responsibilities the government decides that we cannot be given certain rights until we reach a particular age, e.g. students have the right to leave school at 16 years old, and at 18 years old citizens have the right to vote in elections.

GO! **Activity**

Discuss
Discuss with your shoulder partner which government (UK or Scottish) you think sets the age limits associated with certain rights.

Citizens living in a democracy have many political rights and responsibilities that give them the power to participate directly or indirectly in how the country is run.

Figure 1.2: *Declaration of Human Rights*

Political Rights	Responsibilities
Right to freedom of speech and expression: to say and do what you want within the law.	Respect the right of others to express themselves and their points of view. Do not break the law, e.g. do not tell lies or be slanderous.
Right to vote, over the age of 18.	Ensure you use your vote in order to gain appropriate representation.
Right to stand as a candidate in an election, over the age of 18.	To allow others to exercise their rights and accept the result of the election.
Right to campaign, for example, to send a petition, demonstrate etc.	Not pressurise people to support your cause.

⚙ **Think point**

What do you think happens if a citizen does not uphold their responsibilities?

❓ Questions

1. **Explain** what is meant by a democracy.
2. Create a table to show some of the political rights and responsibilities people in the UK have.

Rights	Responsibilities

3. **Explain, in detail**, which right you think is the most important to have in a democracy.
4. **What do you think** the UK would be like if we didn't live in a democracy? **Explain** your answer.

The constitution

A constitution is the rules and fundamental political principles on which a country is governed (run). Some of the principles are about procedures such as how often elections must be held. Others are concerned with the amount of power the government has and therefore specify what those governments can or cannot do.

Unlike most other democratic countries, such as the United States of America and India, the British constitution is not written down in a single formal document. Instead the rights and responsibilities we have as individuals and as a society have come through people

Figure 1.3: *An old poster calling for votes for women*

Make the Link

The EU will be looked at in greater detail in the International Issues section on page 202.

Figure 1.4: *The Union flag*

Make the Link

In History you may learn about the factors that led to the Act of Union.

Word bank

- **Parliamentary sovereignty**

The main legislative body has absolute sovereignty (power) and is supreme over all other government institutions. It may change or repeal any previous legislation.

- **Consensus**

A general agreement, reached by a group as a whole.

- **Referendum**

A vote in which the electorate is asked whether to accept or reject a particular proposal.

- **Motion of 'no confidence'**

A vote in which members of a group are asked to indicate that they do not support the person or group in power, usually the government.

standing up for their rights in the past, such as the suffragettes who fought for the right of women to vote, through acts of parliament and from European law.

Parliamentary sovereignty

Parliamentary sovereignty is the most important principle of the UK constitution.

It makes the UK Parliament at Westminster the supreme legal authority, which means that it can create, change or end any law. However, over the years they have passed laws that limit the application of parliamentary sovereignty. One such law is the devolution of power to the Scottish Parliament.

Scottish Parliament

Until 1707 Scotland had its own parliament and governed itself accordingly. However, the **Act of Union** that year brought about the joining of the Kingdom of England with the Kingdom of Scotland to create Great Britain. Westminster Parliament, where the English Parliament had sat, became the heart of political power in the new 'United Kingdom'.

Ever since then, debate has continued about Scotland's position in the United Kingdom. By the 1970s there was political consensus that political power should be returned to Scotland in some form.

The 1979 referendum

In 1979 a referendum was held in Scotland to establish whether people wanted their own devolved assembly. However, a last minute addition by Labour backbench MP George Cunningham meant that 40% of those eligible to vote (not all of whom would turn out to vote) had to vote in favour in order for a 'Yes' vote to count. In spite of 51.6% of voters voting in favour of the Scottish Assembly, the number was not enough for the proposal to go forward, as this total represented only 32.9% of the registered electorate as a whole.

Figure 1.5: *Calton Hill, Edinburgh, the proposed site for the parliament*

Following the result, the Scottish National Party (SNP) members of parliament submitted a motion of 'no confidence' in the UK government (a Labour-Liberal coalition at that time). The 1979 election led to a Conservative government with Margaret Thatcher as Prime Minister. Throughout the 1980s and 1990s the demand in Scotland for more say in how Scotland was governed grew. After the 1979 referendum defeat a pressure group known as the Campaign for a Scottish Assembly was formed, this led to the creation of the Scottish Constitutional Convention which was to lay the foundations for the re-establishment of the Scottish Parliament.

? Questions

1. What is a constitution?
2. Why is the British constitution different?
3. 'Scotland has a history of popular sovereignty'. **Explain** what this means.
4. What is devolution?
5. What was the outcome of the 1979 referendum?

The 1997 referendum

In the 1997 UK general election campaign, the Labour Party included a referendum on the re-establishment of a Scottish Parliament in their manifesto. Following a landslide Labour victory, in September of that year a referendum was held to re-establish a Scottish Parliament with devolved powers, and to ask whether or not that parliament should have tax-varying powers.

This time the turnout was 60% and 74.3% voted in favour of the establishment of a devolved Scottish Parliament in Edinburgh. In addition to this, 63.5% of voters agreed that a Scottish Parliament should have tax-varying powers.

Establishment of the Scottish Parliament

In 1998 the UK government passed the **Scotland Act 1998**, thereby re-establishing the Scottish Parliament. The first Scottish Parliament election was held on 6th May 1999, leading to the election of 129 Members of the Scottish Parliament (MSPs). There have been three subsequent Scottish Parliament elections since 1999, as of the publication of this book in 2014; the next scheduled election is to take place in 2016.

On Saturday 9th October 2004, in the presence of Her Majesty the Queen, the new Scottish Parliament building was officially opened. The building is located on the Royal Mile in the Holyrood area of Edinburgh, this is why the parliament building is sometimes referred to as Holyrood. In her speech, The Queen described Holyrood as a 'landmark for 21st century democracy'.

Hint

Devolution essentially means the transfer of powers from the UK parliament in London to assemblies in Cardiff and Belfast, and the Scottish Parliament in Edinburgh.

Make the Link

The work of pressure groups will be looked at in more detail later in this Unit on page 70.

Figure 1.6: *Casting votes for a devolved Scottish Parliament*

Word bank

• **Manifesto**
A public declaration of intent, policy, aims, etc., as issued by a political party.

Think Point

The Scottish government has the power to vary (up or down) the basic rate of UK income tax by up to 3p in the pound. If increased, this money could raise millions of pounds for the Scottish economy, yet this power has never been used. Why do you think this is the case?

Figure 1.7: *The entrance to the Scottish Parliament building in Holyrood*

Devolved and reserved powers

The Scotland Act gave the Scottish Parliament the power to legislate (make laws) on a range of issues. These issues are known as devolved matters. However, the UK Parliament has retained the power to make laws on certain issues. These issues, which generally have a UK-wide or international impact, are known as reserved matters.

📖 Word bank

• **Legislate**
To create or pass law

Devolved matters	Reserved matters
Health	The constitution
Education	Benefits and social security
Justice	Immigration
Police and fire services	Defence
Housing	Foreign policy
Local government	Employment
The environment	Broadcasting
Sports and the arts	Trade and industry
Social work	Nuclear energy, oil, gas and electricity
Agriculture	Consumer rights
Many aspects of transport, including roads and buses	Data protection

💥 Make the Link

Education being a devolved power is the reason why you are learning a new curriculum and are studying different qualifications from the rest of the UK.

Figure 1.8: *Education: a power devolved to Scotland*

💥 Make the Link

You will learn more about Justice in Unit 2 and more about Defence and Foreign Policy in Unit 3.

The fact that the Scottish Parliament has the power to make decisions over many devolved matters means that the Scottish people can have a say in these issues. The Scottish Parliament has passed a number of laws that Scottish people are in support of, such as free university tuition and free prescriptions. On the other hand, although the

Scottish Parliament can hold debates on reserved matters it cannot change the law or make decisions on these matters. For example, MSPs debated whether the UK should invade Syria In 2013. However, they had no say on the vote which was held in the House of Commons in London. Many people think it is unfair that the Scottish Parliament cannot pass legislation on reserved matters as they feel that these important aspects of Scottish peoples' lives shouldn't be controlled by Westminster.

> ### Make the Link
> In Geography you will learn about nuclear energy, oil, coal, gas and electricity which are reserved matters.

N5 Legislative Consent Memorandums

Legislative Consent Memorandums can be lodged in the Scottish Parliament by the Scottish government, or by any MSP, giving the Westminster Parliament the power to legislate on a devolved matter. Westminster will not pass bills on devolved matters without first obtaining the consent of the Scottish Parliament. The consent itself is given through a motion (a Legislative Consent Motion), which is taken in the Chamber. This is done because in certain circumstances it can be sensible and advantageous, for example it might be more effective to legislate on a UK basis in order to put in place a single UK-wide regime, e.g. powers for the courts to confiscate the assets of serious offenders. It might also be used when the UK Parliament is considering legislation for England and Wales which the Scottish government believes should also be brought into effect in Scotland, but no parliamentary time is available at Holyrood, e.g. legislation to strengthen protection against sex offenders.

As of October 2013, 131 Legislative Consent Memorandums had been passed by the Scottish Parliament, 39 in the first session (1999–2003), 38 in the second (2003–07), 30 in the third (2007–11) and, when this book was published in 2014, 24 so far in the fourth (2011–16).

> ### Word bank
> - **Bill**
> A draft of a proposed law presented to parliament for discussion.

N5 Anti-social Behaviour, Crime and Policing Bill

Kenny MacAskill, Cabinet Secretary for Justice, lodged a memorandum in relation to the **Anti-social Behaviour, Crime and Policing Bill** that was introduced in the House of Commons on 9th May 2013.

'That the Parliament agrees that the relevant provisions of the Anti-social Behaviour, Crime and Policing Bill, introduced in the House of Commons on 9th May 2013, relating to the abolition of the Police Negotiating Board; dangerous dogs law; and witness protection law; so far as these matters fall within the legislative competence of the Scottish Parliament or alter the functions of Scottish Ministers, should be considered by the UK Parliament.'

N5 GO! Activity

Research
Using the Scottish Parliament website, research Legislative Consent Memorandums that have been lodged recently.

The Scotland Act 2012

In 2011, after the Scottish Parliament election, a request for more powers was made by the SNP government. **The Scotland Act 2012**, which was passed by the UK parliament and received royal assent on 1st May 2012, gives the Scottish Parliament a range of additional powers.

The new powers devolved to the Scottish Parliament include:

- a new Scottish rate of income tax to be in place by April 2016
- new borrowing powers for the Scottish government
- full control of stamp duty land tax from April 2015
- the power to introduce new taxes, subject to agreement of the UK government
- the power to regulate air weapons
- powers relating to the misuse of drugs
- the power to set regulations for the drink-drive limit
- power to set the national speed limit
- powers relating to the administration of elections to the Scottish Parliament
- the act also formerly changes the name of the Scottish Executive to the Scottish Government

Figure 1.9: *The interior of the Scottish Parliament*

? Questions

1. What was the outcome of the 1997 referendum?
2. What are devolved matters? Include some **examples**.
3. What are reserved matters? Include some **examples**.
4. Briefly outline some of the new powers given to the Scottish Parliament by the Scotland Act 2012.

N5 5. **Explain** what a Legislative Consent Memorandum involves.

GO! **Activity**

Class debate: 'The Scottish Parliament has been given enough devolved powers'

Your teacher will now divide your class into two groups. Your challenge is to research either the Proposition's (supporting the motion) or the Opposition's opinion (opposing the motion). Even if you do not agree with the viewpoint that you have been given, a good debater should be able to argue from any perspective.

1. You should try to find evidence from the internet on the powers of the Scottish Parliament. You may wish to focus on:
   - Scotland Act 2012
   - Scotland Act 2008
   - the independence debate (see page 27 for further information)

2. Once you have gathered your evidence, use it to make a valid point.

3. Produce a structured paragraph which uses the 'Point, Explain, Example' structure (see page 240).

You will now all be able to make a contribution to the debate. After everyone has made a point your teacher will invite you to participate in debating the issues that have been raised. Your teacher will explain how the debate is to be structured to allow everyone the opportunity to contribute to the discussion.

Following the debate your teacher may take a vote and may ask the class which side of the debate they now agree with.

Reflect on your learning

Underneath the paragraph you produced above, reflect upon your class debate.

- Has the debate changed your opinion on the topic?
- Did you feel that you were able to contribute in a confident manner?
- What might you change if you were to debate in the future?

The structure of the UK political system

The UK Parliament is based in the Palace of Westminster in the capital city of London. There are three elements that make up the UK Parliament: the House of Commons, the House of Lords and the monarch.

The House of Commons is the part of parliament where 650 elected Members of Parliament (MPs) represent the interests and concerns of their constituents. Parliament has responsibility for checking the work of the government and examining, debating and approving new laws.

The House of Lords is the second chamber of the UK Parliament. It is independent from, and complements the work of, the elected House of Commons. The Lords shares the task of making and shaping laws and checking and challenging the work of the government. Currently, there are about 760 unelected members who are eligible to take part in the

Figure 1.10: *The Houses of Parliament in Westminster, London*

work of the House of Lords. Many members, known as peers, have a political background, some don't. They represent a wide range of professions – in medicine, law, business, the arts, science, sports, education etc.

In the UK, power lies with parliament, not the monarch. However, the monarch does play a role in the processes of parliament, including:

- appointing a government: the day after a general election the Queen invites the leader of the party that won the most seats in the House of Commons to become Prime Minister and to form a government

- in the annual State Opening of Parliament ceremony, the Queen opens parliament in person and addresses both Houses in The Queen's Speech. Neither House can proceed to public business until The Queen's Speech has been read

- during The Queen's Speech, the Queen informs parliament of the government's policy ideas and plans for new legislation. Although the Queen delivers the speech, it is the government who writes it

- meeting with the Prime Minister once a week to discuss current business

- when a bill has been approved by a majority in the House of Commons and the House of Lords it is formally agreed to by the Queen. This is known as the Royal Assent. This turns a bill into an act of parliament, allowing it to become law in the UK

- the Queen dissolves (dismisses) parliament before a general election is held

📖 Word bank

- **Majority**
A number that is more than half of the total.

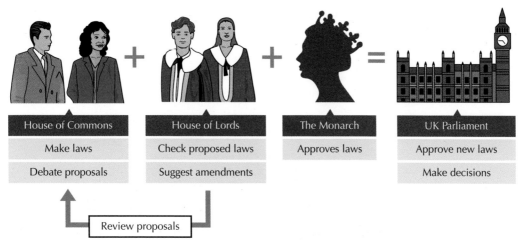

Figure 1.11: *The UK's political structure*

Forming a government

The government runs the country and has responsibility for developing and implementing policy and for drafting laws on reserved matters. After an election, if a party has won more than half the seats in parliament they can form a 'majority government'. This means they find it easier to get bills passed through parliament. Alternatively there may be a 'hung parliament', where no single party has won more than half the seats. In this situation either the party with the most seats forms a 'minority government' or two or more parties can work together to create a 'coalition government'.

UK General Election Results 2010			
Party	**Seats**	**% of vote**	**% of seats**
Conservative	307	36.1	47.1
Labour	258	29	39.7
Liberal Democrats	57	23	8.8
SNP	6	1.7	0.9
Others	22	10.2	3.5
			Turnout = 65.1%

As the 2010 general election resulted in a coalition government, the government at the time of writing in 2014 is made up of Conservative and Liberal Democrat MPs.

The Prime Minister

The leader of the party with the most seats becomes Prime Minister, the head of the UK government, and the person ultimately responsible for all policy and decisions. The Prime Minister:

- oversees the operation of the Civil Service and government agencies, such as the Food Standards Agency

Hint

Government policy is a plan of action that the government proposes to take.

Word bank

- **Implement**
To put something (a decision, plan, agreement, etc.) into effect.

Word bank

- **Coalition**
When two or more political parties work together.

- **Civil Service**
A branch of governmental service in which individuals are employed. They do not work for any particular party, and may work under several different governments throughout their careers.

- appoints members of the government to be in the Cabinet
- is the principal government figure in the House of Commons

The current Prime Minister, in 2014, is David Cameron MP. He is based at 10 Downing Street in London. As part of the coalition agreement, Nick Clegg is his Deputy Prime Minister.

Figure 1.12: *David Cameron and Nick Clegg outside 10 Downing Street*

The UK Cabinet

The Cabinet is made up of the senior members of government. Every Tuesday during parliament, members of the Cabinet meet to discuss the most important issues for the government.

Ministers are chosen by the Prime Minister from the members of the government in the House of Commons and House of Lords. They are mainly responsible for specific government departments, such a health, transport, education etc.

The structure of the Scottish political system

In the Scottish Parliament there are 129 elected Members of the Scottish Parliament (MSPs) who represent the interests and concerns of their constituents. MSPs consider and propose new laws on devolved matters, and can scrutinise government policies by asking ministers questions about current issues either in the Chamber or in committees.

The Scottish Parliament was shaped by four founding principles.

1. That parliament should be **accessible and participative** by being easily accessible to the public and involving the people of Scotland in its decisions as much as possible.

2. That the Scottish government should be **accountable** to the parliament and that both should be accountable to the Scottish people.

3. That parliament should promote **equal opportunities**, everyone should treat all people fairly.

4. That parliament should promote the **sharing of power**, among the Scottish government, Scottish Parliament and the people of Scotland.

The Scottish government

The relationship between the Scottish government and the Scottish Parliament at Holyrood is similar to the relationship between the UK government and the UK Parliament at Westminster.

The Scottish government is the devolved government in Scotland. It is a separate organisation from the Scottish Parliament. The Scottish government is responsible for formulating and implementing policy on devolved matters whereas the Scottish Parliament passes laws on devolved issues and scrutinises the work of the Scottish government.

Figure 1.13: *The Scottish government building in Leith, Edinburgh*

The Scottish government is formed from the party or parties holding the most seats in the Scottish Parliament. The SNP won over half the seats in the 2011 Scottish Parliament election and, when this book was published in 2014, are therefore a majority government. The SNP finds it easier to pass government bills being a majority government than when it was a minority government between 2007-2011.

The First Minister of Scotland

The First Minister of Scotland is the political leader of Scotland and the head of the Scottish government. The First Minister is responsible for the creation and development of Scottish government policy. Additionally, the First Minister promotes and represents Scotland at home and abroad.

MSPs take part in an exhaustive ballot to vote for the First Minister. Under the exhaustive ballot the elector simply casts a single vote for his or her favourite candidate. However, if no candidate is supported by an overall majority of votes then the candidate with the fewest votes is

Figure 1.14: *Alex Salmond and his Cabinet outside Bute House, Edinburgh*

eliminated. Further voting takes place until one candidate has a majority. The winning candidate is then appointed by the monarch. Alex Salmond is the current (as of 2014) and longest serving First Minister of Scotland. He lives at Bute House, Charlotte Square, in Edinburgh.

The Scottish Cabinet

The Scottish Cabinet is chaired by the First Minister who selects members of the government to join. The Scottish Cabinet normally meets weekly at Bute House in Edinburgh.

The Scottish Cabinet operates on the basis of collective responsibility. This means that all decisions reached by ministers, individually or collectively, are binding on all members of the government.

Each government department is run by a Cabinet Secretary who works on behalf of all ministers and all departments in the government to manage Cabinet business and facilitate collective decision-making.

The Presiding Officer of the Scottish Parliament

The Presiding Officer is the MSP who has been elected by other MSPs to chair meetings of the Parliament. The Presiding Officer is supported in their duties by two Deputy Presiding Officers.

The Presiding Officer remains politically impartial in everything that he/she does, which means he or she does not favour any party, even when a member of one. They therefore take the interest of all members equally into account and act on their behalves. The Deputies are also required to act impartially when they are undertaking their official duties.

📖 Word bank

- **Cabinet Secretary**

A member of the Cabinet who runs a particular government department. The role is similar to that of a Cabinet Minister in the Westminster Parliament.

🔵 Activity

Research
Research the names and responsibilities of the current Scottish Cabinet by visiting the Scottish government website at http://www.scotland.gov.uk/About/People/14944/Scottish-Cabinet

---

An interview with Presiding Officer, Tricia Marwick `CASE STUDY`

Q. Can you describe the role of the Presiding Officer?

A. It is a very varied role. I chair proceedings in the Chamber, and also chair the Parliamentary Bureau which sets the business to be discussed in the parliament. I also chair the Scottish Parliamentary Corporate Body, which sets the budget and oversees all the activities within the parliament building. In addition to this, I formally represent the parliament at home and abroad at a range of events and occasions.

Q. How is the Presiding Officer chosen?

A. The Presiding Officer has to be nominated by two other MSPs. The Presiding Officer is then elected, by secret ballot, by all of the MSPs.

Q. Does the Presiding Officer have any political party affiliation?

A. All the Presiding Officers of the Scottish Parliament have given up their political party membership on election as Presiding Officer. There is no legal requirement to do so, however each Presiding Officer to date has chosen to do so to demonstrate the impartiality which is required of the Presiding Officer.

Q. Sometimes MSPs do not follow the code of conduct. What powers do you have to control or punish their behaviour?

A. The parliament passed legislation setting up an independent Commissioner for Ethical Standards in Public Life. This commissioner investigates alleged breaches of the MSPs' Code of Conduct. He reports his findings to the Standards, Procedures and Public Appointments Committee. Following the committee's consideration of the commissioner's report, it then reports to the parliament and the parliament votes on whether the recommended sanction, if any, should be imposed.

Q. What is the difference between the Presiding Officer and the Speaker of the House of Commons?

A. The duties of Presiding Officer and Speaker are very similar.

Q. How do you ensure that you represent the members of the electorate that voted for you?

A. I am still the Constituency Member for Mid Fife and Glenrothes, and continue to represent my constituents by holding surgeries, advocating on their behalf, and supporting local organisations and businesses.

As Presiding Officer I am not permitted to express a view on matters which are, or might come, before parliament, and cannot sign motions or take part in debates. However, I can and do ensure that a constituent's views are made known to the government.

Q. Why did you want to become the Presiding officer?

A. I believed that the parliament needed to review its own procedures and that, with my background in the parliament, I was the best person to initiate and drive forward the reforms.

Q. What is your favourite part of your job?

A. Chairing in the Chamber.

Q. To what extent do you think the Scottish Parliament has achieved its founding principles?

A. Members of the Scottish Parliament are well aware of the founding principles. We constantly strive to make sure that we support and embrace the founding principles.

Figure 1.15: *Tricia Marwick, current (2014) Presiding Officer*

Make the Link

You might like to carry out an interview as research for your Added Value Unit or Assignment; you can find more information on how to do so on page 220.

GO! Activity

Research

Use the case study and the Scottish Parliament website (http://www.scottish.parliament. uk/aboutheparliament/9970.aspx) to create a fact file on the Presiding Officer. Make sure your fact file includes the answers to the following questions:

1. Who is the current Presiding Officer?
2. What are the main roles for the Presiding Officer in the Scottish Parliament?
3. Why does the Presiding Officer give up his or her party political role?
4. Can you name three responsibilities of the Presiding Officer?

Figure 1.16: *The Scottish and UK Parliaments do not always agree on what is best for Scotland*

? Questions

1. **Explain** the role of the House of Commons, the House of Lords and the monarch in making up the UK political structure. You may wish to create a diagram to **exemplify** your points.
2. Briefly **describe** the work of the UK government, the Prime Minister and the Cabinet.
3. Briefly outline the four founding principles of the Scottish Parliament.
4. Outline the differences between the Scottish Parliament and the Scottish government.
5. **Describe** the roles of the First Minister and the Scottish Cabinet.

The relationship between the Scottish and UK Parliaments

The main elements of the relationship between Westminster and Holyrood are set out in a Memorandum of Understanding (MOU). The MOU emphasises the principles of good communication, consultation and co-operation.

During the first two sessions of the Scottish Parliament, the parliament worked in cooperation with Westminster and there was not much conflict. This may have been due to the fact that the Labour party was in power in both parliaments. However, since 2007 there have been different parties in power in Holyrood and Westminster and this has created some conflict between the two parliaments as the two governments have different ideological views about what is best for Scotland.

Legislation issues

The Scottish Parliament has chosen to adopt a different approach to many issues from that applied in England. For example, Scotland does not have tuition fees for those attending Higher Education establishments.

The Scottish Parliament has also clashed with Westminster over reserved policy areas. For example, the UK Trident programme involves Faslane naval base in Scotland storing Britain's fleet of nuclear-powered and nuclear-armed submarines. The continued use of Trident nuclear weapons is opposed by the majority of MSPs. However, because Westminster controls defence legislation (it is a reserved power) MSPs have no say in this matter.

Finance issues

Tax

The Scottish Parliament has the power to raise taxation levels by 3p in the pound. Introducing this tax would mean that the Scottish government would have more money to use for devolved areas.

⚫ Make the Link

Conflict amongst the different political parties will be examined in more detail later in this Unit.

However, this power has never been used; the Labour-Liberal Democrat government in Scotland (1999-2007) and the Labour government in England did not want tax levels in Scotland to be different from the rest of the UK.

The Scotland Act 2012 gives the Scottish Parliament the power to set a Scottish rate of income tax for Scottish taxpayers. From April 2016 Scottish taxpayers and employers will be deducted tax at the rates set by the Scottish Parliament. These rates may be higher, lower, or the same as those which apply in the rest of the UK. Ultimately, the outcome of the independence referendum will have an impact on taxation rates in Scotland.

Annual budget

The Scottish Parliament has the financial power to decide how to spend its annual budget. Most of this money comes from a 'block grant', which comes directly from the UK government. The Scottish people pay taxes on their earnings, which are used to fund the 'grant'. If the UK government decided to reduce the block grant then the Scottish government would have to make cuts in spending in Scotland.

Figure 1.17: *Spending cuts might result if the block grant is reduced*

N5

The Barnett formula is a mechanism used by the UK Treasury to determine the amount of public expenditure allocated to Scotland. For the financial year 2011-12 the budget was approximately £30 billion. Many English people think Scotland gets too much money from the formula as spending per person is higher in Scotland. Some English MPs resent the greater finance Scotland receives under the Barnett formula, which has allowed the funding of various policies such as free prescriptions.

The SNP would like to see the Barnett Formula replaced by 'fiscal autonomy'. This would involve the Scottish Parliament using its full tax-raising powers to allow Scotland to earn and spend its own money. The Prime Minister believes that Scotland should take some responsibility for raising its own finances.

⚫ Make the Link

You will study formulas in Maths.

The relationship between the First Minister and Prime Minster

The relationship between the First Minister and Prime Minister should be one of mutual respect. However, In 2007 when Alex Salmond became First Minister, the then Prime Minister (Tony Blair) refused to acknowledge or even meet with the First Minister before stepping down and passing power to Gordon Brown.

In 2014, the relationship is currently strained due to the fact that both leaders – Alex Salmond and David Cameron – have opposing views about the future of Scotland: the First Minister would like Scotland to re-establish itself as an independent nation and the Prime Minister would like Scotland to remain as part of the United Kingdom.

Alex Salmond: 'our nation is blessed with national resources, bright people and a strong society. We have an independent education

Make the Link

In Geography you may have learned about Scotland's natural resources.

system, legal system and NHS. They are respected worldwide. I believe that if we connect the wealth of our land to the wellbeing of our people, we can create a better country.'

David Cameron: 'the Union works and it works well. Ours is a unique union of nations. It's a union of people too. And together we've achieved so much. We are a family of nations within one United Kingdom. Now is not the time to reduce that relationship to one of second cousins, once removed.'

Figure 1.18: *Alex Salmond and David Cameron meeting In 2012*

Make the Link

In Unit 2 you will learn more about welfare reform.

The First Minister's powers are limited, as he cannot influence decisions made by the Prime Minister nor can he have any control over reserved powers. Despite this, Alex Salmond has made it very clear that he is profoundly against many of David Cameron's policies, such as the continued use of Trident, budgets cuts and the **Welfare Reform Act**.

Ultimately, the UK Parliament has sovereignty and can therefore extend or reduce the areas for which the Scottish Parliament can make laws. However, it is unlikely that powers would ever be taken away from the Scottish Parliament as this would lead to the UK government being unpopular in Scotland.

? Questions

1. **Explain** the relationship between the Scottish and UK Parliaments. Mention legislation and finance issues in your answer.
2. 'The First Minister and Prime Minister don't agree on anything.' Give two reasons why this statement is **exaggerated**.

The future of the UK constitutional arrangement

The idea of Scottish independence has caused major tension between the two parliaments in recent years. The concept of Scottish independence is a constitutional affair that is reserved to Westminster. **The Edinburgh Agreement** is the agreement between the Scottish government and the UK government, signed on 15 October 2012 at St Andrew's House, Edinburgh, of the terms for the Scottish independence referendum in September 2014. Both governments have agreed that they will respect the result.

Figure 1.19: *An independent Scotland separate from the rest of the UK*

The Scottish Independence Referendum (Franchise) Bill was introduced on 21st March 2013. It sets out arrangements for the conduct of the referendum, including the date of the vote and campaign spending limits. The bill states that a referendum will be held on Thursday 18th September 2014. **The Scottish Independence Referendum (Franchise) Bill** was passed on 27th June 2013 giving a person aged 16 or over the right to vote in the referendum.

BALLOT PAPER
Vote (X) ONLY ONCE
Should Scotland be an independent country?
YES ☐
NO ☐

Figure 1.20: *The ballot paper for the September 2014 referendum*

GO! Activity

Group work
In small groups, create a presentation discussing the arguments for and against giving citizens over the age of 16 the right to vote.

- Create a list of the arguments for and against allowing 16 year olds to vote.
- Research the main political parties' stances on the issue of voting at 16.
- Look at voter turnout in countries where 16 year olds have the vote.
- Investigate public opinion on the matter.

The independence debate

Two cross-party campaigns have been established to persuade the people of Scotland which way they should vote in the referendum. The 'Better Together' group will campaign for a 'no' vote whilst the 'Yes Scotland' group will push for a 'yes' vote.

The 'Better Together' campaign promotes the view that Scotland is a better and stronger country as part of the United Kingdom. The campaign was established with the support of the three main pro-union political parties in Scotland: Labour, the Conservative Party and the Liberal Democrats. Alistair Darling, Labour MP, is the head of the campaign.

The 'Yes Scotland' campaign believes that independence will allow Scotland to create a fairer and more prosperous country. The campaign was established with the support of the SNP, The Scottish Greens and The Scottish Socialist Party, as well as the Independent members of parliament. Blair Jenkins OBE (former head of News at BBC Scotland) is the head of the campaign.

GO! Activity

Research
Use the 'Better Together' and 'Yes Scotland' websites (QR codes below) to research the arguments put forward by each side. You can use this information to help you make an informed decision on whether or not you think Scotland should become an independent country.

'Better Together' says…	'Yes Scotland' says …
A strong Scottish Parliament within the UK gives Scotland real decision-making power and a key role in the UK.	Decisions about Scotland's future should be taken by a government that the people want.
As part of the UK we share resources and ideas. The NHS was founded by a Welshman. Partners in these islands are better working together.	Being independent means the revenue from our vast offshore renewable energy will come to Scotland.
The size, strength and stability of the UK economy is a huge advantage for Scotland's businesses. Scotland's largest market is the rest of the UK.	We can work more effectively to attract companies to Scotland, and help businesses already here to grow, allowing us to create more jobs.
Scotland's security will be strengthened as part of the UK. The British Armed Forces are the best in the world. The UK is an important part of the UN, NATO, the EU, and has Embassies around the world.	While the UK government plans to spend £100 billion on new nuclear weapons in the years ahead, we can choose to use our £8 billion share of this money more wisely.

Summary

In this chapter you have learned:

- how the political system operates in Scotland and the UK
- the main rights and responsibilities of citizens in Scotland
- how the Scottish and UK political systems are structured
- the relationship between the Scottish and British political systems
- the ongoing debates regarding the future of Scotland within the United Kingdom constitutional structure

Learning Summary

Now that you have finished the **Introduction to the political system in the UK** chapter, complete a self-evaluation of your knowledge and skills to assess what you have understood. Use the checklist below and its traffic lights to draw up a revision plan to help you improve in the areas you identified as red or amber.

- I can explain what a democracy is.
- I can state the main political rights and responsibilities of citizens in Scotland.
- I can describe how the UK and Scottish governments are set up.
- I can state the role of the Prime Minister and the UK Cabinet.
- I can explain the difference between the Scottish Parliament and the UK Parliament.
- I can state the role of the First Minister and the Scottish Cabinet.
- I can explain the relationship between the Scottish government and the UK government.
- I can explain the relationship between the First Minister and Prime Minster.
- I can discuss the debates about change to the current UK constitutional arrangement, in particular the position of Scotland within the UK.

Examples

In Modern Studies it is essential that you are able to back up any point you make with relevant evidence. When you are considering the statements above try to think of relevant examples for each response. You may wish to note these examples under each statement in your revision notes.

2 Representation

> **What you will learn in this chapter**
> - The names of the different types of political representatives.
> - The work of a MSP in the parliament and constituency.
> - How a constituent can contact their MSP.
> - How local councils are organised in Scotland.
> - The work of a local councillor representing their constituents.

Make the Link

You may have learned about the skills and qualities that are need for specific jobs in subjects like PSE and Business Management.

Representation

Scotland is a representative democracy. A representative is an individual who has been elected to act, speak or make decisions on behalf of other people.

There are different representatives to represent us at different levels of government.

Member of European Union

Member of Parliament (MP)

Member of Scottish Parliament (MSP)

Local Councillors

Figure 2.1: *Representatives at EU, national and local levels*

Word bank

- **Constituency**

An electoral area where a group of voters live.

In the Scottish Parliament elected representatives are called Members of the Scottish Parliament (MSPs). They were elected to represent the people of their constituency.

Activity

Research

Use the Scottish Parliament website to find who your MSPs are. Follow the step-by-step instructions below to do this:

- visit the Scottish Parliament website at http://www.scottish. parliament.uk

- click on: MSPs
- enter your postcode

Once there, answer the following questions:

1. What is the name of the Scottish parliamentary constituency you live in?
2. What is the name of your constituency MSP?
3. What political party is your MSP a member of?
4. What is the name of the Scottish parliamentary region you live in?
5. Write down the names of your seven regional MSPs and which political parties they belong to.

Activity

Discussion

Think, pair, share with your shoulder partner the skills and qualities that you think representatives need to have to make them good at their job. Think about what would make you vote for a candidate and the characteristics they might have.

Hint

You need to know which constituency and region you live in so you can understand who represents you. You will learn more about how MSPs are elected later in this Unit.

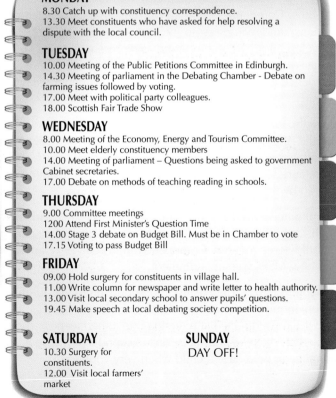

MONDAY
8.30 Catch up with constituency correspondence.
13.30 Meet constituents who have asked for help resolving a dispute with the local council.

TUESDAY
10.00 Meeting of the Public Petitions Committee in Edinburgh.
14.30 Meeting of parliament in the Debating Chamber - Debate on farming issues followed by voting.
17.00 Meet with political party colleagues.
18.00 Scottish Fair Trade Show

WEDNESDAY
8.00 Meeting of the Economy, Energy and Tourism Committee.
10.00 Meet elderly constituency members
14.00 Meeting of parliament – Questions being asked to government Cabinet secretaries.
17.00 Debate on methods of teaching reading in schools.

THURSDAY
9.00 Committee meetings
1200 Attend First Minister's Question Time
14.00 Stage 3 debate on Budget Bill. Must be in Chamber to vote
17.15 Voting to pass Budget Bill

FRIDAY
09.00 Hold surgery for constituents in village hall.
11.00 Write column for newspaper and write letter to health authority.
13.00 Visit local secondary school to answer pupils' questions.
19.45 Make speech at local debating society competition.

SATURDAY
10.30 Surgery for constituents.
12.00 Visit local farmers' market

SUNDAY
DAY OFF!

Figure 2.2: *On Tuesdays, Wednesdays and Thursdays MSPs work in the Scottish Parliament*

The work of MSPs

MSPs work on behalf of their constituents in two main ways:

1. The work they do in the Scottish Parliament.
2. The work they do in their constituency.

Committee work

Committees are small, cross-party groups of MSPs who meet on a regular basis to scrutinise the work of the Scottish government, conduct inquiries into subjects within their remit and examine legislation. There are many committees in the parliament, e.g. the Economy, Energy and Tourism Committee. In January 2012 The Welfare Reform Committee was established in light of welfare changes that were being made by the UK government.

MSPs represent constituents in parliamentary committees by various means.

- Committees have the power to introduce bills (draft laws), which are specific to the committee. These are known as Committee Bills. If there is enough support in parliament Committee Bills are passed and become acts of law.

- When an amendment (change) to a law is being considered or a new law is being created, the bill is sent to the appropriate committee. This gives the committee the chance to scrutinise and propose any changes to the bill before it goes to the parliament.

- Committees conduct enquiries – this is where they investigate issues to find out if there are problems and if changes are needed to bills. Committees can call on outside groups, such as trade unions, and witnesses to present evidence to help them to develop informed opinions and to represent the views of a wide range of people. During this time the questions answered and the evidence given helps the committee understand the issues more clearly.

For example, in 2013 The Justice Committee was seeking evidence as part of the **Victims and Witnesses (Scotland) Bill.** The committee invited all interested organisations and individuals, such as Police Scotland and Victim Support, to submit written evidence to be considered by the committee.

- Committees discuss and write reports for the parliament to consider. Reports will recommend whether the parliament should agree to a bill. Committee reports can have an influence on how MSPs vote in parliament.

For example, in 2013 The Health and Sport Committee published its Report on Inquiry into Teenage Pregnancy in Scotland. The report assessed the work directed at reducing unplanned teenage pregnancy and looked at what else could be done to support young people at risk of pregnancy or who have a child when very young.

Make the Link

In Unit 2 you will learn about new and possible changes to the law. For example, the **Criminal Justice (Scotland) Bill** which sets out the powers of the police.

- When a petition is being examined by the Public Petitions Committee the group must carry out an investigation into what should be done. If the committee finds that the law should be changed it then reports to the parliament and asks for the law to be changed.

- Committees can check the work of the Scottish government by asking Cabinet Secretaries to answer questions and give evidence at committee meetings or enquires. A Cabinet Secretary could be asked to justify money they have spent or received. Minutes (notes) from all committee meetings are available on the Scottish Parliament website and members of the public can sit in on meetings.

> **📖 Word bank**
>
> **• Petition**
> A written request, signed by many people, submitted to authority in support of a cause.

Questions

1. Which days of the week do MSPs work in the Scottish Parliament?
2. **Describe** what is a committee is.
3. **Explain, in detail**, the work of committees in the Scottish Parliament.

N5 4. 'Committees cannot check the work of the Scottish government'. Give one reason to show why this statement is **exaggerated**

The work of MSPs inside the Chamber of the Scottish Parliament

The Chamber is the part of the Scottish Parliament where MSPs are able to debate, discuss and vote on bills. The Chamber is the only part of the parliament where a bill can be passed and become a law. The seats in the Chamber are arranged in a half circle which reflects the desire to promote debate and encourage consensus amongst MSPs.

Figure 2.3: *The Scottish Parliament Chamber*

Figure 2.4: *The House of Commons*

> **GO! Activity**
>
> **Research**
> Using the Scottish Parliament committees webpage: http://www.scottish.parliament.uk/parliamentarybusiness/Committees.aspx (QR code below), create a list of the current committees in the Scottish Parliament. Choose two committees you are interested in and find an **example** of the work that is going on within each committee.
>
>

MSPs can represent constituents in the Chamber by:

- putting forward a motion (idea) to be debated
- speaking and voting in the Chamber
- questioning Ministers and the First Minister
- suggesting an amendment (change) to be made to a bill
- introducing a Members' Bill (according to the parliament's rules every MSP has the right to introduce two bills in the term of the parliament)

Stages of a bill

A major function of the Scottish Parliament is to make laws. All legislation must pass through three basic stages before it can become an act of law:

First stage	The most appropriate committee will scrutinise the bill and take evidence. It will then produce a report that will say whether the committee agrees with the general principles or not. The whole of the parliament will then consider the report and decide whether the bill should proceed to the next stage.
Second stage	If the bill makes it to the second stage it is scrutinised further by committee members or sometimes by all MSPs. Usually a number of amendments will be made at this stage which can results in changes being made to the final legislation.
Third stage	Finally, the bill goes back to the main Chamber and all the MSPs to consider the amended bill. Again, amendments can be made at this point. After a debate MSPs will vote for or against the bill. It will then be scrutinised by law officers to ensure that it falls within the devolved remit of the Scottish Parliament.

Think point

The Chamber in Westminster is set up so that the government faces the opposition. Why do think this is? Which parliament do you think is arranged in the best way?

Make the Link

You may learn more about the minimum pricing of alcohol in subjects which look at health and wellbeing, such as PE and PSE.

Hint

You can watch debates in the Scottish Parliament by accessing the webpage: http://www.scottish. parliament.uk/ newsandmediacentre/30935. aspx

When MSPs are satisfied, the Presiding Officer will seek Royal Assent from the Queen. It is only after the Queen has given her assent that a bill becomes an act of the Scottish Parliament. The power to withhold Royal Assent is permitted but it is not expected that this would happen.

For example, each year the Cabinet Secretary for Finance and Sustainable Growth introduces the **Budget Bill**. The purpose of the bill is to seek parliamentary approval for the Scottish government's spending plans for the financial year. The bill goes through the same three legislative stages as other bills. However, there is an accelerated timescale: no stage 1 report is required and only the Scottish government may lodge amendments to the bill.

Debates

Issues concerning the whole country will be discussed during a debate. MSPs can contribute to debates, particularly if they are of direct concern to their constituents. Debates are useful because solutions to problems can be identified and new bills can be created. During a bill's passage through parliament on its way to becoming an act, MSPs can use the Second Reading to debate the principles or ideas of the bill. During the debating process the issue may be raised by the mass media and attract the public's attention. For example, MSPs debated the **Alcohol (Minimum Pricing) (Scotland) Bill** to make provisions about the price at which alcohol may be sold from licensed premises. The bill received Royal Assent on 29th June 2012.

Voting

At the end of each business day in the Chamber, MSPs need to vote. This is called 'decision time' and the results of the vote can decide whether an issue or bill passes on to the next stage of the legislative process (this depends on the stage of the bill). MSPs must consider the views of their constituents when voting, as well as the view of their political party. In the Scottish Parliament, MSPs vote by electronic keypad and the results can be seen by the Presiding Officer.

GO! Activity

Research

Voting records for all current MSPs are published on the Scottish Parliament website. To find out when and how a MSP has voted in the Chamber:

* go to the Scottish parliament website: http://www.scottish.parliament.uk

* click on 'MSPs' then 'current MSPs'
* choose a MSP
* the information is found under 'parliamentary activities'

N5 Whips

Parties in the Scottish Parliament have 'whips'. A whip is a MSP whose job is to make sure that MSPs vote how their party tells them to. Whips instruct MSPs to vote as a group, regardless of what the MSP's constituents want.

If a MSP ignores these instructions they may find that they are not promoted in the future, or that they might not be reselected as a candidate at the next election. This means if a party has a majority in parliament, and the party whips instruct their MSPs to vote together in a particular way, then it is very likely that the bill would be passed.

Think point

This raises the question as to whether or not MSPs really represent the interests of their constituents. What do you think?

Question Time

Question Time is the main chance for MSPs to question and hold to account the actions of the Scottish government. This is where MSPs can ask questions and raise issues on behalf of their constituents. Question Time is one of the key ways in which parliament can hold the First Minister and individual ministers to account.

First Minister's Question Time (FMQs) takes place every Thursday between 12 and 12.30pm. It is broadcast on the TV, internet and radio by BBC Scotland. The main leaders of the other political parties and some MSPs are able to question the First Minister. The First Minister is therefore directly accountable to the other party leaders. Because FMQs can become quite lively, when the Presiding Officer deems the subject to be exhausted he/she will move on to the next question.

GO! Activity

Homework

Watch First Minister's Question Time online or on the Parliament Channel to see how this process takes place and how the Scottish Parliament is arranged.

Figure 2.5: *Question Time in the Scottish Parliament*

Question Time to Scottish Ministers takes place on a Thursday afternoon. It is a 60-minute session which allows MSPs to ask questions of relevant Scottish ministers on a pre-determined theme for 40 minutes, followed by a general question time lasting 20 minutes. Questions to Scottish ministers can be tabled 8–14 days before Thursday's question time. Questions are randomly selected by the Presiding Officer. For example, the Cabinet Secretary for Health and Wellbeing could be asked about a local hospital closure during this time.

Members' Bills

According to the Scottish Parliament's rules, every MSP has the right to introduce two Members' Bills during one parliamentary session (which is usually four years). These bills may be the result of a constituent contacting their MSP about an issue in an attempt to get them to change the law. Many Members' Bills are unsuccessful, especially if they come from an opposition MSP, but they may impact upon future government legislation. For example Stewart Maxwell, SNP MSP, introduced a bill to ban tobacco smoking in enclosed public places in February 2004. The Labour-Liberal Democrat coalition at first opposed this proposal but were eventually forced to accept the idea after it received widespread support. The coalition eventually published a bill that was passed on 30th June 2005 and the ban came into effect on 26th March 2006.

GO! Activity

Research
Use the internet to find out if your constituency MSP has ever submitted any Members' Bills in the past. If you were to ask your MSP to submit a Members' Bill what would it be about? Think about an issue(s) you feel passionately about – where would you like to see a change in the law?

Members' Bill

On 1st December 2010, the late Margo MacDonald's **End of Life Assistance (Scotland) Bill** was defeated at Stage 1. From the correspondence and comments she received afterwards, Margo believed that most people are convinced of the need for such legislation and for this reason she decided to look again at introducing a bill into the Scottish Parliament. The MSP's **Assisted Suicide (Scotland) Bill** proposes to enable a competent adult with a terminal illness or condition to request assistance to end their life, and to decriminalise certain actions taken by others to provide such assistance. Since the passing of Margo MacDonald, Patrick Harvie MSP will be taking the proposed legislation forward.

Main provisions of the proposed bill:

- it will give any person who meets the eligibility requirements the right to request medication to end their own life
- a qualifying person must be capable (i.e. have the mental capacity to make an informed decision – using the definition established by the **Adults with Incapacity (Scotland) Act 2001)**
- the person must be registered with a medical practice in Scotland
- the person must be aged 16 or over
- the person must have either a terminal illness or a terminal condition
- the person must find their life intolerable
- it will set out a straightforward process for a qualifying person to follow, involving initial registration followed by two formal requests
- it will decriminalise the actions of those who assist a qualifying person to end their own life within the parameters set by the bill
- it will require a trained and 'licensed facilitator' to be present when a qualifying person takes their own life

Figure 2.6: *Margo MacDonald*

GO! Activity

Research

Research a current Members' Bill using the internet. Discuss in small groups the following questions:

- do you **support** the main aim of the proposed bill? **Explain the reasons** for your response
- what do you think are the advantages and disadvantages of the proposed legislation?
- if you were a MSP would you vote for or against this bill? **Explain the reasons** for your choice

---

? Questions

1. Draw a flow chart to show the different stages a bill must pass through before becoming a law.
2. **Why do you think** there are so many stages involved in passing a bill?
3. Create a table showing the work of a MSP in the Chamber of the Scottish Parliament. Use the structure below:

Work of MSP in the Chamber	Explanation	Example

Make the Link

You may have learned about euthanasia in RMPS.

GO! Activity

Group work

In groups, create a role-play exercise demonstrating the work of a MSP in parliament. Choose one example of the work of a MSP from the list below:

- committees
- debating
- voting
- asking a question at Question Time
- creating a Members' Bill

Groups should write and perform a role-play based on their chosen example. All members of the group should be given a part to play to demonstrate their understanding.

The work of MSPs in the constituency

All citizens of Scotland have one constituency MSP and seven regional list MSPs.

For example, Elaine Smith (Labour) is the current (2014) constituency MSP for the constituency of Coatbridge and Chryston. This constituency is in the region of Central Scotland that is currently represented by the following regional list MSPs:

- Clare Adamson (SNP)
- Mark Griffin (Labour)
- Richard Lyle (SNP)
- Margaret McCulloch (Labour)
- Siobhan McMahon (Labour)
- Margaret Mitchell (Conservatives)
- John Wilson (SNP)

All MSPs work in their constituency on Mondays and Fridays.

MSPs can be contacted about issues that are related to devolved matters, such as housing, transport etc.

Figure 2.7: *A Labour constituency office*

GO! Activity

Research
Using the Scottish Parliament website, find out the contact details of your MSPs.

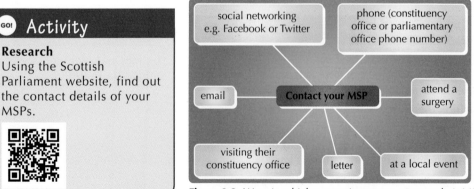

Figure 2.8: *Ways in which a constituent can contact their MSP*

During their time in the constituency MSPs will do a variety of things.

- Mainly work from their local constituency office replying to correspondence, such as letters, emails and phone calls they have received. Constituents have the right to contact their MSPs and MSPs have a duty to respond to constituents and proceed as appropriate. More and more MSPs are using social networking sites such as Facebook and Twitter to reach out to their constituents.

- Hold surgeries. A surgery is when people go along to talk to their MSP face-to-face about problems or issues they might have in the constituency. Issues can be about any devolved matter. Surgeries take place on a regular basis in the constituency and the MSP is duty bound to take up the issue and report back to the constituent with the outcome.

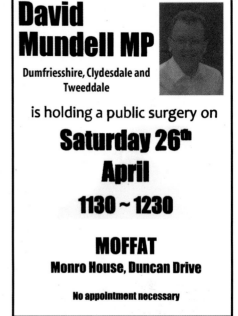

- Attend local meetings. MSPs attend local meetings of local people to find out about things that are of concern to them in the constituency. MSPs might use their influence to talk to business people, the police or council departments.

- Attend local events. MSPs are often asked to local schools, hospitals, factories etc. At these events MSPs can learn about the concerns of their constituents and find out about projects that could affect their constituents.

- Meet with other representatives. MSPs may meet with the MP, local councillors and MEP to discuss issues of common concern in the area or to resolve constituents' issues.

- Organise fact-finding visits. When a constituent raises an issue, the MSP may have to visit somewhere to see first-hand what the problem is. Afterwards, the MSP might arrange more meetings to resolve the problem or raise it as an issue in parliament.

Figure 2.9: *Poster of a MSP's surgery details*

- Contact the mass media. A MSP may also work with the media, such as local TV and newspapers, to highlight an issue within their constituency. The publicity may result in the issue being resolved. Additionally, MSPs will use the media to try to maintain a positive public profile.

? Questions

1. What days of the week do MSPs work in their constituency?
2. List the various ways that a constituent can contact their MSP.
3. Create a table showing the work of a MSP in their constituency. Use the structure below:

Work of MSPs in the constituency	Explanation	Example

4. Copy and complete the below weekly timetable for the work of a MSP. Include the work they do in the parliament and the work they do in the constituency.

Day		Work
Monday	AM	
	PM	
Tuesday	AM	
	PM	
Wednesday	AM	
	PM	
Thursday	AM	
	PM	
Friday	AM	
	PM	

5. Design a webpage, leaflet or poster detailing your MSP's constituency work. You will need to include the following:
   - your MSP's name and their political party
   - how constituents can contact the MSP, e.g. phone number, email address, constituency office details and opening hours
   - examples of the MSP's recent work in the constituency
   - information telling constituents what issues they can contact their MSP about

Local councils in Scotland

Local councils are often referred to as local government or authorities. Local councils provide a range of services and play an important part in the everyday lives of people in Scotland. There are 32 local council areas in Scotland. Glasgow City Council is the largest council with almost 600,000 people and Orkney is the smallest with under 20,000 people.

Each council area is made up of councillors who are directly elected by the residents in the area they represent. These areas are called council 'wards'.

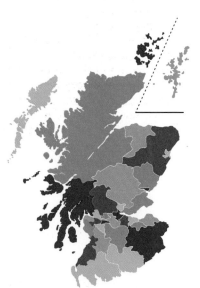

Figure 2.10: *Map of local authorities in Scotland*

Each ward will have three or four councillors and in total there are 1,222 elected councillors in Scotland. For example, in Glasgow City Council there are 21 wards with 79 councillors.

Following the introduction of the **Local Governance (Scotland) Act 2004**, local elections are held using the Single Transferable Vote (STV) system, with this first taking place in 2007. STV asks voters to rank the candidates in order of their preference. This system has produced an entirely new style of politics, and most of Scotland's

Hint

Electoral systems will be covered in more detail later in this Unit on page 46.

GO! Activity

Research
Using the webpage https://www.gov.uk/find-your-local-council find out the following information:

1. Which local authority area do you live in?
2. What is the name of the council ward in which you live?
3. What are the names and political parties of the councillors who represent you?
4. Name the party/parties in control of your local authority.
5. Explain one advantage and one disadvantage of a council being led by a party which has no overall control.

N5

---

local authorities are now either a coalition or led by a party that has no overall control (NOC). NOC means that no single party won a majority of seats.

Local council services

Local government is a devolved matter (see page 14); the Scottish government decides policies and laws in this area and local councils deliver them. For example, the Scottish government decided to increase the provision of free nursery education for three and four year olds by 50% and so local councils needed to employ more nursery teachers.

Local councils are responsible for planning, resourcing and delivering key public services. Mandatory services are those that councils must provide by law, such as education, fire services and social work services. Discretionary services are those that councils do not have to provide but may do if they have enough money. These include recreation services, such as parks and museums.

Since the **Local Government (Scotland) Act 2003** was introduced, local councils have been subject to 'best value' scrutiny by the Scottish Parliament. Local councils have to prove not only that they are seeking the most cost-effective way of providing services, but also that they are providing the highest-quality service too. Councils who do not meet these conditions can be closed down and have their services taken over by the Scottish government.

GO! Activity

Research
Create a fact file on the services your local council offers by visiting their webpage. Your fact file should include the council's name and logo, an explanation of the difference between mandatory and discretionary services, a list of the services provided by the council and appropriate images.

Figure 2.11: *The City of Edinburgh council's website*

Figure 2.12: *Edinburgh Leisure is supported by the local council and run fitness centres throughout the city*

Think point

Think of some advantages and disadvantages of freezing council tax levels.

Local government funding

Every year the Scottish government gives each local authority a fixed amount of money from its annual budget in order to provide its services. The Cabinet Secretary for Finance and Sustainable Growth decides the level of funding each council should receive. In 2012 the Scottish government provided councils with a total funding package worth over £11.5 billion.

Council tax

Councils can raise revenue through council tax. This is the system of local taxation used to part-fund services provided by local authorities. Introduced in 1993, the rate of tax payable is based on the value of residential property. It raises around £1.9 billion every year across Scotland.

The amount that households pay depends on their band (A to H) which is based on the value of their property in 1991.

Although responsibility for setting council tax levels rests with local authorities in Scotland, the Scottish government retains the right to limit the amount of any increase. The Scottish government has worked with authorities to freeze council tax since 2007. This has been done to help households during the recession.

The current Scottish government considers the council tax system to be unfair and intends to consult on options for a replacement local tax based on the ability to pay.

Local councils can also make money by taxing businesses and other properties that are not homes, and through charging people to use their facilities and services such as swimming pools and gyms.

The work of local councillors

The main role of local councillors is to represent the interests of the people in their ward. As most councillors are part-time they do most of their work in the evenings and at weekends.

Councillors find out the views of local people by holding surgeries in their wards. Local people can speak to their councillor who will decide the best course of action to take in order to solve their problem. A local councillor can approach the relevant council department on behalf of the local people. Additionally, councillors can contact other representatives for the area, such as the local MP and MSP, and pass on the concerns of people living in that community.

Councillors have to attend meetings to deal with the major decisions taken by the council. This is a chance for councillors to try to ensure that the decisions made are in the best interests of their constituents.

Councillors may also work on committees wherein small groups of councillors make decisions on behalf of local people. There is usually a committee for each of the various council departments. Committees work to develop new policies for the council or scrutinise existing ones.

Councillors may also be asked to attend local events. During this time they are able to interact with local residents and gain publicity in the media.

N5 Salaries for local councillors were first introduced in May 2007; before this they were able to claim expenses. The basic salary for a councillor from 1st April 2009 is £16,234. A limited number of senior councillors, i.e. those with additional responsibilities such as a committee convenor, receive higher salaries. There are four different salary levels for council leaders, which vary according to the size of the local authority. Salaries from 1st April 2009 are: £27,058, £32,470, £37,880 and £48,704. In addition, councillors are entitled to reimbursement of money spent on travel and subsistence expenses when undertaking council duties.

📖 Word bank

• **Subsistence expenses**

Money paid to an employee to cover cost of work expenses, such as lodging, meals, laundry etc.

? Questions

1. How many local councils are there in Scotland?
2. What is a local councillor?
3. What is the name given to the area which councillors represent?
4. How many councillors will represent each ward?
5. Name the voting system used to elect local councillors.
6. Make a table to show the 2012 Scottish local council elections. Using the table, **make and justify conclusions** using the results.
7. **Explain** why, even though we have a Scottish Parliament, we still need local councils in Scotland.
8. **Explain** what is meant by mandatory and discretionary services. State **examples** of each.
9. What is the main source of funding for Scottish councils?
10. **Describe** other ways in which local councils can make money.
11. **Explain** how local councils operate.
12. Create a diary to show the work of a local councillor.

Summary

In this chapter you have learned:

- the names of the different types of political representatives
- the work of a MSP in the parliament and constituency
- how a constituent can contact their MSP
- how local councils are organised in Scotland
- the work of a local councillor, representing their constituents

Learning Summary

Now that you have finished the **Representation** chapter, complete a self-evaluation of your knowledge and skills to assess what you have understood. Use the checklist below and its traffic lights to draw up a revision plan to help you improve in the areas you identified as red or amber.

- I can list the main types of political representatives I have learned about.

- I can name my local constituency MSP, the party they belong to and at least one of my local councillors and their respective political party.

- I can explain the ways in which MSPs can represent their constituents in committees in the Scottish Parliament.

- I can explain the different ways in which MSPs represent their constituents in the Chamber of the Scottish Parliament.

- I can outline the stages of a bill.

- I can list the ways in which constituents can contact their MSP.

- I can explain the ways in which MSPs represent their constituents in the constituency or region.

- I can explain how local councils in Scotland are organised.

- I can describe the work of a local council.

- I can explain the ways in which local councillors can represent their constituents in their ward.

- I can list the ways a constituent can contact their local councillor.

Examples

In Modern Studies it is essential that you are able to back up any point you make with relevant evidence. When you are considering the statements above try to think of relevant examples for each response. You may wish to note these examples under each statement in your revision notes.

3 Electoral systems

What you will learn in this chapter

- What an electoral system is.
- The main features and outcomes of the electoral system used for Scottish Parliament elections.
- The advantages and disadvantages of the Scottish electoral system.
- The main features and outcomes of the electoral system used for local council elections in Scotland.
- The advantages and disadvantages of the electoral system used for local council elections in Scotland.

Figure 3.1: *Voting: casting a sealed vote*

What is an electoral system?

An electoral system, also known as voting system, is a method used during an election to allow voters to make a choice based on who they wish to represent them. Different electoral systems are used for different elections and can result in very different outcomes.

Scottish Parliament elections

Scottish Parliament elections have fixed four-year terms except if this clashes with the UK election. The 2011 election would have resulted in a 2015 election; however as the next UK election will take place in 2015 it has been extended by one year and the next scheduled election for the Scottish Parliament is now 2016.

The **Fixed-term Parliaments Act 2011** introduced fixed-term elections for the first time to the Westminster Parliament. Under the act a UK Parliament general election will normally be held on the first Thursday in May every five years. The last general election was held on 6th May 2010, therefore the next election is scheduled to take place on 7th May 2015.

The Additional Member System (AMS)

The electoral system used to elect the 129 Members of the Scottish Parliament (MSPs) is called The Additional Member System (AMS). AMS is a hybrid system that combines elements of the First Past the Post (FPTP) system and Proportional Representation (PR). Under the AMS system voters are given two ballot papers.

The constituency ballot paper

The ballot paper to elect constituency MSPs uses the FPTP system. Scotland is divided into 73 constituencies and each constituency elects one MSP.

The constituency ballot paper contains a list of the names of candidates and their political parties who are standing for election. Voters have to put one cross next to the name of the candidate they wish to vote for

📖 Word bank

- **Ballot paper**
A paper used to register a vote.

⚙ Hint

Constituency MSPs are elected by the FPTP system in exactly the same way as MPs are elected to the House of Commons.

on the ballot paper. When the results of the election are counted, the candidate with the most votes is elected as the MSP for the constituency. This is why FPTP is known as a single winner voting system.

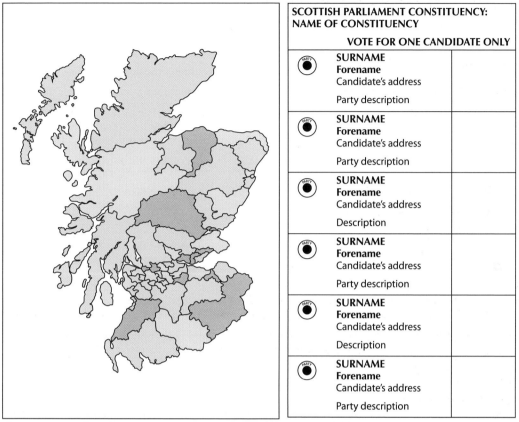

SCOTTISH PARLIAMENT CONSTITUENCY: NAME OF CONSTITUENCY

VOTE FOR ONE CANDIDATE ONLY

SURNAME
Forename
Candidate's address
Party description

SURNAME
Forename
Candidate's address
Party description

SURNAME
Forename
Candidate's address
Description

SURNAME
Forename
Candidate's address
Party description

SURNAME
Forename
Candidate's address
Description

SURNAME
Forename
Candidate's address
Party description

Figure 3.2: *Scottish Parliament 73 constituencies map and constituency ballot paper*

Advantages and disadvantages of the FPTP system

Advantages of FPTP	Disadvantages of FPTP
It is an easy system for voters to understand. FPTP is fair system as the candidate with the most votes wins. For example, in 2011 Alex Salmond won in Aberdeenshire East with about 64% of the vote.	The winning candidate doesn't need to get a minimum number of votes; they only need more votes than any other candidate. This can result in more people actually voting against the winning candidate. For example, in 2011, Bill Kidd (SNP) won the Glasgow Anniesland seat with a majority of just seven votes and 43% of the total votes cast.
There is a strong link between the MSP and the people of the constituency. The MSP is accountable to the voters and have a duty to help them with any problems.	Many votes do not make a difference, especially in constituencies where a candidate wins with a large majority. This can lead to voter apathy. In the 2011 election for the Scottish Parliament around four million people had the right to vote. Almost 51% of the population turned out to vote compared to almost 54% in 2007.
It can discourage candidates from extremist parties as it is very hard for them to be elected, even if they do achieve a sizeable number of votes. For example, the British National Party has never won a seat in the Scottish Parliament.	It is unfair on candidates from smaller parties as they usually do not receive enough votes to secure a seat in parliament. Only the SNP, the Scottish Labour Party and the Scottish Conservative Party had candidates in all constituencies. The Scottish Green Party only contested regional seats.

The regional ballot paper

The second ballot paper uses a form of PR to elect 56 additional members to the Scottish Parliament. Scotland is divided into eight parliamentary regions, each comprising a number of whole constituencies. The initial regions for the parliament were the same as the European Parliament constituencies. Each region elects seven regional MSPs.

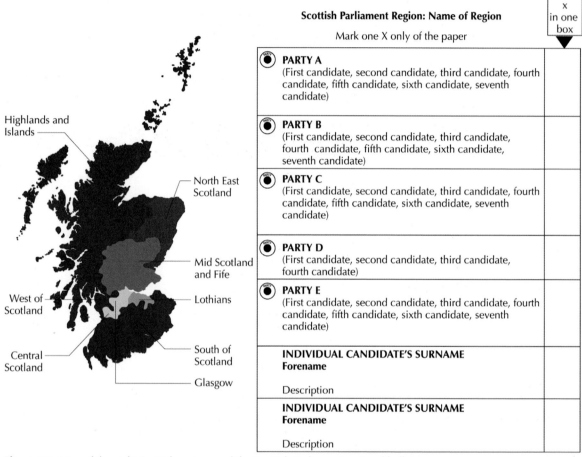

Figure 3.3: *Map of the eight Scottish regions and the Scottish Parliament regional ballot paper*

On the regional ballot paper, voters indicate their choice by placing an 'X' next to their preferred party or individual candidate to represent the region. The votes are counted for each political party. As a system of PR is in place, the percentage of votes a party receives is then converted into seats. The formula takes into account the number of regional votes that a party has received and the number of constituency seats it has already won – this helps to make the overall result more proportional.

For example, if the SNP received 40% of the vote then they get around 40% of the seven seats. 7 × 40% = 3 MSPs

Regional MSPs are selected from lists compiled by the parties. Each party produces a list of candidates numbered one to seven before the election. If a party receives three MSPs through the regional vote then the candidates numbered one to three on the list become MSPs. This is why regional MSPs are sometimes referred to as Party List MSPs.

If a regional seat becomes vacant, the next candidate on the party list becomes a MSP. For example, in August 2013 David McLetchie, Conservative list MSP for the Lothians region, died. He was replaced by Cameron Buchanan who was the next name on the Conservative Party list for the region.

This is different from a constituency MSP resigning or dying, as this would trigger a by-election. In the Dunfermline by-election, after the resignation of Bill Walker MSP in 2013, Labour candidate Cara Hilton won after beating the SNP candidate by almost 3,000 votes.

Summary of the make-up of the Scottish Parliament

1 constituency MSP for each constituency	73 constituencies = 73 constituency MSPs
7 regional list MSPs for each region	7 MSPs x 8 regions = 56 regional list MSPs
	Total MSPs = 129 Therefore a political party needs to secure **65 seats** to win an overall majority in Holyrood.

GO! Activity

Discuss
Think, pair, share with your shoulder partner what type of individuals you think political parties might put at the top of their Party List?
Why do you think this might be the case? (Hint – it might be useful to think about female candidates, or candidates from an ethnic minority.)

? Questions

1. Name the electoral system used to elect MSPs.
2. How many ballot papers are Scottish voters given?
3. **Explain, in detail,** how constituency MSPs are elected to the Scottish Parliament.
4. List some advantages and disadvantages of electing constituency MSPs using FPTP.
5. **Explain, in detail,** how regional MSPs are elected to the Scottish Parliament.
6. Can you **explain** why by-elections are not held to replace regional MSPs?
7. Copy out the summary of the make-up of the Scottish Parliament.

The outcome of AMS

After the 1999 and 2003 Scottish Parliamentary elections, the Labour Party and the Liberal Democrats formed a coalition in the Scottish Parliament. By joining forces they had a majority of MSPs and formed the Scottish Executive (now called the Scottish Government). After the 2007 elections, however, the SNP won more seats than any other party, but only by one seat – they did not have an overall majority. The SNP decided to form a minority government, which meant that every time it wanted to pass legislation it had to agree with the other parties in the parliament on an issue-by-issue basis. The SNP argue that this approach led to more consensus politics in the third Scottish Parliament electoral term (2007–11).

The 2011 Scottish Parliament Election Results					
Party	Constituency MSPs	Regional MSPs	Total MSPs	% of votes	% of seats
SNP	53	16	69	44.7	53.5
Labour	15	22	37	29	28.7
Conservative	3	12	15	13.15	11.6
Liberal Democrats	2	3	5	6.55	3.9
Green	0	2	2	2.2	1.6
Margo MacDonald	0	1	1	0.45	0.8
					Turnout= 50.6%

Figure 3.4: *SNP leader Alex Salmond, jubilant after the historic 2011 election result*

The results of the 2011 election were historic because for the first time in the history of the Scottish Parliament one party, the SNP, were able to achieve an overall majority. AMS was designed to prevent this from ever happening – indeed, one of the many advantages often cited of AMS is the fact that it produced governments that need to work in coalition, be that formally, as with the Labour-Liberal alliance from 1999, or more informally, as in the SNP's 2007–11 term.

The 2007 Scottish Parliament Election Results					
Party	Constituency Seats	Regional Seats	Total Seats	% of votes	% of seats
SNP	21	26	47	33	36.4
Labour	37	9	46	31	35.7
Conservative	4	13	17	16	13.2
Liberal Democrats	11	5	16	14	12.4
Green	0	2	2	2	1.6
Independent	0	1	1	0.5	1
					Turnout = 51.7%

Think point

Try to think of some disadvantages and advantages of AMS.

It is clear to see that under AMS the percentage of votes a party gains is closely related to the percentage of seats they gain in parliament. In both elections The Greens had a better chance of being elected and doing well out of AMS as they only fielded candidates in the regional election. This is because their votes were spread out geographically rather than being concentrated in specific constituencies.

The Conservatives also gained under AMS. They have only one MP from a Scottish constituency in Westminster, yet when this book was published in 2014 they had the third largest group of MSPs in Holyrood.

GO! Activity

Use your skills

Using only the results from the Scottish Parliament elections, what **conclusions** can be drawn about AMS?

You must make and justify a **conclusion** about each of the following headings:

- fairness in representation – do all political parties receive a proportionate (equal) number of seats in relation to the number of votes secured?
- overrepresentation of parties – which parties do well under AMS?
- underrepresentation of parties – which parties do not do well under AMS?
- trends/patterns over time – has support increased or decreased for some parties?

The advantages and disadvantages of AMS

Advantages of AMS	Disadvantages of AMS
AMS is a fair system because there is a link between the number of votes a party receives and the number of seats it gets. This results in fewer wasted votes and should improve turnout.	AMS is more difficult for voters to understand. In the 2007 election there was a lot of confusion – around 140,000 ballot papers were not filled out properly and were therefore disqualified.
AMS usually results in a coalition government. Some people think that coalition governments are more representative of the way people have voted.	Coalition governments may be less stable than a majority government. If the coalition parties disagree over too much, the coalition can be torn apart and the government can fall.
AMS prevents large parties from getting more seats than the share of the vote they received. This has prevented Labour from potentially governing Scotland permanently. PR helps smaller political parties gain seats and representation in the parliament.	AMS is unfair to larger parties. Parties that win a lot of constituencies lose out on seats from the regional lists. For example, in 2007 Labour won only nine regional members because they performed well on the constituency vote.
AMS gives voters greater representation. It is a way of keeping the link between voters and their constituency representative as well as giving voters additional representatives who are accountable to them in their region.	Scottish voters have eight representatives, very often from different political parties. This can lead to confusion about who is responsible for what and who they can go and see if they have a problem.

? Question

Explain the advantages and disadvantages of AMS. Use the election results above and your knowledge of AMS to give examples to support as many of your points as possible.

Figure 3.5: *The sign points to a polling station, where voters can cast their vote*

Local council elections in Scotland

Scottish local government elections are a matter devolved to the Scottish Parliament under the **Scotland Act 1998**. The Scottish government is responsible for setting the rules for the conduct of local government elections. Local authorities themselves are responsible for organising and conducting these elections in their own areas.

Legislation in 2009 moved local elections to two consecutive five-year terms to prevent local government and Scottish parliament elections being held on the same day. Therefore the current term (when this book was published in 2014) runs from 2012-2017 and thereafter the term will revert to a four-year term. Local government elections elect local councillors who represent the voters who live in the council area. In May 2007 the Single Transferable Vote (STV), a form of PR, was first used in Scotland. Before 2007, councillors had been elected using the FPTP electoral system.

N5 How does STV work?

Within the 32 local councils in Scotland, each council is divided into areas called 'wards', often referred to as 'multi-member constituencies'. Under STV, constituencies are normally larger than they were under FPTP, however each elects several representatives; depending upon its size up to four councillors are elected for each ward.

Under STV, voters rank candidates in order of preference by marking '1', '2', '3' and so on next to the names of candidates on a ballot paper. A voter can rank as many or as few candidates as they like or just vote for one candidate. It is simple for the voters to cast their votes, but it is complicated to count the votes in the STV system.

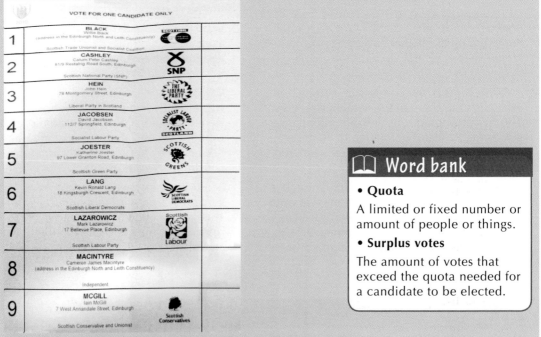

> ### 📖 Word bank
>
> • **Quota**
> A limited or fixed number or amount of people or things.
> • **Surplus votes**
> The amount of votes that exceed the quota needed for a candidate to be elected.

Figure 3.6: *A STV ballot paper as used in the 2012 local council elections*

Each candidate needs a minimum number of votes to be elected. This number is calculated according to the number of seats and votes cast, and is called a quota. The

N5 quota is calculated by dividing the number of votes cast by one more than the number of seats available, and then adding one.

$$\left(\frac{\textit{Votes cast}}{\textit{Number of seats available} + 1} \right) + 1 = \textit{Quota}$$

E.g. in a four-member constituency where 150,000 votes were cast, a candidate would require 30,001 votes in order to be elected:

$$\left(\frac{150,000}{5(4\,\textit{seats} + 1)} \right) + 1 = 30,001$$

The first preference votes for each candidate are added up and any candidate who has achieved this quota is elected. If a candidate has more votes than are needed to fill the quota, that candidate's surplus votes are transferred to the remaining candidates. Votes that would have gone to the winner instead go to the second preference listed on those ballot papers.

If candidates do not meet the quota, the candidate with the fewest first preference votes is eliminated and the second preference votes are transferred to other candidates. These processes are repeated until all the seats are filled.

The outcome of the 2012 local council elections

Party	Councils		Councillors	
	Total	+/−	Total	+/−
SNP	2	+2	424	+57
Labour	4	+2	394	+58
Conservative	0	0	115	−16
Liberal Democrats	0	0	71	−80
Green	0	0	14	+6
Scottish Socialist Party	0	0	1	0
Independent	3	0	0	0
British National Party	0	0	0	0
Independent Community and Health Concern	0	0	0	0
Liberal	0	0	0	−1
Residents Association	0	0	0	0
Respect	0	0	0	0
Socialist	0	0	0	0
UK Independence Party	0	0	0	−1
Others	0	0	201	−22
No Overall Control	23	−4		

(continued)

Figure 3.7: *Voters cast their vote in private voting booths*

In the 2012 local council elections the SNP overtook Labour and became the party with most councillors across Scotland. Labour made gains from 2007, whilst the Liberal Democrats lost seats and fell behind the Conservatives.

For the first time since the introduction of the STV, the SNP won majority control of two councils (Angus and Dundee City), from no overall control in 2007. Labour also won majority control of two councils from no overall control, while retaining majority control over two councils (Glasgow City, North Lanarkshire, Renfrewshire and West Dunbartonshire). Independent councillors retained majority control over the three island councils of the Western Isles, Shetland and Orkney. The 23 other councils remained under no overall control.

The advantages and disadvantages of the STV system

Advantages	Disadvantages
Fewer votes will be wasted as a number of candidates will be elected in each constituency. This means that a variety of parties may win some representation. This may encourage more people to vote if they know that their vote will count.	STV is a complicated system for voters to understand. This may stop people from voting because they do not understand how candidates are to be elected.
There is greater choice for voters as they can choose between different candidates from the same party. This means that less effective candidates will not be guaranteed election and keeps elected politicians on their toes as there are no longer 'safe seats', where established politicians can, in some case, rely on being re-elected.	Each constituency being able to elect a number of representatives may cause confusion. If a voter has a problem, it may be difficult to work out which representative to consult. Furthermore, larger constituencies may result in less representation of local issues.
STV gives smaller parties a greater chance of getting elected, resulting in a more diverse range of views being represented. For example, many Green Party and Independent candidates were elected to Scotland's councils in 2007 when STV replaced FPTP as the electoral system.	Some people argue that coalitions are fractious and prone to disharmony. This is because coalitions include parties with different beliefs which therefore may not always agree on policy. For example, in Stirling Council, after the 2007 election, the Labour-Liberal Democrat coalition collapsed within a year following a series of disagreements on policy. The SNP then formed a minority administration but after the 2012 election the Labour Party (with eight councillors) and the Conservative Party (with four councillors) created a coalition.
Following the 2012 elections a single party has overall control in only six councils. This has resulted in many multi-party coalitions across Scotland's councils, leading to a broader spectrum of opinion being represented in local government and more consensus-based politics as parties with opposing views have to find common ground with one another.	

? Questions

1. How often do local council elections usually take place?
2. Name the electoral system used to elect local councillors.

N5
3. **Describe, in detail,** how the STV works.
4. 'In the 2012 local council elections no political party won more councils than they had in 2007. Also, all political parties saw a decrease in the number of councillors they won'.

   Using the table above give one reason why each statement is **exaggerated**.
5. **Explain, in detail,** some advantages and disadvantages of STV.

Figure 3.8: *A Labour-Conservative coalition was the way forward for Stirling Council in 2012*

Summary

In this chapter you have learned:

- what an electoral system is

- the main features and outcomes of the electoral system used for Scottish Parliament elections

- the advantages and disadvantages of the Scottish electoral system

- the main features and outcomes of the electoral system used for local council elections in Scotland

- the advantages and disadvantages of the electoral system used for local council elections in Scotland

Learning Summary

Now that you have finished the **Electoral systems** chapter, complete a self-evaluation of your knowledge and skills to assess what you have understood. Use the checklist below and its traffic lights to draw up a revision plan to help you improve in the areas you identified as red or amber.

- I can explain what is meant by an electoral system.

- I can state how often Scottish Parliament elections are held.

- I can name the electoral system used to elects MSPs to the Scottish Parliament.

- I can describe the features of the electoral system used to elect MSPs.

- I can explain what is meant by proportional representation.

- I can outline when by-elections are held.

- I can explain the outcome of recent Scottish Parliament elections.

- I can explain the advantages and disadvantages of the AMS.

- I can state how often local council elections are held in Scotland.

- I can name the electoral system used to elect local councillors in Scotland.

- I can describe the features of the electoral system used to elect local councillors. (N5 only)

- I can explain the outcome of the last local council elections in Scotland. (N5 only)

- I can explain the advantages and disadvantages of the STV system. (N5 only)

Examples

In Modern Studies it is essential that you are able to back up any point you make with relevant evidence. When you are considering the statements above try to think of relevant examples for each response. You may wish to note these examples under each statement in your revision notes.

4 Participation

What you will learn in this chapter

- The meaning of participation.
- The rights and responsibilities associated with taking part in elections.
- The main political parties in Scotland.
- How to stand as a candidate for election.
- About election campaigns in Scotland.
- How to vote in elections.

Participation

The word 'participate' means 'to take part'. As Scotland is a democracy, people can participate in making decisions for the country and try to influence representatives.

There are various ways to participate, such as:

- voting in elections
- joining a political party
- standing as a candidate
- contacting a representative, e.g. at a surgery
- signing a petition
- contacting the media, e.g. writing to a newspaper
- taking part in a protest or demonstration
- joining a pressure group
- joining a trade union

Figure 4.1: *Joining a protest or demonstration is one way to partici- pate in a democratic country*

Make the Link

You may have learned about pressure groups and trade unions in Business Management.

Voting in the UK

One of the most important ways people can participate in a democracy is by voting. Voting usually takes place at election time when the whole country is given the opportunity to choose who they want to represent them. In Scotland we have the right to vote in elections for local councils, the Scottish Parliament, the Westminster Parliament, and the European Parliament.

Citizens have the right to vote when they are:

- 18 years of age or over on polling day
- a British citizen, a Commonwealth citizen or a citizen of the Irish Republic (and resident in the United Kingdom)
- on the electoral register (see below)

Figure 4.2: *British citizens have the right to vote*

Figure 4.3: *Citizens who are in prison cannot vote*

Hint

Many people think that members of the Royal Family are not able to vote. This is not the case – however, in practice, most choose not to do so because it would be considered unconstitutional.

The following citizens do not have the right to vote:

- anyone under 18 years old
- people who are visiting the UK
- those who are in prison
- anyone found guilty within the previous five years of electoral malpractice
- under common law, people with learning disabilities or a mental illness if, on polling day, they are incapable of making a reasoned judgement

The responsibilities associated with voting

Each year the local council sends every house in the UK a list of people registered to vote at that address. The form should contain the names of those who live in the house and are eligible to vote. You can register to vote from the age of 16. These names are then submitted to become part of what is known as the 'electoral register'.

If an individual is unable to vote in person they may choose to have someone vote on their behalf. This is called a proxy vote. Alternatively, a voter may choose to apply to make their vote by post. Postal voting takes place before election day, so that the results can be counted with the others.

The responsibility of voting lies with the individual voter. Voters should use their vote wisely when selecting a candidate/party to best represent their interests.

Turnout

Voter turnout is the percentage of eligible voters who cast a ballot in an election. It is often used as an indicator of how engaged or disengaged with democracy the people are; for many, turnout is viewed as the most important measure of the health of a democracy.

Figure 4.4: *Voters turning out to vote at their polling station*

Scottish Parliament elections	Turnout
1999	59%
2003	49.4%
2007	50.6%
2011	51.7%

Voter turnout at Scottish parliament elections is usually over 50%. This is lower than turnout at UK general elections but higher than other elections. For example, turnout in the 2010 UK general election was 65.1%, up from 61.4% in 2005, but down compared to 1950 when it was 83.9%.

Scottish local council elections	Turnout
1999	58.1%
2003	49.1%
2007	52.8%
2012	39.1%

The fact that Scottish Parliament and local council elections used to be held on the same day made it difficult to judge the interest of voters in local elections. Turnout in 2012 was the lowest for Scottish local council elections since the restructuring of local government in 1974. However, the figures are not as low as they are for European Parliament elections. The first ever European Parliament election in 1979 recorded a UK turnout of 32.7%. The lowest reported turnout in the UK was 24.4% in 1999 and the highest was 38.5% in 2004. Turnout again fell in 2009 to 34.5%.

Compulsory Voting

CASE STUDY

The right to vote is a freedom fiercely sought by people all over the world, yet in some countries, for example Australia, voting is not a choice, it is compulsory. Under such a system voters are obliged to vote in elections or attend a polling place on voting day, although once there they can choose not to use their vote. Additionally, many voters spoil their ballots – they either mistakenly or intentionally submit a ballot that is blank or improperly filled in and so cannot be counted in the final tally. If an eligible voter does not attend a polling place he or she may be punished by methods such as a fine or community service.

Think point

The fine for failing to attend a polling place in Australia is the equivalent of just over £10. Do you think this is a reasonable punishment for not voting?

Make the Link

You will learn about different types of punishments in Unit 2.

Why should we use our right to vote?

Our right to vote is important and we should use it because:

- it will ensure that Scotland and the UK stay democratic
- it ensures that people are represented democratically at local, national and European level
- it allows us to hold representatives to account
- if we do not then unpopular parties may pass laws which we do not want
- it allows the government to gain an understanding of what the public want
- if representatives do not do what voters want, voters can elect someone else the next time
- people have fought and died in the past to win us the right to vote

Make the Link

In History you may have learned how the suffragettes fought for a woman's right to vote. You may also have studied dictatorships such as Nazi Germany; you will learn more about dictatorships in Unit 3.

- people in dictatorships do not have the right to vote, we should appreciate our rights
- if you don't vote you don't have the right to criticise what the government does
- if the turnout is very low those elected may not represent the views of the electorate

? Questions

1. Make a list of those who have the right to vote in elections.
2. Make a list of those who do not have the right to vote in elections.
3. **Describe** the responsibilities associated with the right to vote.
4. What is voter turnout?
5. **Explain** what is meant by compulsory voting.
6. Copy and complete the following spider diagram.

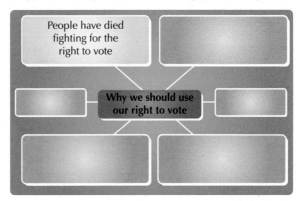

7. In your opinion, do think it is important that people use their right to vote? Give reasons to **support** your answer.
8. Voter apathy is when there is lack of concern, enthusiasm or interest by voters at election time. Can you think of any reasons why voters might be apathetic? Give examples to **support** your point.

GO! Activity

Homework
Conduct a survey amongst eligible citizens, such as family members, teachers etc, to find out the reasons why they did or did not vote in the 2011 Scottish Parliament election. Display your results in a suitable way, such as in a bar graph or pie chart.

Make the Link

More information about conducting a survey can be found on page 223.

In Maths you will have learned how to report findings in different ways.

Political parties in Scotland

A political party is a group of people who have the same ideas about running the country. They join together to try to win elections. The party that wins the most seats during an election usually becomes the government and they will work to make their polices the laws that the people of the country have to live by. Political parties are always working to gain support so that when the next election takes place voters are more likely to vote for them.

The main political parties in Scotland are:

- The SNP
- The Labour Party

- The Scottish Conservative Party
- The Liberal Democrat Party
- The Scottish Green Party
- Independent candidates

Each political party has their own ideology (ideas and ideals) based on how they think about the world.

N5 A political spectrum is used to classify ideologies in terms of their position on a scale.

Left wing	Centre	Right wing

Political parties on the left wing have beliefs that are usually progressive in nature, they look to the future, aim to support those who cannot support themselves, are idealist and believe in equality. Left wing supporters believe in taxation to redistribute wealth and are also in support of things like the National Health Service (NHS) and social security. In Scotland and the UK the main left wing parties are the SNP and the Labour Party.

Political parties on the right wing have beliefs that value tradition, they believe in equity, survival of the fittest, and economic freedom. They typically believe that businesses shouldn't be regulated (controlled), and that we should all look after ourselves. Right wing supporters believe they shouldn't have to pay for someone else's education or health service. In Scotland and the UK the main right wing party is the Conservative Party.

At the centre of the political spectrum there is the belief that tradition is important but change should be supported if most people want it; the government should play a role only in that it improves the lives of citizens. The Liberal Democrats are the political party most commonly seen as holding the centre ground.

Nowadays, political parties have moved either to the 'centre-left' or 'centre-right', meaning most mainstream parties are neither very left wing, nor very right wing. This may be because there is not mass public support for a political change resulting in a significant shift of society either strongly to the left or the right.

Figure 4.5: *Political parties often align themselves to the left or right of the political spectrum*

📖 Word bank

• Social democratic

The use of 'democratic' means to achieve socialism. Socialism involves the means of production (the facilities and resources for producing goods) and distribution of goods being owned collectively or by a centralised government that often plans and controls the economy.

Beliefs of Scotland's main political parties

Scottish National Party (SNP) **SNP☓**	The SNP is a social democratic political party that has gained considerable support across Scotland. The party is committed to achieving independence for Scotland and has campaigned for many decades on this issue. In the 2011 Scottish Parliament election, the SNP won a landslide victory and became the first party to form a majority government in Scotland.
The Scottish Labour Party Scottish Labour	The Scottish Labour Party is a centre-left political party that traditionally gains most of its support from working-class voters. The party has links with many trade unions in Scotland. The party stands for 'social justice, strong community and strong values, reward for hard work, decency and rights matched by responsibilities'. The party came second in the 2011 Scottish Parliament election making them the opposition party.
The Scottish Conservative Party Scottish Conservatives ☓	The Scottish Conservative Party is a centre-right political party that traditionally gains most of its support from middle- and upper-class voters. The party says it 'stands for freedom, enterprise, community and equality of opportunity as it is a party of choice, responsibility, localism, low taxation and strong but limited government'. The party won 15 seats in the 2011 Scottish Parliament election making it the third largest party in Scotland.
The Scottish Liberal Democrat Party **SCOTTISH LIBERAL DEMOCRATS** www.scotlibdems.org.uk	The Scottish Liberal Democrat Party is a centre-left political party. The party says it 'exists to build and safeguard a fair, free and open society, in which we seek to balance the fundamental values of liberty, equality and community and in which no-one shall be enslaved by poverty, ignorance or conformity'. In the 2011 Scottish Parliament election the party won five seats.

❓ Questions

1. Name the main political parties in Scotland.
2. **Explain** what is meant by an ideology.
3. **Describe** what politics parties on the left wing, right wing and centre believe in.

What is a manifesto?

Before an election, political parties produce a document called a manifesto. This is an outline of the policies (plan or course of action) they promise to introduce if they are elected to form the government. These promises can be outlined under specific policy areas, such as education, health, justice etc.

Below you will find a table giving the key points from each of the main party's manifestos from the 2011 election.

SNP
- Maintain the council tax freeze throughout the next parliament.
- Attempt to generate 100% of Scotland's electricity from renewable sources by 2020.
- Legislate to give Scotland a referendum on independence.
- Continue offering free university tuition to Scottish students.
- Maintain high police numbers.

Scottish Labour Party
- Introduce Scottish Living Wage of £7.15 an hour, starting in the public sector.
- Abolish youth unemployment and aim to create 250,000 jobs by 2020.
- Compulsory six-month jail sentences for people convicted of knife-carrying.
- Two-year council tax freeze.
- Reinstate the proposed rail link between Glasgow Central station and Glasgow International Airport, which was cancelled in 2009.
- Continue offering free university tuition to Scottish students.

Scottish Conservative Party
- A council tax freeze during the period 2012-2013.
- Re-introduce prescription charges at 2009 standards (£5 for a single item).
- Consider building new nuclear power stations, but not on new sites.
- Bring in Variable University Graduate Fee, with no more than £4,000 being paid annually per student.
- Replace community service with short prison sentences.

Scottish Liberal Democrats
- Continue offering free university tuition to Scottish students.
- Aim to create 100,000 new jobs through selling Scottish Water, which would generate £1.5 billion for investment purposes.
- Oppose moves to create a centralised Scottish police force.
- Maintain the Scottish bus pass, but bring the qualifying age up to 65.
- Reform the council tax.

Scottish Green Party
- Bring in large-scale ecosystem restoration projects.
- Replace council tax with land value tax.
- Continue offering free university tuition to Scottish students.
- Focus on bringing restorative justice within Scotland's justice system.
- Abolish the Forth Replacement Crossing.

GO! Activity

Group work

Select one of the political parties in Scotland from the list below:

* SNP
* Scottish Labour
* Scottish Conservatives
* Scottish Liberal Democrats
* Scottish Greens

Use the manifesto proposals above and the internet to make notes on the key policies of one of these parties. Once you have done this you should take part in 'political speed dating' with your classmates:

* divide a double page into four and in each corner write down the names of the main parties
* the class should be split into two groups
* Group One students should stay in their seats and Group Two should rotate as many times as possible so that each Group Two student spends time with each Group One student
* in the time allocated by your teacher you should share as many policies with each other as you can. You should write these policies on your page so that by the end you are more informed about the views of different political parties

How do you become a candidate in an election?

Standing as a candidate in an election is another way that individuals can participate in politics in Scotland. To become a candidate an individual must be aged over 18 years old and be a British citizen. A nomination form needs to be signed by 10 voters from that constituency. The papers must be returned along with a £500 deposit to the Returning Officer (who manages the election in the constituency). Candidates do not need to be a member of a political party.

The main parties have their own selection methods, usually involving local party members voting for a candidate to stand for election. Once the candidate has been chosen, 10 party members sign the candidate's nomination papers and the political party usually pays the deposit. The deposit is refunded provided that the candidate gains 5% or more of the total valid votes cast in the constituency.

The election campaign

Before an election can take place, an election campaign is rolled out. An election campaign is when candidates and their parties try to persuade voters to choose them on election day. During the election campaign candidates are competing against each other to win votes.

Becoming a member of a political party is another way to participate in politics. Many people pay annual membership fees or make donations to the political party that they feel closely represents their views and beliefs. Party members can attend local meetings and

Figure 4.6: *Senior members of the SNP join a candidate on the campaign trail*

sometimes national conferences. In addition to this, party members offer assistance to candidates by canvassing voters on the campaign trail. The major political parties will have many supporters to help do this – if you look on each of the main political parties' websites you will notice that you can sign up to volunteer for the next election campaign.

These parties also have a large campaign budget to help them get elected. Each candidate and their supporters need to get their message across to as many people as they possibly can. They try to persuade voters that their party's policies would be the best for their area and for Scotland as a whole.

Figure 4.7: *An election candidate canvassing door-to-door*

Hint

Positive publicity in the media can help a candidate gain votes.

Make the Link

You may have taken part in a short performance in Drama or Media Studies.

The methods used by candidates and their supporters include:

- putting up posters around the constituency with party promises, candidate's name and picture on them
- canvassing voters by talking to people in the street and knocking on the doors of houses of constituents
- handing out leaflets containing manifesto policies
- putting a loud speaker on a car and driving around the constituency talking about policy
- holding public meetings to discuss policies and meet voters
- attending debates with other prospective candidates
- visiting local business, schools etc
- organising media events – TV, radio and newspaper interviews
- political parties can create Party Election Broadcasts which can be shown on TV during the election campaign
- keeping a blog and/or updating social networking sites whilst on the campaign trail
- organising transport to take people to the polling station on election day
- trying to persuade people at the last minute at the entrance to the polling station

Figure 4.8: *Party leaders attending a televised debate*

GO! Activity

Group work

In small groups, choose a political party and create a Party Election Broadcast. To be successful in this task your group must:

- refer to the name of the political party you have chosen throughout
- mention policies from the party's manifesto
- the party's policies should be compared to those from other political parties
- use persuasive language throughout to persuade voters to choose your party

❓ Questions

1. **Explain** what a manifesto is.
2. Using the manifesto promises decide which party you would vote for. Give reasons to **justify** your choice of party. **Explain** why you did not choose the other parties.
3. Briefly **explain** the process involved in standing as a candidate for election.
4. Make a spider diagram to show the various methods a candidate and their supporters may use during an election campaign.
5. Which method of campaigning **do you think** is the most effective and why?

Election day

- Scottish elections usually take place on the first Thursday in May of a specific year.

- Voting normally takes place at a polling station between the hours of 7am–10pm. Polling stations are usually primary schools or community centres which are easy for local constituents to access.

- Those who are eligible to vote are listed on the electoral register and receive their polling card in advance of election day (see page 58 for more information about registering to vote).

- Voters should take their polling card to the polling station, where their name will be checked on the electoral register by the polling clerk (though taking the card is not mandatory, it can help speed-up the process).

- The polling clerk gives the voter their ballot paper(s). You cast your vote in secret in a polling booth.

- Voters go into the polling booth and mark their preference(s) on the ballot paper.

- Ballot papers should then be placed in a locked ballot box.

- Once the polling stations have closed the ballot boxes are taken to the town hall where they are opened and counted.

- Once all the votes have been counted and verified the winner is announced.

📖 Word bank

- **Polling card**
A card sent to all registered voters shortly before an election. The card gives information about the election and the voter such as the date of the election, the location of the polling station, opening and closing times and the name, address and electoral number of the voter.

- **Polling clerk**
A person who checks the electoral register to confirm that the voter is eligible to vote in a certain polling station.

- **Verified**
Confirmed as correct.

Figure 4.9: *Locked ballot boxes being taken away for counting*

🔵 Activity

Show your knowledge

Create a story board showing a step-by-step guide to what happens on election day. You should include words and pictures to show that you fully understand the process.

Referenda

Voting in a referendum is another way to participate in politics in Scotland. A referendum is a vote that is held when the government wants to find out what the electorate thinks about a particular subject. Voters are usually asked to respond either 'yes' or 'no' to the question being asked. The outcome of the referendum will depend upon how the majority of voters voted.

The Alternative Vote (AV) referendum, as part of the Conservative-Liberal Democrat coalition agreement, was held on Thursday 5th May 2011. The referendum asked the UK electorate whether they wanted to change the electoral system used to vote for Westminster MPs from the present FPTP system to the AV method. AV is a preferential voting system in which voters rank the candidates in order of preference rather than voting for a single candidate. The proposal to introduce AV was rejected by the electorate with 68% of voters voting no.

Think point

If you could have participated in the AV referendum, what way do you think you would have voted and why?

Summary

In this chapter you have learned:

- the meaning of participation
- the rights and responsibilities associated with taking part in elections
- the main political parties in Scotland
- how to stand as a candidate for election
- about election campaigns in Scotland
- how to vote in elections

Learning Summary

Now that you have finished the **Participation** chapter, complete a self-evaluation of your knowledge and skills to assess what you have understood. Use the checklist below and its traffic lights to draw up a revision plan to help you improve in the areas you identified as red or amber.

- I can explain what participation means.
- I can state the various ways people can participate in a democracy.
- I can list those who do and do not have the right to vote in elections.
- I can describe the rights associated with voting in elections.

- I can explain what is meant by voter turnout.

- I can suggest why voter turnout is not as high as it was in the past.

- I can state the arguments for and against compulsory voting.

- I can outline why people should use their right to vote.

- I can explain what a political party is.

- I can list the main political parties in Scotland.

- I can explain what an ideology is.

- I can describe the political spectrum that exists in Scotland.

- I can explain what a manifesto is.

- I can describe the manifesto policies of the main political parties during the 2011 Scottish Parliament election.

- I can explain the process involved when standing as a candidate for election.

- I can describe the methods used by candidates and their supporters during an election campaign.

- I can outline the process that takes place on election day.

- I can explain what a referendum is.

Examples

In Modern Studies it is essential that you are able to back up any point you make with relevant evidence. When you are considering the statements above try to think of relevant examples for each response. You may wish to note these examples under each statement in your revision notes.

5 Influence

What you will learn in this chapter

In this section students will make a choice of a group which influences decision makers on a Scottish basis. They will choose either trade unions OR pressure groups OR the media. We will focus here on trade unions and pressure groups.

- The purpose of pressure groups and trade unions.
- The aims of pressure groups and trade unions.
- The methods pressure groups and trade unions use to influence decision making in Scotland.

Pressure groups

> **Make the Link**
>
> You may have studied pressure groups in Business Management and/or History.

A pressure group is a group of individuals working together in pursuit of a common cause. Pressure groups try to influence public policy through their actions in support of that cause.

> **GO! Activity**
>
> **Discuss**
> With your shoulder partner, create a list of the different pressure groups you have heard of, e.g. the World Wide Fund for Nature (WWF).

Members of pressure groups join together because they have similar views on a specific issue or a range of issues linked to a theme. Pressure groups are not political parties and do not want to become the government. It can be difficult for individuals on their own to influence policy and political decisions and a group of like-minded people working together can have more impact and can be more successful in getting their concerns heard by the government, the general public, and the mass media.

There has been a dramatic increase in the number and range of pressure groups in recent years. There are many reasons why this happened; one main reason may be because more people have chosen to become politically active through their membership of groups, organisations and associations of various kinds rather than through voting and joining political parties. Pressure groups include registered charities, trade unions, faith-based organisations, professional and business associations, and community groups.

Figure 5.1: *The World Wide Fund for Nature (WWF) logo*

Types of pressure groups

Pressure groups can differ greatly from one to another; one way is that they can be local, national or even international in their focus. As a result of this, pressure groups vary in size from very small groups with only a handful of members who want to deal with a local issue, to very large organisations with millions of members all over the world.

Local pressure groups

Group	Aims
Aberdeen Wildlife Trust	Inform the citizens of Aberdeen on wildlife topics or particular species through workshops and events.
Glasgow Against ATOS	Committed to opposing the Department of Work and Pension's treatment of sick and disabled people through the Work Capability Assessments carried out by the French company ATOS.
Friends of the River Kelvin (FORK)	A society formed to build public awareness and commitment to the care and maintenance of the Kelvin and its tributaries.

Figure 5.2: *Pressure groups can focus locally or globally*

Communities Opposed to New Coal at Hunterston (CONCH)   [CASE STUDY]

Communities Opposed to New Coal at Hunterston (CONCH) had been campaigning since 2009. 22,000 people lodged objections to Ayrshire Power's plans for a coal-fired station at Hunterston making it the most unpopular proposal in Scottish planning history. The group used various methods to draw attention to their cause: they contacted MSPs, used the mass media and local events such as Sand Art to create giant sand drawings in support of the campaign. In June 2013, Ayrshire Power formally withdrew their plans for a coal-fired Power Station at Hunterston.

Figure 5.3: *Sand Art created to support the CONCH campaign*

Figure 5.4: *The Scottish Campaign for Nuclear Disarmament logo, also used internationally as a peace sign*

National pressure groups

Group	Aims
Shelter Scotland	A charity that works to alleviate the distress caused by homelessness and bad housing.
Scottish Society for the Prevention of Cruelty to Animals (SSPCA)	Scotland's animal welfare charity encourages kindness to animals. Their aim is to prevent cruelty through education, investigate abuse, rescue animals in distress and find animals new homes.
Scottish Campaign for Nuclear Disarmament (SCND)	The SCND works for the abolition of all nuclear weapons in Britain as a step toward the global elimination of these weapons of mass destruction.

International pressure groups

Group	Aims
Greenpeace	Aims to defend the natural world and promote peace by investigating, exposing and confronting environmental abuse, and championing environmentally responsible solutions.
Amnesty International	A campaigning organisation whose purpose it is to protect people wherever justice, fairness, freedom and truth are denied.
Save the Children	The organisation works in 120 countries to save children's lives. They fight for children's rights and to help them fulfil their potential.

Hint

There are many pressure groups in Scotland who aim to influence political decision making (especially because the Scottish Parliament has a number of devolved powers). Therefore, UK-based pressure groups will often have a designated Scottish section that deals with issues in Scotland.

Make the Link

In Geography you may have looked at these international pressure groups, or ones similar to them.

Activity

Research
Use the internet to research examples of other local, national and international pressure groups.

Figure 5.5: *Amnesty International supporters marching for their cause*

DAILY NEWS

world - business - finance - lifestyle - travel - sport

Philippines Typhoon Appeal

A significant contribution to the Philippines Typhoon Appeal is to be made by the Scottish government.

Following the devastating typhoon that ripped through the Philippines (in 2013) and the launch of the appeal by the Disasters Emergency Committee (DEC), External Affairs Secretary Fiona Hyslop has announced that the Scottish government will donate £600,000.

Following the announcement Ms Hyslop said:

"The devastating pictures from the Philippines can't fail to touch the hearts of all who see them. The Scottish Cabinet discussed the situation this morning and today we are pledging a donation of £600,000 to the Disasters Emergency Committee in Scotland's Philippines Typhoon Appeal."

"The Scottish government funding will help our aid agencies support those affected including through the supply of clean water and medical supplies – essential if we are to avoid disease getting hold and making a tragic situation even worse."

"As well as the Scottish government's donation I urge the people of Scotland to dig

Figure 5.6: *Damage caused by the typhoon*

deep to help support our aid agencies responding to the devastation caused by Typhoon Haiyan."

Chair of the Disasters Emergency Committee in Scotland, Norman McKinley, said,

"We greatly welcome the Scottish government's support, which will enable us to make a huge difference to so many people who have lost everything overnight"

[Source: http://news.scotland.gov.uk/News/Hyslop-announces-600-000-funding-for-Philippines-612.aspx]

Insider and outsider groups

Insider groups are regularly consulted by the government and operate inside the decision making process. The degree of how regularly they are consulted, on what matters, and how seriously their opinions are taken varies depending on the group. For example, MENCAP Scotland – a group representing people with mental health disabilities – works closely with the Scottish government to make an impact on mental health issues or policies.

Outsider groups have to work outside the governmental decision-making process and, therefore, have fewer opportunities to determine the direction of policy. For example, PETA Scotland – People for the Ethical Treatment of Animals (Scotland) – aims to protect the rights of all animals. Through public education, research, special events, celebrity involvement and protest campaigns, the group tries to get the Scottish government to create new legislation.

Figure 5.7: *PETA logo*

Insider groups	Outsider groups
Access to policymakers	No/limited access to policymakers
Usually have a high profile	May have a low profile
Have mainstream goals	Radical goals
Tend to have financial stability	Tend to have a lack of financial stability
Strong leadership	Strong grassroots support

Cause and interest groups

Cause (also known as promotional) groups are made up of individuals who share similar concerns about particular issues with the aim of changing opinions and attitudes. For example, ASH Scotland – Action on Smoking and Health (Scotland) – work to eliminate the harm caused by tobacco.

Interest (also known as sectional) groups are concerned with the interests of a particular section of society and usually represent the interests of their members, such as professional organisations and trade unions. For example, the FBU Scotland – Fire Brigades Union (Scotland) – is the voice of firefighters and the fire and rescue service in Scotland.

> **🧠 Think point**
>
> Some pressure groups prefer to be outsider rather than insider groups. Why do you think this is the case?

Cause groups	Interest groups
Promote a cause	Defend interests
Open membership	Closed membership
Focus on concerns that affect the masses – a group for the people	Focus on concerns that affect specific groups – a group for certain individuals
Benefit others or wider society	Benefits members only
Members usually make donations	Members usually pay fees

? Questions

1. **Explain** what a pressure group is and why they exist.
2. Outline the reasons why people might join a pressure group.
3. Create a spider diagram to show examples of the pressure groups you know of. Divide the diagram into three focus areas: local, national and international.
4. **Describe** what an insider pressure group is. Include an **example** of a Scottish insider pressure group in your answer.
5. **Describe** what an outsider pressure group is. Include an **example** of a Scottish outsider pressure group in your answer.
6. Create a table to show the main differences between insider and outsider groups.
7. **Explain** what a cause group is. Include an **example** of a Scottish cause pressure group in your answer.
8. **Explain** what an interest group is. Include an **example** of a Scottish interest pressure group in your answer.
9. Create a table to show the main differences between cause and interest groups.

🧠 Hint

Not all groups fit neatly into these categories, and some groups fit into more than one category.

🔵 Activity

Show your knowledge
Using the pressure groups you have researched, identify whether they are insider or outsider groups, and whether they are cause or interest groups.

Methods used by pressure groups

The methods pressure groups use tend to reflect the area they are interested in. A pressure group generally tries to gain as much publicity as possible for its cause. Attention from the mass media can encourage more people to join and provide the pressure group with the ability to draw direct attention to their cause.

⚫ Make the Link

You may have learned about the mass media in Media Studies.

Figure 5.8: *Attracting TV and other media to a cause helps it to reach a wider audience*

Demonstration

Pressure groups can make direct contact with the public by inviting members to march through the streets holding signs and banners, handing out leaflets and using loudspeakers publicising their aims. If lots of people attend the event this normally attracts widespread media coverage and can influence the government.

Figure 5.9 *Pro-independence campaigners in Edinburgh*

Figure 5.10 *There are various forms of mass media available to pressure groups*

Figure 5.11 *Petitions are a useful tool in showing public feelings*

For example, in September 2013 thousands of pro-independence campaigners marched through the streets of Edinburgh in support of an independent Scotland.

Using the mass media

Due to developments in the mass media such as the internet, social networking and 24/7 news, pressure groups have the opportunity to use the mass media to great advantage. Increasingly, pressure groups are using social networking sites such as Facebook and Twitter to build support for their cause and put pressure on decision makers. Using a hashtag when campaigning on Twitter makes it easier for people who might be interested in the cause to find information about it. Pressure groups may even use a well-known celebrity to publicise their cause.

For example, in June 2013 the Equality Network created a new campaign video called 'It's Time' to encourage people to back the introduction of same-sex marriage in Scotland. The video features Scottish celebrities including Brian Cox, Lorraine Kelly, Alan Cumming and The Proclaimers.

Pressure groups that have the support of the media and the wider public have more chance of pressurising the government into taking the pressure group's advice. If the government is seen to be responding to public opinion they may gain support from the media.

For example, Citizens Advice Scotland was allocated additional funding from the Scottish government to help them cope with the increasing demand for help from hard-hit families as a result of Westminster's cuts. Some Scottish newspapers supported the government's decision.

Petitions

Pressure groups will try to convince the relevant policy maker about the strength of public feeling on an issue by collecting as many signatures as possible from people who support their cause. The Scottish Parliament encourages responsible participation in the democratic process and the use of the Public Petitions Committee in the Scottish Parliament has been very popular. In Scotland, you only need one signature to introduce a petition, whereas in Westminster, you need 100,000. E-petitions are carried out entirely online.

Between 1999 and 2006, 449 petitions were submitted to the Scottish Parliament Public Petitions Committee with only one signature.

Leaflets and posters

The creation of promotional materials draws attention to a campaign and can persuade ordinary people to take action themselves, e.g. by writing to the relevant representative. For example, groups such as the SSPCA and Sense Over Sectarianism use controversial and powerful images on their posters to get attention for their cause.

Contact or lobby representatives

Representatives, such as MSPs or MPs, meet with members of the pressure group and listen to the arguments being put forward. The representative may be able to influence decision makers. They could also attempt to introduce laws that support the aims of the pressure group.

Shelter Scotland's 'Banish the Bedroom Tax Monster' Campaign involves lobbying the Scottish government to express their opposition of the under-occupancy charges applied to those who claim housing benefit and have a spare bedroom(s).

Professional lobbyists

Professional lobbyists are people whose job it is to contact government decision makers and persuade them to change the law. For example, wealthy pressure groups like the British Dental Association (Scotland) can employ people to do this. The lobbyist does not have to necessarily agree with the cause for which they are lobbying.

Public meetings

Groups attempt to get as many people as possible to attend meetings publicising the aims of the pressure group. Pressure groups can invite influential people to speak in support of their cause at the meeting.

Both the 'Better Together' and 'Yes Scotland' campaigns organised public meetings across Scotland in the build up to the independence referendum.

Figure 5.12: *Professional lobbyist*

Figure 5.13 *Pressure groups use public meetings to voice their opinions*

Direct action

This is action that affects the government or the running of the country. Direct action is often (but not necessarily) illegal. Stunts, strikes, blockades, boycotts and sit-ins are all examples of direct action.

The Scottish Campaign for Nuclear Disarmament (SCND) often holds blockades at Faslane naval base.

Show your knowledge
Create a mind map to show the various types of action that pressure groups can take. You should research further **examples** of pressure group actions in order to exemplify each of the methods.

Figure 5.14 *Protests are common at Faslane*

GO! Activity

Research
Use the internet to research a pressure group you are interested in. Create a poster/ leaflet/ social networking page that can be used to inform the general public about the group. Include information about the following:

1. The pressure group's name.
2. When the group was formed.
3. Why it was set up.
4. What it aims to achieve and whether it has been successful.
5. Real **examples** of the methods the pressure group uses.

⚙ Hint

The founding principles of the Scottish Parliament were discussed on page 20.

Figure 5.15: *Freedom of expression*

Rights and responsibilities of pressure groups

The founding principles of the Scottish Parliament give pressure groups the opportunity to directly influence government policy, this is because the Scottish Parliament encourages responsible participation in the democratic process.

Pressure groups have rights and responsibilities when participating in the democratic process. Their rights allow them to use certain methods to make the public and government aware of their views, but these rights are also balanced by responsibilities. The responsibilities pressure groups have usually determine the way they can behave in particular situations.

The right to freedom of expression is regarded as one of the most important human rights. Many of the rights that pressure groups have are based on the principle of freedom of expression.

Rights	Responsibilities
The right to free assembly (protest) allows group members to meet to discuss and promote their views.	The organiser needs to tell the police in writing six days before a protest is held. The police must be informed of the date and time of the protest, the route, and the names and addresses of the organisers. Protesters must behave within the law.
The right to criticise (comment on negatively) the government or other organisations.	Not to tell lies about people or organisations. If the group is slanderous (tells lies that will harm the reputation of another) it is going against defamation laws and could be sued.
The right to promote their cause using methods such as the mass media, leaflets, posters etc.	To give accurate information. If the laws of libel are broken then the pressure group can find itself in trouble. Misrepresenting their cause can damage a pressure group's reputation.

📖 Word bank

• **Defamation**

The action of damaging the good reputation of someone.

• **Libel**

A false publication, as in writing, print, signs, or pictures, that damages a person's reputation.

❓ Questions

1. **Explain, in detail,** four methods used by pressure groups to influence the Scottish government. Include **examples** of Scottish pressure groups in your answer.

2. Which method **do you think** is the most effective way to influence the Scottish government? Give reasons to **support** your answer.

3. Which method **do you think** is the least effective way to influence the Scottish government? Give reasons to **support** your answer.

4. **Describe, in detail,** the rights and responsibilities that pressure groups have.

5. 'Pressure groups are good for democracy'.

   Give one reason to **support** and one reason to **oppose** this statement.

GO! Activity

Show your knowledge

Choose a pressure group that you are interested in. Write a letter to a person of power and influence, asking them to support the pressure group. For example you could write to:

- the head of the local council or a relevant local councillor if your issue is a local matter
- the First Minister or a relevant MSP if your issue is a devolved matter
- the Prime Minister or a relevant MP if your issue is a reserved matter

Remember the different powers that each representative has. You could ask them to introduce a Members' Bill, or ask a question at Question Time or simply post a tweet in support of the pressure group.

Before you start writing, plan the organisation of your letter, ensure you use the correct layout. Use the table below to help you.

Technique	Purpose	Aim of writing
To persuade	To give reasons to persuade others to think again/change their actions.	To persuade the government to stop taking a particular action.
To argue	To weigh up what's fair and unfair in different situations.	To explain your reasons for wanting the government to end a particular action: do this through the use of counter-arguments.
To advise	To suggest what others should do	To offer sympathy, explaining that you want to stop others from feeling the way they do; to advise them on how they might use their experiences to help others.

Trade unions

Trade unions are organisations that aim to represent employees by helping them to achieve common goals and to protect themselves against employers. Trade unions communicate with employers about a large range of issues such as pay, health and safety, pensions, and discrimination. Around 30% of workers in Scotland (and the UK) belong to a trade union and this covers a wide array of professions from cleaners to footballers.

Figure 5.16: *Trade unions allow common goals to be met*

GO! Activity

Discuss

With your shoulder partner, create a list of the different trade unions you know of. An example might be the National Union of Rail, Maritime and Transport Workers (RMT).

Examples of trade unions include:

- Unison Scotland is Scotland's largest public service union. It represents staff who provide public services, such as NHS workers etc.
- Scottish Unite represents members from every type of workplace, such as construction and IT
- The Educational Institute of Scotland (EIS) is the largest teaching union in Scotland
- Equity Scotland is a trade union for professional performers and creative practitioners in Scotland

To participate in trade union activities workers need to join a union appropriate to their profession and pay a membership subscription. Members can then:

- attend union meetings in the workplace and discuss issues such as pay and working conditions. Collective bargaining may then take place.
- ask the union advice when they have a problem in the workplace, e.g. if they are being asked to do a job they are not trained for
- promote equal rights and fight discrimination that may exist for some members, such as women and ethnic minorities
- vote in ballots held by the union. Sometimes these ballots will be to decide whether or not the union should take industrial action. At other times the ballot may be to elect a new representative within the union such as a shop steward
- stand as a candidate in an election to become a union representative, also known as a shop steward
- take part in a form of industrial action, such as a strike
- receive legal advice and representation on professional matters and benefits such as discounts from specific companies

Why do some people decide not to join a union?

- An individual might be self-employed or work for their family business and have no need to join a union.
- Some employers have non-union agreements forbidding workers from joining a union.
- The cost of joining and remaining a member could be too high, especially for low-paid or part-time workers.
- Some well-paid workers do not see the point as they are happy with their conditions of employment.
- Employees who are not members can enjoy the benefits of pay rises and better working conditions negotiated by the unions without joining.

Make the Link

You may have learned about trade unions in History.

Word bank

- **Collective bargaining**
A process of negotiations (talks) between employers and the union aimed at reaching agreements on pay and working conditions.

Figure 5.17 *RMT logo*

Figure 5.18 *UNISON logo*

incorporating the Variety Artistes' Federation

Figure 5.19 *Equity logo*

Figure 5.20: *Striking is one option open to union members*

GO! Activity

Homework

Conduct a survey of adults who work to find out how many of them are a member of a trade union. You should also find out what union they are a member of and their reason for being part/not part of a union. Display your results in a suitable way, such as a table or bar graph.

Make the Link

In Maths/Numeracy you should have learned how display information in graphs.

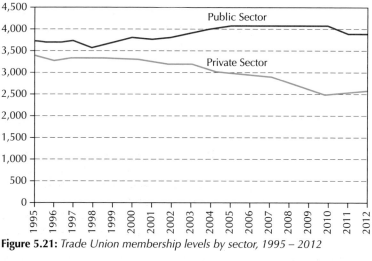

Figure 5.21: *Trade Union membership levels by sector, 1995 – 2012*

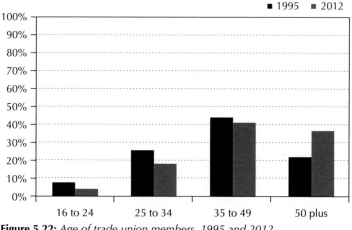

Figure 5.22: *Age of trade union members, 1995 and 2012*

Word bank

• **Public sector**

The part of the economy concerned with providing basic government services, such as the police, teachers etc.

• **Private sector**

The part of the economy run by private individuals or groups, usually as a means of enterprise for profit.

GO! Activity

Use your skills

Trade union membership has changed over the years. Using the information in Figures 5.21 and 5.22, make **conclusions** about each of the following:

- trade union membership levels in the public sector between 1995 to 2012

- trade union membership levels in the private sector between 1995 to 2012

- the age of trade union members between 1995-2012

What is industrial action?

If a trade union believes that its members are not being treated fairly and negotiations with employers are not working then it might decide to take industrial action. Industrial action is any action taken by employees to put pressure on employers. Trade union members have the right to vote on whether or not to take industrial action. If a majority of members agree then action is usually taken by all members. However, if an individual member decides they do not want to take part in industrial action then they do not have to. Taking industrial action shows the general public that a dispute (disagreement) is going on between the employer and the trade union.

Actions taken by trade unions

Type of industrial action	Description
Go slow	Employees perform their duties, but at a slower pace. By doing this they aim to reduce productivity and cost the employer money. This is one of the least disruptive forms of industrial action but it may to lead to further action being taken. In 2009 thousands of postal workers deliberately took their time in sorting the mountain of mail that had built-up following strikes.
Overtime ban	Employees limit their working time to the hours specified in their contracts, refusing to work any overtime. Because there is no breach of contract by the employees there is less chance of disciplinary action by the employer. An overtime ban can have a significant impact on industries that normally operate outside of regular office hours, such as emergency services, public transport, or retail. The Public and Commercial Services Union (PCS) conducted an overtime ban from 1st July to 31st August 2013. The industrial action was agreed when members were balloted. The aim was to cause maximum problems for the employer unless they agreed to negotiations with the union. See case study below for further action taken by the PCS union.
Work to rule	Employees do no more than the minimum required by the rules of their contract which has the effect of slowing down production. This action is less susceptible to disciplinary action as employees are simply obeying the rules. For example, a teacher who is working to rule may refuse to supervise the canteen at lunchtime if it is not written into their contract that they have to do this. See the newspaper article on page 85 for more information on work to rule.

(continued)

Type of industrial action	Description
Strike	This involves a work stoppage caused by the mass refusal of employees to perform their duties. Strike action can be short term, usually one day; selective, only one group within an organisation is taking part; or long term, until the end of the dispute. The longer a strike goes on the more damaging effect it has on employers.
	A strike is the most serious form of industrial action. Workers usually form a picket line outside of their workplace during the strike in order to persuade fellow employees and the public to support them by not crossing the picket line. During an official strike employees are not paid.
	For example, in 2012 members of the Prison Officers Association in Scotland went on strike and protested outside their prisons to show their opposition to the pensionable age being raised to 68 years.

Figure 5.23: *Striking workers form a picket line outside their workplace*

Make the Link

The Police Act, 1919 outlawed police membership of unions and industrial action. You will learn more about the police in Unit 2.

Word bank

• **Picket line**

A boundary established by workers on strike, especially at the entrance to the place of work, which others are asked not to cross.

• **Keynote speech**

A speech addressing the main issues.

Trade unions need to be able to influence decision makers in order to achieve their aims and represent their members. They can do this in a number of ways which can be similar to the methods used by pressure groups:

- trade unions can lobby politicians. This is when they directly try to persuade MSPs to make decisions in their members' favour. Trade unions such as the EIS can sometimes achieve success for their members by lobbying the government. Additionally, trade unions can sponsor a MSP. This is when they donate money to a politician they think is favourable to their cause. This can help a MSP in an election and aid the trade union's cause
- trade unions can also organise demonstrations where keynote speeches are made to rally support. For example, teaching unions such as the EIS and Scottish Secondary Teachers Association (SSTA) have organised large demonstrations to show their opposition to government budget cuts
- trade unions can create petitions, including e-petitions, and submit them to the Petitions Committee. Ultimately, actions taken by trade unions are aimed at attracting media attention in support of their cause

? Questions

1. What is a trade union?
2. Why do employees join trade unions?
3. Why do some employees choose not to join a trade union?
4. **Explain** what is meant by industrial action?
5. Create a spider diagram to show the main types of industrial action.
6. **Describe, in detail,** the main types of industrial action that can be taken by trade unions. Include some **examples** of Scottish trade unions in your answer.

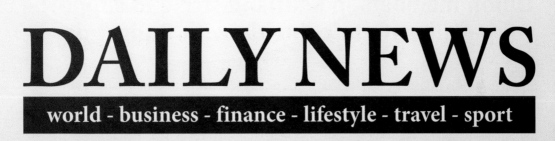

DAILY NEWS

world - business - finance - lifestyle - travel - sport

Secondary school teachers vote for work to rule over pension plan dispute

Members of a teachers' union will work to rule from mid-May to protest against changes to pension plans.

The Scottish Secondary Teachers Association (SSTA) says its members will only work for their contracted 35 hours a week from Monday, May 14.

But general secretary Ann Ballinger said there would be no teacher walk-outs and no school closures during the action.

Ms Ballinger said: "Teachers are paid for 35 hours. The tasks they are instructed to undertake must be capable of being completed within that timescale.

"SSTA members will be adhering to that timescale and to the principle of a fair day's work for a fair day's pay."

A ballot found that 85% of the union's members who voted were in favour of the industrial action.

A Scottish Government spokesman said: "Discussions with trade unions, including SSTA, and employer group representatives on long-term reforms of public sector pensions have begun.

"These discussions need to be carefully considered but also mindful of the time constraints we face as a result of the limitations set by the UK Government."

[Source: http://news.stv.tv/scotland/ 97568-secondary-school-teachers-vote-for-work-to-rule-over-pension-plan-dispute/]

? Questions

1. What type of industrial action did members of the SSTA take in 2012?
2. What did this action involve union members doing?
3. Why were union members taking industrial action?
4. What was the union doing on behalf of its members?

DAILY NEWS

world - business - finance - lifestyle - travel - sport

Union members in Scotland strike in support of pay dispute to coincide with Budget day

Workers at the National Museum of Scotland, Ministry of Defence and Edinburgh Sheriff Court were among the strikers.

Striking union members in Scotland have come out in "strong" support of a dispute about pay, pensions and working conditions.

Timed to mark Budget day at Westminster, the action will hit Scottish government, parliament and tax offices, the Public and Commercial Services (PCS) union said.

About 85 per cent of members at HM Revenue and Customs office in East Kilbride were taking part in the 24-hour strike, according to PCS Scotland officer Joy Dunn.

"Anecdotally, we're hearing it's been very strong across the country. We're getting encouraging feedback from picket lines," she said.

The union, which has about 30,000 members in Scotland, said up to 250,000 workers across the UK are expected to join the walkout.

As well as core government agencies, the strike involves workers at job centres, border patrols at ports and airports, and courts.

Members of the PCS Union hold a strike outside the Glasgow passport office.

Some MSPs supporting the strike refused to enter Holyrood which continued with ordinary parliamentary business.

Elaine Smith, Labour MSP for Coatbridge and Chryston, said: "PCS's strike today is particularly pertinent on the day George Osborne will outline more austerity measures that will make the rich richer and everyone else poorer.

"The Labour and trade union movement has fought for decades for the rights of workers and we should not now allow current Westminster and Holyrood governments to take those rights away."

Green party co-leader Patrick Harvie said: "SNP ministers have imposed a further real-terms pay cut which, along with increased pension contributions, means yet further raids on the pockets of people working to deliver the public services we all depend on.

"The Scottish government likes to blame the UK coalition but the truth is we have the power in Scotland to end this unfair squeeze."

The Holyrood government estimated that 1283 workers from their core and main agencies are on strike, which is about 18 per cent of government staff.

"Main Scottish government and agency buildings have remained open and arrangements are in place to ensure essential business continues," a spokeswoman for the government said.

Business in the Welsh Assembly was cancelled because Labour and Plaid Cymru members would not cross a picket line.

[Source: http://www.dailyrecord.co.uk/news/scottish-news/union-members-scotland-strike-support-1774515]

? Questions

1. What type of industrial action did members of the PCS union take in 2013?
2. Why were union members taking industrial action?
3. How many members of the PCS took industrial action?
4. Name some of the different government agencies whose workers took industrial action.

Rights and responsibilities of trade unions

Trade unions have rights that they are entitled to but they also have responsibilities which they must adhere to. Trade unions and their members have a responsibility to act within the law at all times.

Figure 5.24: *Rights are only guaranteed if the trade union fulfils their responsibilities*

Rights	Responsibilities
To ballot members to see if the majority of members are in favour of taking industrial action.	To hold a secret ballot and inform members of the outcome. Once the decision is confirmed the union must inform the employer. Advance notice must be given in the outcome of a strike being held. In October 2013 university staff across Scotland went on strike over a pay dispute. The industrial action was co-ordinated among the University and College Union, Unison and Unite.
To take industrial action in order to protect the rights of the workers.	To ensure that all forms of industrial action are peaceful and within the law. In October 2013 pupil support assistants working for Glasgow City Council went on strike over a dispute about extra duties such as healthcare and the administration of medicine. The pupil support assistants held a peaceful demonstration outside of the Glasgow City chambers.
To form a picket line outside the workplace. The Code of Practice on picketing says usually there should be no more than six people outside an entrance to a workplace	Must not break the rule around lawful picketing. For example, pickets must not prevent people from going to work or doing their usual work if they want to do so.
To try to attract new trade union members.	Not to pressurise anyone into joining a trade union. No employer or employment agency may require an employee to join a trade union or be a member of a specific trade union.
Trade unions can ask employers to make changes to employees' conditions of employment.	Trade unions must not make unreasonable demands, e.g. they should not ask for a 100% pay rise for employees. Scottish local government trade unions, such as the GMB and Unison, have asked for all councils to pay staff the Living Wage (£7.65). The unions have launched a campaign for a £1-an-hour local government pay rise that would see all council employees paid the Living Wage.

The work of a shop steward

One of the most important people in a trade union is the shop steward (sometimes called union representative). The shop steward is an employee who has been elected by the union members to represent them. The shop

Figure 5.25: *The shop steward can accompany the employee to meetings with management*

steward is elected by a secret ballot. He/she is the first person a member will go to in order to seek help or advice about a problem at work.

Shops stewards represent members by helping to find solutions to their problems. When union members have a problem it is the shop steward they turn to. Shop stewards might need to help sort out problems with issues such as equality in the workplace. The shop steward will take the problem up with the employer on behalf of the members or the shop steward will advise members on how to take the matter further.

The shop steward can represent the member during meetings with the employer. This could involve dealing with worker disciplinary hearings, accompanying workers during management interviews, negotiating with employers over worker concerns such as pay, overtime, holidays and health and safety, and finally raising issues with management formally or informally. The member can request that their shop steward be present to aid them. If a member needs legal advice they can receive this by contacting the union.

The shop steward will attend union meetings and share information with members. Meetings are usually held at the union headquarters where union matters are discussed and voted on. He/she will let members know what was discussed by holding a meeting, distributing leaflets and newsletters, sending emails, or by maintaining the union notice board, e.g. putting up posters etc. Members have the right to approach the shop steward to discuss union meetings.

Shop stewards continually try to recruit new members. Increasing and maintaining trade union membership is important to ensure the union continues to support its members. A shop steward can do this by actively persuading people to join the union, distributing leaflets and putting up posters, and encouraging membership around the workplace.

? Questions

1. **Explain, in detail,** the rights and responsibilities of trade unions.
2. **Describe** the ways in which employees can participate in how their trade union is run.
3. What is a shop steward?
4. How do union members choose their shop steward?
5. What problems might a member go to a shop steward with?
6. How can the shop steward represent the members of the union?

GO! Activity

Research
Use the internet to research a trade union you are interested in. Create a poster/leaflet/social networking page that can be used to inform the general public about the group. It should include the following information:

1. The trade union's name.
2. When the group was formed.
3. Who the group represents.
4. The aims of the trade union.
5. Real examples of the industrial action the trade union has used.
6. An overall **conclusion** as to how well the trade union represents its members.

Summary

In this chapter you have learned:

- The purpose of pressure groups and trade unions
- The aims of pressure groups and trade unions
- The methods pressure groups and trade unions use to influence decision making in Scotland

Learning Summary

Now that you have finished the **Influence** chapter, complete a self-evaluation of your knowledge and skills to assess what you have understood. Use the checklist below and its traffic lights to draw up a revision plan to help you improve in the areas you identified as red or amber.

- I can outline the purpose of pressure groups.

- I can explain the aims of different pressure groups.

- I can describe the different methods pressure groups can use to achieve their aims and influence the Scottish government.

- I can describe the rights and responsibilities of pressure groups when trying to influence decision making in Scotland.

- I can outline the purpose of trade unions.

- I can explain the aims of different trade unions.

- I can describe the different methods trade unions can use to achieve their aims and influence the Scottish government.

- I can describe the rights and responsibilities of trade unions when trying to influence decision making in Scotland.

- I can explain the ways shop stewards can represent their members.

Examples

In Modern Studies it is essential that you are able to back up any point you make with relevant evidence. When you are considering the statements above try to think of relevant examples for each response. You may wish to note these examples under each statement in your revision notes.

Crime and the law in the United Kingdom

In Unit 2 there is a choice of topic; you can study **either** social inequality **or** crime and the law. In this book we will be looking at **crime and the law**.

Level 3 and 4 experiences and outcomes relevant to this topic

The Social Issues in the United Kingdom topic naturally builds upon the knowledge already secured in the third and fourth level experiences and outcomes, and in particular:

✤ I can gather information and use it to investigate. **SOC 4-16b**

✤ I can understand how the media affects attitudes. You may have covered how the media affects what people think of crime and criminals. **SOC 3-17b**

✤ I can understand the rights and responsibilities of people in society. **SOC 3-17a**

✤ I can understand how decision-making bodies (like the government) make laws. **SOC 4-18a**

Outcome and Assessment Standards

National 4 (*Social Issues in the United Kingdom*)	**National 5** (*Social Issues in the United Kingdom*)
Outcome 1	**Outcome 1**
1 Use a limited range of sources of information to make and justify decisions about social issues in the United Kingdom, focusing on either social inequality or crime and the law by:	**1 Use a range of sources of information to make and justify decisions about social issues in the United Kingdom, focusing on either social inequality or crime and the law by:**
1.1 Making a decision using up to three sources of information.	1.1 Making a decision using between two and four sources of information.
1.2 Briefly justifying a decision using evidence from up to three sources of information.	1.2 Justifying, in detail, a decision based on evidence from between two and four sources of information.
	1.3 Showing an awareness of alternative views.
Outcome 2	**Outcome 2**
2 Draw on a straightforward knowledge and understanding of social issues in the United Kingdom, focusing on either social inequality or crime and the law by:	**2 Draw on a detailed knowledge and understanding of social issues in the United Kingdom, focusing on either social inequality or crime and the law by:**
2.1 Giving straightforward descriptions of the main features of a social issue which draw on a factual knowledge of either social inequality or crime and the law.	2.1 Giving detailed descriptions of a social issue which draws on a factual and theoretical knowledge of either social inequality or crime and the law.
2.2 Giving straightforward explanations relating to a social issue in the United Kingdom.	2.2 Giving detailed explanations relating to a social issue in the United Kingdom.

Social Issues in the United Kingdom

6 What is crime?

What you will learn in this chapter

- What crime is.
- Types of crime.
- Causes of crime.
- What drives people to commit crimes.
- What impact crime has on individuals, communities and society.

What is crime?

Figure 6.1: *The scales of justice*

A crime is any action that breaks the law of the land. Laws are passed by the UK Parliament in Westminster, the Scottish Parliament in Holyrood and the European Parliament in Brussels. Any individual who does something that a law forbids has committed a crime. Anyone who commits a crime may be punished for this action.

The figures published by the Scottish government in June 2013 show that the total number of crimes recorded by the police decreased by 13% between 2011–12 and 2012–13. In 2012–13, the Scottish police recorded 273,053 crimes, 41,135 fewer crimes than in 2011–12. These figures suggest that crime is not getting any worse in Scotland.

📖 Word bank

- **Law of the land**

Historically the rules of the kingdom, but today the principles of justice in a given place.

⋮ Make the Link

You will have learned about how laws are made in Unit 1. The area of law and order is mostly devolved to the Scottish Parliament, however Westminster can make laws on some criminal activity, for example drug use.

GO! Activity

Research

Working individually, use the internet to research the crime levels in Scotland for the last ten years. Provide a written one-page report to your teacher: you may wish to include graphs and other visual ways of presenting the information. In your report you may wish to consider:

- have crime levels increased or decreased overall?
- have violent crime levels increased or decreased?
- what percentage of crimes are solved?
- are crime levels higher in certain areas in Scotland?
- any other information you think is relevant

The Scottish government website has an area dedicated to crime and justice which may help you with this (QR code below).

Figue 6.2: *Police officers on duty*

Laws

Laws are necessary in society to ensure that everyone's rights are protected and their safety is ensured. This means that laws alter over time to keep up with changes in society – something that may have been illegal in the past may now be considered acceptable by law; for example, abortion and same-sex marriages were both once illegal but today they are not.

? Questions

1. What is a crime?
2. Using **evidence** from the written information above, make a **conclusion** about crime in Scotland.
3. Name any laws that have changed recently. You may be able to think up some recent **examples** of your own.

As laws are designed to protect everyone's rights, different laws apply to different age groups. You can be held responsible for a crime as young as age eight in Scotland (although you cannot be prosecuted until age 12) so it is very important to know which laws apply to you.

GO! Activity

Research
Using the internet, investigate the laws and rights relevant to each age in Scotland. Use the information to create a leaflet for someone your age explaining the laws that are applicable to them.

You should find out the age that you can:
- be held responsible for a crime
- be sent to prison
- hold a passport
- buy a pet
- buy alcohol
- buy cigarettes
- and any other relevant law

Extension
Are there any laws that are different in Scotland to the rest of the UK?

📖 Word bank

- **Prosecuted**
When a person is formally charged with a crime and legal proceedings begin.

🧠 Think point

Do you think eight is old enough to be criminally responsible? Do you think 12 is old enough to be prosecuted for a crime? Your teacher may ask you to debate the criminal age of responsibility.

Word bank

- **Motivation**
A reason for doing something.

- **Homophobia**
Negative feelings and actions towards homosexual (gay) people.

Make the Link

In the USA many states have the death penalty, which was abolished in the UK in 1965. You may study the death penalty in RMPS.

Types of crime

The Scottish government divides crime into three main categories:

- crimes against the person
- crimes against property
- other crimes

Within these categories there are many types of crime.

Crimes against the person – violent crimes and sexual offences

Murder
Murder is the unlawful premeditated killing of one human being by another. Premeditated means the murder was planned in advance. People found guilty of murder face the most serious of punishments and will have to spend time in prison. If the murder is found to be motivated by racism, homophobia or religious beliefs then the sentence is often even more severe.

Activity

Class debate: 'The death penalty should be reintroduced in the UK'
Your teacher will now divide your class into two groups. Your challenge is to research either the Proposition (supporting the motion) or the Opposition (opposing the motion) opinion. Even if you do not agree with the viewpoint that you have been given, a good debater should be able to argue from any perspective.

You should try to find evidence and opinions from the internet on the death penalty. You may wish to focus on the following:

- have any individuals been found innocent after their death?
- do you believe in the saying 'an eye for an eye'?
- how the death penalty should be carried out

Once you have gathered your evidence, use it to make a valid point. Produce a structured paragraph which uses the 'Point, Explain, Example' structure (see page 240).

You will now all be able to make a contribution to the debate. After everyone has made a point your teacher will invite you to participate in debating the issues that have been raised. Your teacher will explain how the debate is to be structured to allow everyone the opportunity to contribute to the discussion.

Reflect on your learning
Following the debate your teacher may take a vote and may ask the class which side of the debate they now agree with. Underneath your paragraph reflect upon your class debate.

- Has the debate changed your opinion on the topic?
- Did you feel that you were able to contribute in a confident manner?
- What might you change if you were to debate in the future?

Assault

When someone is hit or beaten this is called assault. Individuals found guilty of assault will face serious punishment, including possible stays in prison or a young offenders' institution. As with murder, if the attack is found to be motivated by racism, homophobia or religious beliefs the punishment is likely to be more severe.

Figure 6.3: *The punishment for assault is often very serious*

DAILY NEWS

world - business - finance - lifestyle - travel - sport

Woman jailed for racist assault

A woman who launched a racist attack on an African woman after a four-day drinking binge has been jailed for more than two years.

Eileen Kennedy, 28, and 16-year-old Paige Bain assaulted Umaimi Musa, from Sudan, in Glasgow, on September 3 2012.

The teenager also assaulted Ms Musa's Congolese friend Mary Marandran.

As the women were sitting in a playpark they heard the phrases "F****** black African" and "F*** brings you to this country?" from one of the two accused before they were set upon.

Procurator Fiscal depute Mark Allan, told the court that Kennedy and Bain demanded Ms Musa's mobile phone.

Mr Allan said Ms Musa was punched on the head, which caused her to fall to the ground. He added: "Once on the ground, she was repeatedly punched on her head and body, her hijab was pulled from her head and she was robbed of her mobile telephone."

The incident was captured on CCTV, which was shown to the court and the camera operator alerted the police as the incident happened.

Passing a sentence of two years and six days, sheriff Kenneth Mitchell told Kennedy: "There is no place at all in a modern Scotland for this sort of behaviour."

[Source: http://news.stv.tv/west-central/208055-woman-launched-racist-attack-on-african-woman-after-drinking-binge/]

📖 **Word bank**

• **Procurator Fiscal**
A public prosecutor in the Scottish court system.

GO! Activity

Research

Research assault cases in Scotland. Try to find at least three different cases where different punishments have been given. **Do you think** prison should be an automatic sentence for racist attacks?

Figure 6.4: *It is illegal to carry a knife in Scotland*

Figure 6.5: *White-collar crime*

Rape and sexual assault

Rape is when someone forces another person to have sex against their will. A large proportion of rape victims are women but men can be victims of rape too. Sexual assault is any sexual contact that is not wanted by any individual. Punishments given out for rape are sometimes considered to be too lenient.

Knife crime

Knife crime is mentioned regularly in the media, perhaps due to the devastating effects injury caused by it can have. It is often portrayed as a type of crime usually committed by young people. Laws have been made stricter recently to try and clamp down on knife crime; for example, the maximum sentence in Scotland for anyone found guilty of carrying a knife is now five years, up from four years previously.

Domestic violence

Domestic violence applies to violent or aggressive behaviour in the context of a family or relationship. This can also include child abuse. Domestic violence may include emotional and/or physical abuse and may have long lasting impacts on an individual's life. Research has shown that on days when there are Old Firm (Celtic v Rangers) football matches there is a spike in domestic violence; often a lot of alcohol is drunk at these matches, and this suggests that there is a link between alcohol and domestic violence.

Crimes against property

Housebreaking

Housebreaking is when an individual has had to break locks or another secure device in order to access the property; the offender may then proceed to steal items from the household.

Theft

This can include anything from theft from an individual in the street or on public transport, to shoplifting. People convicted of theft face various consequences depending on the value of the goods stolen and whether the individual is a repeat offender or not.

Damage to property

Damage to property is often referred to as vandalism. Vandalism is deliberately causing damage to property or deliberately causing fires. Vandalism and anti-social behaviour can often go hand in hand.

Other crimes

Anti-social behaviour

Anti-social behaviour incorporates many elements of vandalism and fire raising. Anti-social behaviour refers to crimes that affect local communities and make people feel unsafe in their own local area, or even their homes.

White-collar crime

White-collar jobs are defined as those carried out by individuals working in office environments. Sociologist Edwin Sutherland defined white-collar crime as 'a crime committed by a person of respectability and high social status in the course of his occupation'. These are crimes such as bribery, corruption, fraud and embezzlement (embezzlement is when an individual uses someone else's money that has been entrusted to them to meet their own needs).

Blue-collar crime

Blue-collar jobs are defined as manual jobs that often involve labouring or unskilled work, and that are usually low paid. People who work in blue-collar jobs are often from deprived inner city areas that lack opportunities. Blue-collar crimes are likely to be those described above, e.g. crimes against property or crimes against the person.

Figure 6.6: *Car crimes can include vandalism and theft*

Traffic crime

Crimes such as speeding or driving without insurance are common types of traffic crime. Although some people might think these crimes are less serious than others mentioned above, they can often lead to more serious offences like death by dangerous driving. Driving whilst under the influence of alcohol or drugs is also a traffic crime.

Alcohol crime

Alcohol crimes are actions committed whilst under the influence of alcohol. Alcohol can lower inhibitions and people may do things they wouldn't normally do when sober. Drunkenness, breach of the peace, or drinking underage can all be punished by police.

Figure 6.7: *Speeding is driving faster than the speed limit*

Drug crime

All illegal drugs are put into one of three categories, according to how dangerous they are. Different drugs affect people in different ways; if a drug is not Class A that does not mean it is safe and it can still have severe consequences.

What crimes are most/least common?

Serious crimes, such as rape, assault and murder make up only 6% of all crimes recorded. White-collar crimes are also uncommon.

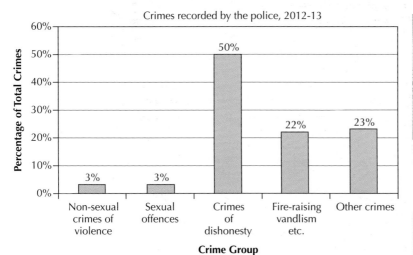

Crimes recorded by the police, 2012-13

Figure 6.9: *Crimes recorded by the police by percentage*

Figure 6.8: *Graffiti is one kind of vandalism*

The most common types of crime are those of dishonesty (i.e. offences such as burglary or robbery) with acts that damage property, such as vandalism, coming second. Young people are most likely to be involved in these types of crime due to boredom and peer pressure.

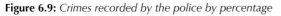

> **Hint**
>
> Youth crime might be a very interesting topic to investigate for your Added Value Unit or Assignment.

Make the Link

Drugs laws are a reserved issue. You will have learned about reserved and devolved matters in Unit 1.

Word bank

- **Intent**

Having planned to do something.

Figure 6.10: *Illegal drugs in their various forms*

Hint

The Frank website (http://www.talktofrank.com) has a lot more information on drugs.

Make the Link

In RMPS you may study the ethical and moral issues surrounding drug use.

Activity

Discuss
Read the newspaper article with a shoulder partner. **Do you think** the sentence was fair? Why might some people argue that prison was not the best option for these criminals?

Questions

1. Create a spider diagram showing the types of crime and give **examples** of each.
2. What is the difference between blue-collar crime and white-collar crime?
3. Using the **evidence** in Figure 6.9 make a **conclusion** about the most common category of crime.
4. Use Figure 6.9 to create a pie chart of crime in Scotland.

Drugs

The three categories of drugs are Class A, Class B and Class C.

Class of drug	Maximum sentence for possession
Class A These drugs have the most harmful effects. These drugs include: heroin, cocaine, ecstasy and LSD.	Up to seven years in prison with an unlimited fine.
Class B These drugs are considered less dangerous than Class A drugs but they can still be harmful. These include: speed, cannabis, mephedrone and some amphetamines.	Up to five years in prison with an unlimited fine.
Class C These drugs are considered the least dangerous in comparison to the others, but they are still illegal. These include: ketamine, GHB and some tranquilisers.	Up to two years in prison with an unlimited fine.

The above table refers to the maximum sentences that can be given for being convicted of possessing drugs; it is also possible that a lesser sentence will be given. Often the type and length of punishment that someone receives will depend on their previous criminal history. If they have no previous convictions, possession of a Class C drug may result only in a formal warning, whereas possession of a Class A or Class B drug will be much more likely to result in harsher punishments.

Different sentences apply to the offences of supplying and dealing drugs which carry much harsher punishments. The maximum sentences for intent to supply drugs are up to life in prison and/or an unlimited fine for a Class A drug, and up to 14 years in prison and/or an unlimited fine for a Class B or C drug.

Recently, there have been a lot of cases involving 'legal highs'. These are substances that have similar effects to illegal drugs but which are not controlled under the **Misuse of Drugs Act** as of yet; new substances are often not banned because there is currently not enough research about them to do so. 'Legal highs' cannot be sold as 'drugs' and so are often labelled as things like plant food to bypass the law. Although these drugs are still 'legal' that does not mean they are not dangerous. In fact, the number of deaths linked to 'legal highs' has more than doubled in the last four years.

? Questions

1. Using the table above, **explain** the different drugs classifications and the relevant punishments.
2. **Do you agree** with different classifications for different drugs?

GO! Activity

Use your skills

Use the information above and additional research to **support or oppose** the statement 'drug crimes are ruining communities all over Scotland'. You should produce two written paragraphs to support your decision.

You should think about:

- levels of drug crime in certain places
- how the crimes impact on the local community
- weather any other crimes are linked to the drug use

It may be helpful to carry out a survey in your local community. Information on how to prepare a questionnaire can be found on page 223.

DAILY NEWS

world - business - finance - lifestyle - travel - sport

Cocaine couple jailed over £100,000 haul

A mum shocked to find cocaine with a street value of more than £100,000 had been stored in her home wept today as she was jailed for two years.

Jo-Anna Wallace, 21, had begged not to be separated from her baby daughter when, at an earlier hearing, she admitted being concerned in the supply of the drug.

Unusually, judge Lord Pentland allowed her and partner Lee Middlemass, 25, to remain on bail pending sentence - so that they could spend more time with their three-month old child.

But today the judge dismissed a plea to allow her to do community service - saying the court would be failing in its duty.

"What sort of message would that send to society and, in particular, to persons further up the drug chain who might be tempted to prey on vulnerable individuals," he said.

Second-hand car dealer Middlemass, who had also admitted being concerned in the supply of cocaine, was jailed for three years and nine months.

The prosecutor said it was accepted that Middlemass was "the principal actor" and Wallace was simply allowing the flat to be used - although benefiting from any profit made by her partner.

Sentencing the couple, Lord Pentland said the motive had been money.

"Neither of you seen to have taken into account the enormous damage Class A drugs cause in communities throughout the country."

[Source: http://www.edinburghnews.scotsman.com/news/crime/cocaine-couple-jailed-over-100-000-haul-1-3146939]

Alcohol

Alcohol is a legal drug but it can also lead to health problems and offences. There are currently many laws relating to the sale and consumption of alcohol, some of which apply to the whole of the UK and others which are specific to Scotland. The Scottish government also plans to make more changes to the current laws.

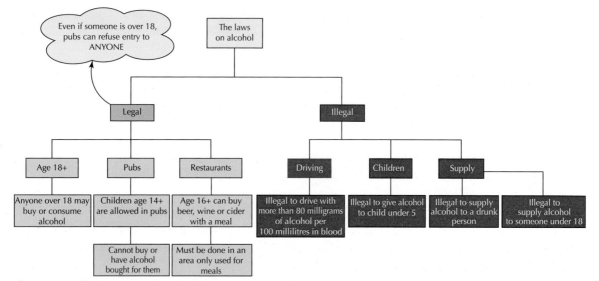

Figure 6.11: *The law surrounding alcohol*

Figure 6.12: *Alcoholic drinks come in many forms*

The **Licensing (Scotland) Act 2005** (in force 2009) stipulates the following rules around buying and selling alcohol:

- no proof, no sale – people who want to buy alcohol must be able to show proof of their age, such as a driving licence or passport

- responsible sales – people selling alcohol must not serve people who are drunk

- no 'happy hours' – prices must be set 48 hours in advance and must remain the same for 72 hours

- it is illegal to buy alcohol for under-18s – anyone doing so can be fined up to £5,000 and/or receive a three-month prison sentence

Changes to alcohol laws
Discount deals

Discount deals have already been banned in supermarkets. A provision of the **Licensing (Scotland) Act 2005,** introduced in October 2011, placed restrictions on how alcohol could be displayed and promoted. Sales of alcohol have dropped in Scottish supermarkets since the ban; many argue this will improve the health of the Scottish public. If this ban was introduced in pubs and clubs this may also decrease sales and reduce drunk and disorderly behaviour.

Minimum pricing for alcohol

The Scottish government passed the **Alcohol (Minimum Pricing) (Scotland) Act 2012** and plans to introduce a minimum price of 50p per unit of alcohol.

Arguments for minimum pricing	Arguments against minimum pricing
A higher minimum price will mean that the government will collect more tax from alcohol sales; this could help the NHS pay the bills that come about as a result of alcohol abuse, like liver disease.	The minimum price will affect those on low incomes the most. There is already a lot of tax on alcohol.
It may discourage younger drinkers from drinking too much.	A higher minimum price could encourage people to switch to dangerous illegal 'home brews' and replacement alcohol.
People may go out to a pub and spend money there, rather than drinking cheap alcohol from supermarkets in their house, meaning local businesses will profit.	It will be an easy way for supermarkets to increase their profits by increasing their prices more than the tax demands.

GO! Activity

Class debate: 'There should be a minimum price for alcohol'
Your teacher will now divide your class into two groups. Your challenge is to research either the Proposition (supporting the motion) or the Opposition (opposing the motion) opinion. Even if you do not agree with the viewpoint that you have been given, a good debater should be able to argue from any perspective.

You should try to find evidence and opinions about the topic from the internet. You may wish to focus on the following questions:
- would a minimum price for alcohol help the health of Scotland?
- would other crime levels be reduced?
- would anyone be negatively impacted by a minimum price?

Once you have gathered your evidence, use it to make a valid point. Produce a structured paragraph which uses the 'Point, Explain, Example' structure (see page 240). You will now all be able to make a contribution to the debate. After everyone has made a point your teacher will invite you to participate in debating the issues that have been raised. Your teacher will explain how the debate is to be structured to allow everyone the opportunity to contribute to the discussion.

Reflect on your learning
Following the debate your teacher may take a vote and may ask the class which side of the debate they now agree with.

Underneath your paragraph reflect upon your class debate:
- has the debate changed your opinion on the topic?
- did you feel that you were able to contribute in a confident manner?
- what might you change if you were to debate in the future?

Why do alcohol laws matter?

The Scottish government's Scottish Health Survey 2012 (http://www.scotland.gov.uk/Publications/2013/09/4693/1) reported that:

- 40% of 15 year olds drink on a weekly basis
- approximately 25% of 16–24 year-olds drink more than the recommended safe limit of 2–3 units per day for women or 3–4 units per day for men. 1 unit is roughly equal to of a half-pint of beer
- liver disease in 20–30 year olds has increased, with more deaths
- drink-driving: it is estimated that 5% of accidents and 15% of deaths are related to alcohol (2010)
- drunk and disorderly: there were 36,000 notices of drunk and disorderly in 2011
- other offences: in 2009, 938,000 offenders were estimated to be under the influence of alcohol when they committed a crime. The National Probation Service reported that 'alcohol is a factor related to a lot of crimes including many assaults, murder and rape cases (between 50 and 80%)'

? Questions

1. **Explain** the current laws relating to alcohol.
2. Using the table on page 101, summarise the arguments for and against minimum pricing of alcohol.
3. 'Alcohol is not a major factor in criminal behaviour'. Explain fully why the person who made this statement could be accused of being **selective in the use of facts**.

Road traffic offences

The Scotland Act 2012 made changes to road traffic offences, for example the Scottish Parliament now has full control of speed limits.

There are a number of road traffic offences, including driving whilst under the influence of alcohol or drugs. In 2009, 30 fatalities and 920 casualties were estimated to be due to drink-driving in Scotland. The Scottish government recently lowered the blood alcohol limit (the amount of alcohol a person is legally allowed to have in their blood whilst in charge of a vehicle) to the equivalent of approximately one pint of beer; however, many argue that it is much safer not to drink at all when driving. Below are the current road traffic laws and punishments.

Road Traffic Acts 1988 and 1991

Offence	Punishment
Driving without tax or MOT	Maximum £1,000 fine
Driving without a licence	3–6 points on driving licence Maximum £100 fine Possible disqualification
Driving without insurance	6–8 points Maximum £5,000 fine Possible disqualification

Figure 6.13: *A speed camera can capture images of cars breaking the speed limit*

Speeding on non-motorway	3–6 points Maximum £1,000 fine Possible disqualification
Speeding on motorway	3–6 points Maximum £2,500 fine Possible disqualification
Refusing breath test	4 points Maximum £1,000 fine Possible disqualification
Driving with excess of alcohol or drugs	4 points Maximum £5,000 fine Disqualification
Failure to stop and/or report an accident	5–10 points Maximum £5,000 fine Possible disqualification

Road Safety Act 2006

Offence	Punishment
Driving while using hand-held mobile phone	3 points £60 fine
Causing death while unlicensed, disqualified or uninsured	Up to 2 years in prison
Causing death by careless or inconsiderate driving	Up to 5 years in prison

DAILY NEWS

world - business - finance - lifestyle - travel - sport

Driver kills elderly woman

Gary McCourt, 49, was found guilty of killing Audrey Fyfe in Edinburgh when he hit the back wheel of her bike.

Mrs Fyfe, from Joppa, died two days after being struck by McCourt at the junction of Portobello Road and Craigentinny Avenue on August 9, 2011.

McCourt was convicted of causing death by careless driving and sentenced to 300 hours of community service and banned from driving for five years.

After McCourt was found guilty, it emerged that in 1985 he had hit and killed 22-year-old cyclist George Dalgity on Regent Road in Edinburgh, for which he served two years in jail.

[Source:http://news.stv.tv/east-central/225213-family-of-audrey-fyfe-lodge-complaint-against-drivers-sentence/]

GO! Activity

Show your knowledge
Create a poster encouraging people not to drink and drive. It should mention the punishments that can be received for drinking and driving.

📖 Word bank

• **Socialised**

The way someone learns to behave in order to fit in with their group.

• **Social scale**

The structure of a society, usually with the richest people at the top and the poorest at the bottom.

Make the Link

If you study Sociology you may have learned about the causes of crime and the arguments of nature versus nurture.

Figure 6.14: *Peer pressure can lead to disruptive behaviour*

? Questions

1. **Describe** the law on alcohol and driving.
2. **Explain** the legal consequences of driving under the influence.
3. Using the newspaper article above, summarise the case of dangerous driving and the punishment given. Give **your opinion** on whether the punishment was fair.

Causes of crime

People are responsible for their own behaviour. However, some factors in life may increase the chances of people acting irresponsibly. This relates to the way in which people are socialised and depends upon the way they are brought up, the peer group they belong to and the role models they may or may not have. Some groups in society are, however, statistically more likely to break the law than others. Those most likely to break the law and commit crime are white, working-class males under the age of 25.

Peer pressure/gang culture

The need to follow what everyone else in your group of friends is doing can be very powerful. If a person does not do what the rest of the group does they can face threats or even exclusion from the group and the fear of 'not fitting in' often encourages people to commit acts they wouldn't otherwise. For example, if an individual is involved with underage drinkers or other criminals there is a danger of giving in to the pressure of this group. In many communities there are groups of young males at the lower end of the social scale who live in areas with very high crime rates. Some youngsters will commit crime to draw attention to themselves and to win popularity within a group. Frequently, rival gangs can form and this can increase levels of crime. It is also often the case that young males in these gangs may be labelled as 'trouble-makers'; sociologists argue that treating people as criminals means that they will continue to behave like criminals because no one expects anything different. Gang related behaviour can often be linked to poverty and geographical location.

Figure 6.15: *Abandoned and burnt-out cars littering the landscape*

Poverty

Poverty remains a substantial problem in Scotland, and when this book was published in 2014 the ongoing effects of the recent recession had made this worse. A report claimed that poverty levels in Scotland in 2013 were worse than they had been at any time during the previous 30 years, with 29% of people unable to afford three or more necessities for basic living such as money for a winter coat and shoes, a warm dry home, or the ability to eat an adequate diet.

Most people living in poverty do not break the law, but some do. Poverty can lead to boredom; this may encourage some people to commit crimes to give them something to do. Poorer families may not be able to afford activities and basic material goods, meaning crime becomes more attractive as a means to meet these needs.

Some people in poverty see a future of low pay or unemployment and know this will never allow them to have a fancy car, a big house or designer clothes. This is often linked to the type of communities poorer families and individuals live in – with few amenities nearby and cut off from the areas of wealth that might offer better paid jobs, better schools and a route out of poverty. As a result poorer families often feel frustrated and trapped in their environment. One way to solve this is to turn to crime in order to pay for the lifestyle they cannot afford legally.

Many in poverty also feel socially excluded.

Social exclusion

The government describes social exclusion as what 'happens when people or places suffer from a series of problems such as unemployment, discrimination, poor skills, low incomes, poor housing, high crime, ill health and family breakdown.' As a result, individuals do not feel like they are part of society. This may be due to a lack of education leading to an inability to secure well-paid employment and may also be linked to poor facilities in certain areas.

People who feel excluded may then turn to crime as a way of dealing with their situation or as a way of being able to take part in society. Many feel that we live in a very materialistic society where status is measured by what people 'own'; it is often the case that individuals feel they need to have certain possessions such as the latest tablet computer or smartphone in order to 'fit in'. People may feel that they have to steal or commit other crimes in order to feel as good as their friends or the people around them.

Social exclusion is often linked to geographical location and poverty.

Poor role models

'How young people learn what is acceptable and normal behaviour' is referred to as socialisation. If this process breaks down then young people may turn to criminal behaviour and this can be passed down through generations, from parents to children, through learned behaviour.

Make the Link

You may cover absolute poverty in developing countries in Geography.

Word bank

- **Facilities**

Places provided for a useful purpose like schools, leisure facilities, other recreational activities and housing.

- **Materialistic**

Caring about things more than people.

Figure 6.16: *Lack of money and greed for money can lead to crime*

Word bank

• **Organised crime**

Widespread criminal activities controlled by a structured hierarchy of people.

• **Lucrative**

Producing a great deal of profit.

• **Sink estates**

A council housing estate, often on the edge of town, with high levels of poverty.

• **Deprivation**

The damaging lack of the basic necessities in life.

• **Poverty cycle**

A set of factors or events by which poverty will continue without help from outside.

• **Underachievement**

When someone's poor performance does not match their ability.

Figure 6.17: *Kids can escape poverty through education*

Hint

The best descriptions of causes of crime show the links *between* the causes.

Learned behaviour such as family break-ups, absent parents (particularly fathers), and criminal friends can lead to skewed values of what is right and wrong, and crime can become 'normal' behaviour.

Children require good role models who hold good moral values and do not advocate crime in order to cope in the wider world and, when these are lacking, children may require support from social services and mental health services. Statistics show that children who access these services are more vulnerable to becoming involved in crime.

The lack of role models can often be linked to geographical location.

Greed

In order to 'fit in' individuals may feel the pressure to steal the latest gadgets or become involved in other criminal activity. Although they may not be doing it entirely to survive, some may feel that theft is the only way to 'fit in' with the rest of society.

Some people are career criminals who make their living from organised crime. The drug trade (the importing, manufacturing and selling of drugs) can often be a very lucrative trade where some can make vast amounts of money, far more than is necessary to survive. This can be described as greed.

Geographical location

Rural areas and suburbs have a lower crime rate than inner city areas and 'sink estates'. The wealth of an area is an important factor in crime levels; the highest levels of violent crime occur in the poorest areas. Drug and alcohol abuse is more common in these areas, which often see crimes being committed while under the influence or to fund a habit.

Due to the high levels of unemployment in inner city areas, many young people in poorer areas find themselves with time on their hands but nothing to do due to the lack of facilities in the area. When hanging around with no real purpose the opportunity to get involved in a crime such as vandalism, fighting or joyriding can be difficult to resist.

The culture and values in many inner city communities or 'sink estates' can also contribute to crime levels as many may see criminal behaviour as 'acceptable' because of the role models they are surrounded by.

The geographical location that an individual finds themselves in may also be linked to poverty.

Lack of education

In areas of deprivation some people experience a low level of education. In areas of high poverty, often formal education is not valued and is not seen as a route by which young people can escape from the poverty cycle. People may not do well at school, possibly due to truancy or underachievement. As a result they cannot get a good job that will give them good pay, leaving them unable to escape the cycle of poverty. This can then lead to status frustration, where individuals feel they are stuck in a certain 'rut' in society and unable to escape the poverty cycle. This may encourage individuals to turn to crime.

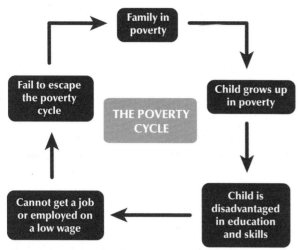

Figure 6.18: *The cycle of poverty*

Alcohol and drugs

The British Crime Survey (2009) reported that as many as 80% of all crimes that are committed have alcohol misuse or drug abuse as their root cause. In 2008–9, 938,000 offenders admitted to being under the influence at the time of their offence. Crimes such as assault, violence, petty crime and breach of the peace are frequently fuelled by alcohol and drugs. Alcohol and drugs can lower inhibitions and encourage people to make decisions they wouldn't when sober.

Those who are addicted to Class A drugs, such as heroin or cocaine, find that their habit becomes very expensive – sometimes running into hundreds of pounds a week. Many addicts are therefore forced to turn to crimes such as robbery or prostitution in order to get money to pay for their drugs.

There are often higher levels of drug and alcohol abuse in poverty stricken areas.

? Questions

1. 'People are responsible for their own actions, their circumstances do not matter. If someone commits a crime it is their own responsibility.'
   Do you agree with the statement? Give reasons for you answer.

2. **Explain, in detail,** why alcohol and drugs can cause criminal behaviour.

3. Why do some people suggest that higher crime levels are linked to poverty?

4. 'Everybody has the opportunity to escape the cycle of crime'. Explain why the person who made this statement may be accused of being **selective in the use of facts**.

Impact of crime

Crime impacts on victims, criminals, local communities and businesses.

Victims of crime suffer the immediate impacts such as physical harm and loss of or damage to property. The 'aftermath' (fear of crime) often

GO! Activity

Show your knowledge
Create a mind map of the different causes of crime. Try to show the links between the causes. Use each of the different bold headings to create a different point of information. It may be useful to use different colours to show the different reasons and the links between the causes.

GO! Activity

Show your knowledge
Imagine you have to summarise the causes of crime in a tweet to a friend. This means you can only use 140 characters, what would you say?

Make the Link

In Social Education you may examine the causes of youth crime in your area. You may also have looked at the riots in England in 2011 in other subjects.

Figure 6.19: *The impact of crime can have a shattering effect on lives*

far exceeds the immediate impact. Research carried out by Victim Support in 2005 found that fewer than 1% of victims said that their physical injuries were the most upsetting part of their experience of crime. The prevalence of crime can also cause distress to the wider society through the fear of crime.

A criminal record may mean that criminals face the consequences of their actions for the rest of their lives. Businesses affected by crime may experience a negative impact on their profits or even ability to continue trading. All criminal activity represents a cost to the Scottish government ranging from police wages to the cost of prison.

Victims

The chance of being a victim of a crime is not the same for everybody in society, some groups are more likely to be victims of a crime than others. For example, statistically, young people face higher risks of crime than older people. The Scottish Crime and Justice Survey 2011–12 found that around a quarter of 16–24 year olds had been victims of crime compared with only 9% of those aged 60 or older. Evidence also suggests that repeat victimisation affects poor people the most: 4% of victims experience 44% of crime.

Women are less likely to be victims of crime than men. This may be due to a number of factors; men are more likely to be involved in gang activity and more likely to be involved in alcohol-related offences. Around 4% of males were either perpetrators or victims of violent crime in 2011–12 compared to only 2% of women.

Criminals

Any individual who commits a crime has to accept the consequences of their actions. If convicted, a criminal will have a criminal record which may have to be declared when applying for jobs and may decrease the amount of employment opportunities available to them. A lot of employers will not hire individuals who have a criminal record and those with convictions may end up trapped in low paid, temporary, part-time or zero-hour contract work.

Individuals may then be trapped in the cycle of poverty and therefore feel forced to commit more criminal acts in order to survive. Criminals may also have to spend time in prison away from their friends and family and, while this may be necessary for punishment, it may also impact negatively on friends and family as they are separated from their loved one.

Business

Crimes such as shoplifting and fraud cost businesses in the UK billions of pounds each year. According to research done by the Scottish Business Resilience Centre in 2012, the cost of business crime in Scotland was over £5 billion. To try and prevent crimes such as shoplifting, many companies employ security guards, others attach 'anti-theft tags' to expensive goods and many increasingly use recording devices such as CCTV. All of these added security methods cost a business money.

📖 Word bank

- **Repeat victimisation**

When the same person or group suffers from crimes or incidents over a period of time.

- **Convict**

To find someone guilty of committing a crime.

💥 Make the Link

We use a lot of statistics in Modern Studies; you will probably cover how statistics can be misleading in Maths.

Figure 6.20: *A criminal record can make life very difficult*

A third of all crime related to business is now committed using the internet. Internet crime mainly involves thieves stealing highly confidential business data such as customers' personal information. Gaining access to this type of information can result in thieves getting rich very quickly. UK companies such as banks, insurance companies and energy suppliers have recently been the victims of internet crime. Again, installing extra internet security can cost businesses greatly.

The Scottish and UK governments have tried to combat the increase in internet crime by setting up special internet crime units. The Scottish Business Crime Centre works with businesses and aims to use the latest security technology to catch internet thieves.

Figure 6.21: *Criminals can operate online to steal customers' private, often financial, details*

Country

The cost of crime in Scotland and the UK as a whole is very large. The cost of putting criminals through courts and punishing them has to be supplied from taxes which otherwise could have been spent on other public services.

Often losses due to theft are passed on to customers as businesses have to increase their prices to make up the loss. Insurance payments increase for businesses and individuals, impacting negatively on the economy as people have to spend more money on insurance and therefore have less money to spend on other things.

When crime rates are high, countries look unstable to the rest of the world and their currency can decrease in value.

In addition to this we must consider the cost of treating victims of violence through the NHS and Victim Support services. Victim Support reported that in 2010 £2 billion was spent treating victims in the UK.

> **Make the Link**
>
> You may cover the cost of criminal activity to businesses in Business Management.

> **Activity**
>
> **Discuss**
> With your shoulder partner, create a bullet pointed list of the impact of crime on victims, individuals, the economy and community. You should use the information above to help you.

> **Make the Link**
>
> In Unit 3 you will learn about the cost of crime to the international community.

Summary

In this chapter you have learned:

- the different types of crime
- the causes of crime
- the impact of crime on society

Learning Summary

Now that you have finished the **What is crime?** chapter, complete a self-evaluation of your knowledge and skills to assess what you have understood. Use the checklist below and its traffic lights to draw up a revision plan to help you improve in the areas you identified as red or amber.

- I can understand that crime is any action that breaks the law of the land.

- I can understand that the laws in Scotland are made by the UK Parliament in Westminster and the Scottish Parliament in Holyrood.

- I can list the many different types of crime according to the government statistics.

- I can group the different types of crime under the headings: crimes against the person, property and other crimes.

- I can describe how crime levels in Scotland have fallen in recent years for almost all crimes.

- I can understand that the current alcohol laws were introduced in 2005 but there are changes underway.

- I can list the three different classifications of drug laws: Class A; Class B; Class C with each carrying different punishments.

- I can describe how the Road Traffic Laws were set out in the Road Traffic Acts of 1988 and 1991 and the Road Safety Act of 2006.

- I can list crime's many causes and how they interlink with one another.

- I can describe how criminal activity impacts on the individual, victims, local businesses and society.

Examples

In Modern Studies it is essential that you are able to back up any point you make with relevant evidence. When you are considering the statements above try to think of relevant examples for each response. You may wish to note these examples under each statement in your revision notes.

7 Convicting criminals

What you will learn in this chapter

- The role of the police.
- The courts system in Scotland.
- Sentencing.
- The youth justice system in Scotland.

The role of the police

Police Scotland is the national police force of Scotland. It was formed on 1st April 2013 when the eight territorial police forces and the Scottish Crime and Drug Enforcement Agency joined together to produce one force. By bringing together expertise from across the country Police Scotland hopes 'to improve service delivery to individuals and local communities in Scotland.' Police Scotland hopes that by combining resources they will be able to work more efficiently and save money. In 2013, Police Scotland had 17,436 police officers, 5,637 police staff and 1,404 special constables.

Police Scotland's first Chief Constable is Stephen House. As Chief Constable he is responsible for dealing with the financial side of policing and deciding on Scottish policing priorities. To help him in his duties, and to represent the different areas in Scotland, he has 14 local area police commanders who identify the police priorities for each area. Each division will have its own team of response officers and community officers, and teams for local crime investigation, road policing, public protection and local intelligence. The Chief Constable is also supported by an executive team of Deputy and Assistant Chief Constables.

Police Scotland has a number of national specialist divisions. For example, the Specialist Crime Division is responsible for major crime investigation, public protection, organised crime, counter-terrorism, intelligence and safer communities. These divisions mean that when a serious crime takes place, or if public safety is under serious threat from organised criminals, the most professional response is available regardless of where you live. Police Scotland is attempting to effectively bring together the investigative teams from all over Scotland.

What do the police do?

The **Police (Scotland) Act 1967** lays down the general functions of the police. These duties did not change with the introduction of Police Scotland.

Activity

Discuss
With your shoulder partner, discuss what life would be like without the police. Try to come up with six points.

Figure 7.1: *An illuminated sign outside a police station*

POLICE SCOTLAND
Keeping people safe

Figure 7.2: *The Police Scotland logo*

Hint

Many local initiatives are continuing under Police Scotland; your teacher may encourage you to investigate initiatives in your local area.

Make the Link

In Unit 3 of this textbook you will study terrorism and the impact it has had on the world in more detail.

Figure 7.3: *A person can be detained by the police for up to 24 hours*

Word bank

• **Charge**

An official statement by the police that they believe someone guilty of a crime.

• **Warrant**

A document that allows the police to enter premises or arrest a suspect.

Make the Link

In History or RMPS you may study cases when police have used unreasonable force, for example in Nazi Germany or Rwanda.

The duties of the police

- maintain law and order
- detect crime
- prevent crime
- protect the public

Police Scotland state they will uphold these duties by continuing with the values of integrity, fairness and respect. In order to carry out these duties the police have a number of powers.

Powers of the police

Stop and question a suspect or witness

The police can stop any individual to ask what they are doing and where they are going. They can ask questions about a particular incident or general questions.

Search a person suspected of having an offensive weapon, stolen property or drugs, or of being a terrorist

Although police can question anyone they can only search a person if they have good reason, for example if they suspect them of carrying an illegal weapon. After the September 11th terrorist attacks on the USA in 2001, the police are also allowed to search anyone suspected of being a terrorist.

Detain a person at a police station for 24 hours for questioning without charging them

Police can keep people at a police station and question them for 24 hours, although a single 'session' of questioning cannot go on for more than six hours. If all questions are not answered then the police can apply for an extension of 12 hours. For a terrorist offence police can apply for a maximum of 14 days extension without charge.

Arrest a person and charge them with a crime that they have seen them committing or for which they have reliable witness and evidence

Usually the police will have a warrant to arrest a suspect but there are circumstances where an arrest is made on the spot. This would include someone caught committing a crime, running away from a crime scene or carrying out dangerous or threatening behaviour.

Enter a building with a warrant, **or without one if they hear a disturbance, are pursuing a criminal or suspect it is a drug den**

In order to enter a building the police must have reasonable grounds to believe a suspect or evidence is on the premises. If you are arrested the police have the right to enter any premises where you were during or immediately before the arrest. The police obtain a warrant by asking the courts to issue one.

Use reasonable force in pursuit of their duties

Police have the duty to use persuasion wherever possible, but when that is not successful they can use force. Police have batons and pepper spray as part of their regular issue kit. They are able to use force in pursuit of arrest, to protect themselves, or to protect other members of the public.

Issue fixed penalty notices (fines)

Police have the power to issue fines for certain offences, for example driving without a seatbelt or littering. The police issue these fines on the spot rather than going through the court system, which would take much longer.

Other police bodies

There are a number of other police bodies who operate in Scotland, including:

- British Transport Police – police force of the railways providing a service for rail operators, their staff and passengers
- Ministry of Defence Police – provide security within Ministry of Defence property across Britain (e.g. the nuclear submarine base at Faslane)
- Civil Nuclear Constabulary – provides protection for nuclear materials on designated UK nuclear licensed sites and in transit
- United Kingdom Border Agency – an agency of the Home Office tasked with protecting the UK's border, also in charge of immigration

Approaches to policing

Proactive policing

Police will target known criminals, especially those involved in organised crime, using informants and local intelligence to try and prevent any serious crimes from happening in the first instance. Proactive policing is likely to involve the use of modern technology such as phone bugging, CCTV and email hacking.

Zero tolerance

All crimes will be dealt with by a high-profile police presence. Sometimes surveillance will be carried out in order to target crime hot-spots (places where a crime often takes place) in advance of a police presence being deployed; often this tactic is used to combat alcohol-related crimes in city centre areas. Under a zero tolerance initiative, any individuals caught carrying out the crime in question will often be given the most severe punishment available rather than a police warning.

Figure 7.4: *Littering can result in an on-the-spot fine*

> **Make the Link**
>
> The nuclear base at Faslane is a controversial subject; you may have discussed arguments surrounding this base in Unit 1.

> **Hint**
>
> Your school will have a community police officer known as a 'campus officer'. You might want to interview him or her for your Added Value Unit or Assignment.

> **Word bank**
>
> - **Informant**
> A person who offers useful information.
>
> - **Local intelligence**
> Information received from people in the nearby area.

Police: zero tolerance for parade louts

Police have warned marchers in today's Orange Order parade through Glasgow city centre that officers will take a 'zero tolerance' approach to sectarian behaviour and drinking in public.

Some 8000 marchers from 182 lodges marched from George Square to Glasgow Green, accompanied for the first time by 800 professionally trained stewards paid for by the Orange Order.

Police arrested 32 people - six for sectarian offences.

[Source: http://www.heraldscotland.com/news/home-news/ police-zero-tolerance-for-parade-louts.14244612]

Figure 7.5: *Community support officers*

📖 Word bank

- **Partner agencies**

Other organisations working to meet the same goal.

Figure 7.6: *CCTV cameras are seen more and more around our towns and cities*

⚙ Hint

Some people think 'bobbies on the beat' are more effective than CCTV cameras because an actual police presence may make people think about their actions more than a camera.

Community policing

Police attempt to build a relationship with the local area through education, neighbourhood watch schemes and 'bobbies on the beat'. A recent initiative saw all schools have a campus police officer employed, at least on a temporary basis. Community policing is designed to build trust and therefore to help solve problems more easily or prevent problems from arising in the first place.

Police Scotland uses a combination of approaches to policing in order to achieve the best possible outcome. Recently they have increased their use of CCTV and community policing in order to try and increase police presence in local communities.

Police initiatives

Initiative on violence

One of the first initiatives launched by Police Scotland is designed to fight violence, disorder and anti-social behaviour. Despite overall levels of violence decreasing, Police Scotland is concerned that violence in the home is increasing. To combat this, Police Scotland is implementing a national campaign against violence and is working with partner agencies to tackle such crimes. They will encourage people to reduce their alcohol intake in an attempt to decrease alcohol-related violence. The initiative also aims to target well-known offenders and problem locations in order to try to reduce both alcohol-related violence and domestic violence. Police Scotland plans to use intelligence to prevent violent crime by removing weapons, drugs and alcohol from well-known violent crime hot-spots.

❓ Questions

1. **Describe** Police Scotland. How is it different from the previous system?
2. What are the main duties of the police?
3. Choose the three most important powers of the police. **Explain** why you think they are important.
4. Write a paragraph on the different approaches to policing.
5. **Explain** the aims of the 'initiative on violence'.
6. Which approach(es) to policing does the 'initiative on violence' use? **Justify** your answer.
7. Which other police bodies operate in Scotland?

CCTV

CCTV is used to detect crime as it is happening, to try and deter the public from committing crimes in the first place and in the hope that the public will feel safer in their communities. It is thought that if someone can see a CCTV camera they are less likely to carry out a crime, such as theft or assault, as they know the film of the incident could be used to prove their guilt.

CCTV footage of a crime can be used as evidence in court. CCTV camera operators can also report crimes as they are happening allowing the police to intervene. Police officers and local councils believe that CCTV is an effective way of preventing crime; this can be seen in the widespread network of CCTV surveillance monitoring Scotland's towns and cities which has trebled in the past ten years to comprise more than 4,000 cameras.

The biggest rise in CCTV use has been in Aberdeen where 680 cameras were in use in 2012 compared with 482 in 2011. Some people think CCTV is an invasion of privacy and that it does not actually help the police to do their job; they believe that more police officers on the street would make people feel safer and prevent crime from occurring in the first place. However, others think CCTV is crucial in fighting crime; they argue that the police can't be everywhere and CCTV can be the eyes and ears of police officers: in Edinburgh, figures show CCTV resulted in 1,806 camera-assisted arrests in 2012. Others would suggest that CCTV doesn't work on its own but can work in partnership with other methods.

GO! Activity

Discuss
With your shoulder partner, discuss the advantages and disadvantages of CCTV for police use in Scotland.

❓ Questions

1. Give one advantage of CCTV **using evidence** from the information above.

2. Give one disadvantage of CCTV **using evidence** from the information above.

3. 'CCTV is useless, it has not helped the police solve any crimes and the public hate it'.

   Explain why the person who made this statement may be accused of being **selective in the use of facts**.

4. Give at least one advantage of using an internet search as a source of information for an investigation into CCTV.

5. Give at least one disadvantage of using an internet search as a source of information for an investigation into CCTV.

6. Suggest another research method that you could use to investigate CCTV. **Explain** why it would be a good method.

Convicting criminals

Scotland has long had a unique court and criminal justice system that is very different to that within the rest of the UK. The main difference is that Scottish courts allow the 'not proven' verdict. This is used when there is not sufficient evidence to prove a person guilty but there remains suspicion that they are not entirely innocent. Some people think the not proven verdict is unfair as it leaves the accused without the label of 'innocent'.

The **Criminal Proceedings etc. (Reform) (Scotland) Act 2007** created six sheriffdoms in Scotland:

- Glasgow and Strathkelvin
- Grampian, Highlands and Islands
- Lothian and Borders
- North Strathclyde
- South Strathclyde, Dumfries and Galloway
- Tayside, Central and Fife

Court system

Each sheriffdom contains one or more Sheriff Courts and a number of Justice of the Peace Courts. The High Court of Justiciary is based in Edinburgh but travels around major towns and cities.

When a crime is committed, and the police have charged someone with a criminal offence, the details are sent to the Procurator Fiscal who looks at the evidence and decides whether or not to go ahead with prosecution. If the Procurator Fiscal decides that the case should proceed then those accused will appear before one of three courts: the Justice of the Peace Court, the Sheriff Court, or the High Court of the Justiciary (known as the High Court). In these courts it is decided whether the accused is guilty, not guilty or not proven. Then, if necessary, a sentence will be handed out. Each court deals with different offences depending on the seriousness of the crime, and either solemn or summary procedure can be used.

Justice of the Peace Courts

Justice of the Peace Courts were created by the **Criminal Proceedings etc (Reform) (Scotland) Act 2007** to replace District Courts. The process brought all the courts under the control of the Scottish Court System rather than local authorities, and this was intended to streamline the system.

Figure 7.7: *The entrance to the Sheriff and Justice of the Peace Courts in Edinburgh*

📖 Word bank

• Summary procedure

Trial before a Sheriff or Justice of the Peace and no jury.

• Solemn procedure

Trial before a Sheriff or judge and a jury of 15 people.

Justice of the Peace Courts are the lowest level of criminal court and therefore handle relatively minor crimes such as breach of the peace, minor assaults, minor road traffic offences and animal cruelty. Justice of the Peace Courts operate a summary procedure which consists of a lay magistrate (Justice of the Peace) and no jury. A lay magistrate (Justice of the Peace) is appointed from within the local community and is not usually a legally qualified judge, however they will have been trained in criminal law and procedure. When the court is in session lay magistrates have access to lawyers who can advise them on law and procedure. The maximum sentences that a lay magistrate can impose in a Justice of the Peace Court are custodial sentences of up to 60 days, and fines of up to £2,500.

Sheriff Courts

Each sheriffdom has a Sheriff Principle who is in charge of all of the Sheriff Courts in the area and of ensuring that all 'court business is carried our efficiently'. For example, the current (2014) Sheriff Principle of North Strathclyde is Sheriff Principle Bruce A. Kerr QC.

The Sheriff Court deals with more serious offences committed within the sheriffdom. As the crimes tend to be more serious, the Sheriff Court may use summary procedure or solemn procedure depending on the case. Under summary procedure, the sentencing powers are limited to three months imprisonment, unless there are previous convictions, or a fine of £5,000. Under solemn procedure, the Sheriff can impose a prison sentence of up to three years or an unlimited fine, unless previous laws define a maximum fine for the offence. If a Sheriff ever feels that a harsher punishment is called for then they can refer the case to the High Court for sentencing, where a more severe punishment may be handed out.

The High Court of the Justiciary

The High Court is Scotland's highest criminal court. This court only conducts trials under solemn procedure and a legally trained judge and a jury of 15 men and women. A jury is chosen from the list of people on the electoral register; anyone who is over 18, has lived in the UK for at least five years since the age of 13, and is not currently ineligible can be summoned for jury duty.

The High Court usually sits in Edinburgh but also travels to different parts of Scotland; it has permanent buildings in Glasgow and Aberdeen and uses the Sheriff Court buildings in Stirling, Oban, Inverness, Dundee, Perth, Dumfries, Jedburgh and Ayr. The High Court deals with the most serious of crimes such as treason, murder, rape, armed robbery, drug trafficking, sexual offences involving children and certain offences under the **Official Secrets Act**. In difficult cases, such as a highly public murder trial, there may be three judges sitting. The High Court has unlimited sentencing powers in terms of imprisonment and fines.

Figure 7.8: *Bruce A. Kerr QC, Sheriff Principle of North Strathclyde*

📖 Word bank

- **Custodial**
A sentence consisting of containing the offender, usually in a prison.

- **Sheriff Principle**
The senior legal authority for the local area.

- **Ineligible**
Legally or officially unable to be considered for a position.

⠿ Make the Link

You may have taken part in a mock trial using solemn procedure in English, or other subjects.

GO! Activity

Show your knowledge

Complete simple diagrams showing the crimes, procedures and sentencing of the three criminal courts. The High Court has been done for you below.

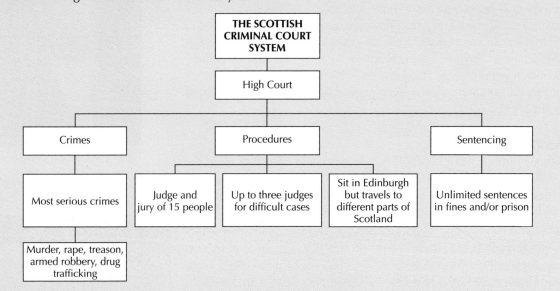

Extension

Research local and national newspapers to find a recent example of a case that has been heard in each of the courts. Summarise the procedure followed, the verdict and the sentence given.

📖 Word bank

- **Court of Session**

The highest civil (as opposed to criminal) court.

- **Appeal**

When someone who has been convicted of a crime asks for the decision to be reviewed. This is only allowed in certain cases.

Civil courts and the right to appeal

The civil court settles disputes between people about non-criminal matters. This court sits in Parliament House in Edinburgh and acts as a Court of Session. In some cases, convicted criminals may have the opportunity to appeal their conviction or their sentence and the Court of Session deals with appeals from any of the other three courts in Scotland. Any appeal heard here can be referred on to the House of Lords in London, where the case may be heard and the decision overturned.

❓ Questions

1. What is solemn procedure?
2. What is summary procedure?
3. If a criminal is unhappy with their conviction, which court may they appeal to?

Scottish youth justice system

Scotland has a unique Children's Hearing system that is very different from juvenile justice systems elsewhere in the UK and the rest of the world. Children (those under 16 years old) are only considered for prosecution in court for serious offences such as murder, an assault that would put a life in danger or serious road traffic offences that can lead to disqualification from driving. This means that all other offences are dealt with by the Children's Hearing system. However, the Children's Hearing system does not just deal with criminal offences, it also deals with children who:

- are beyond the control of their parent/guardian
- are exposed to 'moral danger'
- have been a victim of an offence, e.g. abuse
- have experienced neglect from parents
- are involved in drug or alcohol abuse
- have failed to attend school

Figure 7.9: *Entrance to the High Court of Justiciary building in Glasgow*

The Children's Hearing System

In 2013, Children's Hearing Scotland took over the running of the 32 local authority (council) panels used previously and created one National Children's Panel for Scotland with approximately 2,700 volunteers supported by 22 Area Support Teams. This was intended to streamline the system and to try to combat the high turnover of volunteers as well as some other things the system had previously been criticised for. This national body is in charge of the recruitment, selection, appointment, training, retention and support of all panel members.

Figure 7.10: *Protecting the child*

How the Children's Hearing system works	
Step 1	Referral to the Children's Reporter.
Step 2	Initial investigation is carried out – three possible outcomes.
Step 3	Referred to a hearing in front of the Children's Panel – one of three decisions will then be made.

A referral may be made to the Children's Reporter by the police in criminal cases, or by a social worker, health or education services, a member of the public or the child themselves. When the reporter receives the original referral they will carry out an initial investigation, which would involve things like collecting witness statements from teachers, police, social workers etc. Once this initial investigation has been carried out the reporter has three options:

1. If they think the problem is under control by the family they will take no further action.

2. They may refer to the local authority who can offer extra support such as counselling, usually involving the support of a social worker.

3. Or, if it is decided that compulsory supervision methods are needed, they may arrange a hearing of the Children's Panel.

📖 Word bank

- **Moral danger**

When a child is in need of protection from parents or guardians who behave in an immoral or wrong way.

- **Children's Reporter**

The person who is employed to make decisions about a young person to help them sort their problems out.

- **Compulsory supervision methods**

The social worker assigned to the child, along with others (e.g. the child's school), will work out a plan to improve the child's situation.

Figure 7.11: *Supporting the child*

> ### 📖 Word bank
>
> • **Grounds for referral**
>
> Reasons to send the child on to the next stage of the process, e.g. lack of parental care.

The Children's Hearing

The purpose of a hearing of the Children's Panel is to decide on the measures of care that are in the best interests of the child. In cases where a crime has been committed the hearing is not usually about deciding on a 'punishment', it more often about helping the child move away from the criminal behaviour.

The people who sit on Children's Hearings are known as the Children's Panel. They are volunteers and come from a wide range of occupations and backgrounds and they all have experience of, and an interest in, helping and supporting children. Members are trained for their role with the Children's Panel and all panels must contain a mix of men and women.

The hearing is designed to support the child. The young person must always be present during the meeting, along with a person of their choosing. The parents/carers will attend and there are also three panel members present at the meeting who have to discuss and decide the next steps that should be taken. The meeting takes place in the young person's local area in order to encourage the young person to feel comfortable. The panel receives reports from the young person's social worker and sometimes the school. Everyone has the opportunity to look at the reports and discussion will be centred around the 'grounds for referral'. The young person has to agree to the grounds they have been given during the hearing; if they do not agree then they may be referred to one of the adult courts.

The hearing normally lasts around an hour and then a decision has to be made by the three panel members about the next steps. The panel can make three decisions:

1. Firstly, that they don't need to do anything about the grounds for referral and decide not to take it any further. This is called 'discharging the case'. This might be because things have improved for the young person at home or school and the panel members don't feel that the young person needs to come back to another hearing.

2. Secondly, they may decide that more information is needed to help them make a decision about what is best for the young person, and they can decide to continue the hearing at a later date. They would then ask the reporter to carry out further investigations.

3. Thirdly, they may agree that compulsory measures of supervision are needed to help the young person, and can make a Compulsory Supervision Order.

A Compulsory Supervision Order is a legal document that means that the local authority is responsible for looking after and helping the young person. It can state where the young person must live and other conditions that must be followed. It may be necessary to put the young person into secure accommodation (a place they cannot leave) because there is suspicion that they could hurt themselves or others if they are left in their own home. They may also be fitted with an electronic tag to stop them from entering certain areas. To place a child on a Compulsory Supervision Order is a very serious decision and is not taken lightly by the Panel Members. A Compulsory Supervision Order must be reviewed at another hearing within a year.

Figure 7.12: *The people who would attend a Children's Hearing*

Craig's Story

CASE STUDY

Craig was 15 when he first got into trouble with the police. He had become involved with a local gang and in a short space of time had committed 15 offences. He had been vandalising the local area, and had started drinking and smoking cannabis.

Craig was living with his mum and her new boyfriend. His mum's boyfriend had a criminal record and a history of drug misuse.

The police caught Craig and referred him to the Reporter. His mum was very upset and angry with him. The Reporter decided it was important that Craig went to a Children's Hearing.

At his hearing, Craig said he was really sorry for getting involved with the gang. He said he had been showing off and trying to impress them. He also stated he was unhappy at home.

The Panel Members made a Compulsory Supervision Order. His mum was happy as she wanted him to stay away from the gang and she later left her boyfriend. They also put in a condition that he attend a special drugs awareness programme for teenagers.

As part of his Compulsory Supervision Order, Craig was placed on a work experience programme which then offered him the opportunity to train to become a mechanic. Craig has not been in trouble with the police since.

Activity

Discuss

Discuss with your shoulder partner how the Children's Hearing system helped Craig. Write a short summary of the positive changes Craig made.

Activity

Group work

With your shoulder partner, make up a quiz on the youth justice system in Scotland. Then test your classmates to see how much they've learned. Your quiz should have at least 10 questions; you might wish to make them multiple choice. Your teacher will want to see that you also have answers to the questions to show your understanding.

Proposals for change

The Children's Hearing system is sometimes criticised because 60% of cases are to do with the welfare and care of children which some argue would be better dealt with elsewhere. Some critics see the hearing system as a 'soft' way of dealing with criminal behaviour and they believe it does not prevent crime in later life. There are also a lot of changes in staff members on the Children's Panel and some children feel intimidated by having to appear in front of one, so the truth is not always uncovered. Because of these criticisms the Scottish Prisons Commission has recommended 'Youth Hearings' for 16 and 17 year olds. Under proposals these would deal exclusively with criminal cases of 16 and 17 year olds. They would be structured more like an adult court rather than a supportive panel and the focus would be on giving the appropriate punishment. However there would also be support to tackle the causes of crime and prevent youngsters from reoffending.

? Questions

1. Why might a young person be referred to the Children's Hearing system?
2. **Describe** the steps of the Children's Hearing system. Include the possible options available at each stage.
3. What is a Compulsory Supervision Order?
4. **Explain** how the Compulsory Supervision Order benefitted Craig.
5. What changes have the Scottish Prison Commission recommended to the current Children's Hearing system?

Sentencing

Scottish courts have a range of sentencing powers available to them. The majority (61% in 2011) of all convictions result in a financial penalty. Most of these are fines, however those convicted can also be ordered to pay a compensation order to the victim. The traditional way of dealing with criminals is by placing people in prison where they are physically confined and usually deprived of a range of personal freedoms. In 2012 the number of convictions resulting in a custodial sentence increased 3% to 15,880. This is still lower than in previous years and equates to 15% of all convictions.

A custodial sentence is most frequently used for crimes involving violence, including rape and sexual assault. The average length of a custodial sentence in 2011–12 was 284 days (over nine months), one week higher than it was in 2010–11.

Figure 7.13: *A judge's gavel and soundboard for use in court*

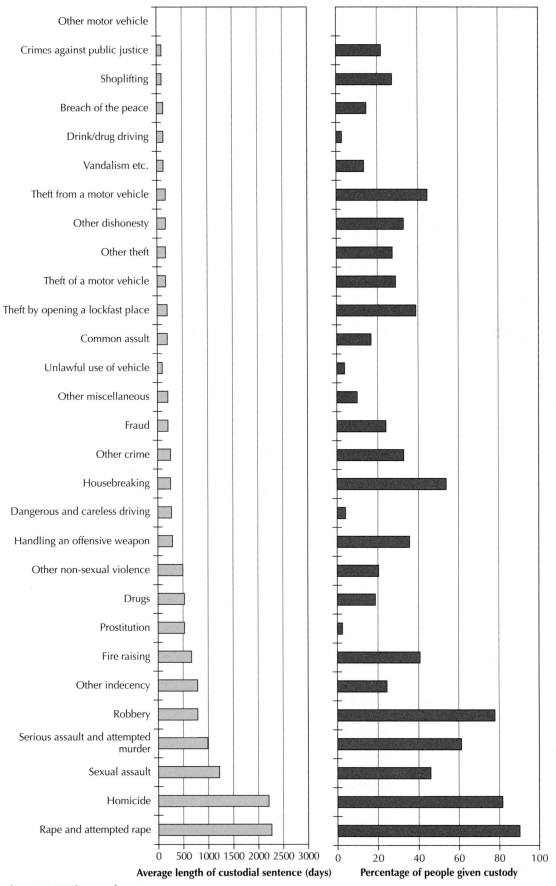

Figure 7.14: Crimes and sentences

Figure 7.15: *What purpose should being behind bars serve?*

Custodial sentences

For anyone over the age of 21 a custodial sentence means a stay in prison. For women, the Scottish female prison is Cornton Vale. If a young person between the ages of 16–21 is given a custodial sentence then they will attend a young offenders institution such as Polmont Young Offenders.

- The Scottish Prison Service (SPS) manages prisons in Scotland.
- The SPS is an agency of the Scottish government and was established in 1993.
- The SPS has 14 publicly managed prisons and two privately managed prisons with over 8,000 prisoners in total.
- The purpose of the SPS is to:
  - ensure criminals are kept in secure custody
  - care for prisoners
  - deliver opportunities that attempt to reduce reoffending once a prisoner returns to their community. They aim to do this by offering education programmes, training and drug rehabilitations

There is debate over what the role of prisons should be; some feel it should only be to punish, and to protect society from criminals. They would argue that the reduction of civil liberties will deter criminals from committing crimes again as they will not want to go back to prison. Others suggest that prisons should help criminals to prevent future reoffending. Short prison sentences are shown to be least effective: in 2011 offenders who were released from a custodial sentence of three months or less had the highest reconviction frequency rate compared to those who were released from longer sentences.

The below table shows the arguments surrounding whether prisons work or not.

Prisons work:	Prisons don't work:
Retribution: crime needs to be punished, people should know society will punish serious offences.	**Overcrowding:** too many people are sentenced to six months or less. Many people are in prison for non-payment of fines. In June 2013 prison numbers reached a record high with nearly 8,154 people in jail in Scotland.
Protection: society must be protected from murderers, rapists, terrorists, persistent offenders.	**Expense:** it costs over £30,000 per year per inmate to keep people in prison. Alternatives to prison such as electronic tagging are much cheaper.
Deterrence: shows that society has rules that should not be broken. Fear of punishment stops more crimes happening.	**Unjust:** most people in prison are working-class. Middle- and upper-class people are less likely to go to jail, perhaps because people with a higher income can afford better legal representation.
When in prison offenders will be removed from their normal surroundings. This may give them a **chance to change**.	Three out of four prisoners reoffend. 90% of Barlinnie Prison inmates are **repeat offenders**, usually committing the same type of crime. First time offenders are exposed to habitual criminals; people in prison may learn how to commit more serious crimes.

Proposals for change

The Scottish Prisons Commission wants to end prison sentences of less than six months and introduce more non-custodial sentences instead. In February 2011, a presumption against sentences less than three months was introduced. The Commission believes this will have many benefits to the prison service including:

- lessening the problem of prison overcrowding
- reducing the cost to the taxpayer
- preventing reoffending and improving behaviour by not allowing minor offenders to mix with other more serious offenders in prison
- stopping families from being negatively affected by having a relative in jail
- freeing up money for prison rehabilitation, which currently lacks money and staff to keep it going and make it effective

Non-custodial sentences

One of the key challenges for the Scottish justice system is dealing with low-level offenders who commit crimes that cause havoc, disturbance, upset and fear in communities such as vandalism and arson. For many that are convicted the punishment is a short prison sentence; however, if the aim is to prevent repeated offending the evidence shows that prison is not working for these types of offenders. In order to try to reduce reoffending, alternatives to prison have been used by the courts.

Figure 7.16: *Reducing the number of custodial sentences will mean a saving for the taxpayer*

Fine

A fine is a sum of money paid by the convicted person to the court. This could be paid in one lump sum or paid in instalments over a longer period of time. If the convicted person fails to pay the fine they may be sentenced to a prison stay as an alternative. Fines allow individuals to continue living their lives and do not have the same stigma attached to them as a stay in prison.

> 📖 **Word bank**
>
> • **Prison rehabilitation**
> Programmes within the prison that prepare the prisoner for returning to life outside in a productive way.

Community Payback Orders (CPOs)

The new Community Payback Order came into effect on 1st February 2011. Courts can impose one or more of a range of requirements, depending on the nature of the crime and the issues that need addressed in order to stop reoffending. When sentencing the offender to a CPO, the court could require them to:

- carry out hours of unpaid manual work in the community
- be subject to periods of supervision where they would have to report to a local police station or probation officer
- comply with specific conduct requirements, such as not attending certain areas or associating with certain individuals
- pay compensation to the victim(s)
- participate in alcohol, drug or mental health treatment interventions

Figure 7.17: *Paying a fine is a common non-custodial sentence*

Figure 7.18: *Working in a vegetable garden or allotment to grow produce for the community: paying it back*

At the same time, tougher punishments have been introduced to deal with those who do not carry out their order properly, for example a prison sentence.

CPOs mean offenders are being punished by being sent out to improve streets and neighbourhoods to repay communities for the damage caused by their crimes; at the same time, CPOs address the issues that can influence repeat offending behaviour, such as drug or alcohol addiction. The work they carry out may also help the offenders gain valuable experience that they can use in order to apply for a job. Some examples of unpaid work being carried out by offenders across Scotland include:

- clearing pathways of snow or ice
- building eco-plant areas for school children
- repainting community centres or churches
- cleaning beaches
- growing vegetables and distributing the produce to care homes and local charities

DAILY NEWS

world - business - finance - lifestyle - travel - sport

Poster girl for community payback plan sent back to jail

A woman who posed with justice minister Kenny MacAskill to promote the government's policy on alternatives to custody has been sent back to prison.

Cheryl Ferguson admitted breaching the terms of her community service order by repeatedly failing to turn up for appointments or carry out unpaid work.

The 29 year old from Dundee was given the original order last March after she admitted stealing sweets, hair accessories and a children's craft kit from an Asda store.

Ferguson was hailed as a model reformed offender thanks to community sentences,

but at Dundee Sheriff Court it emerged she had committed two further crimes since the order was made.

A spokesman for Dundee City Council, which runs the women's project that Ferguson helped front, insisted the scheme does have a positive effect.

He said: 'The project has had success in breaking a cycle of repeat offending.

"Given the level of offending this individual had before, there has been a positive impact through the project."

[Source:http://news.stv.tv/tayside/223064-community-payback-poster-girl-cheryl-ferguson-back-behind-bars/]

DAILY NEWS

world - business - finance - lifestyle - travel - sport

Community benefits from offenders' payback scheme

Removing 65,000 illegally dumped tyres, spending over 3,700 hours clearing snow during severe winter and gardening for over 20,000 hours to provide fresh fruit and vegetables to local elderly residents ...

These are just some of the ways offenders have paid back the community for crimes they committed.

North Lanarkshire Council hosted an event focussing on the new Community Payback Orders. Father Kelly of St Brigid's RC Church in Newmains said: "The service has transformed the grounds of the parish. It's continuing and is going from strength to strength. I'm delighted with the work being carried out."

"People don't always fully recognise the benefits that projects involving offenders bring," explained Mary Fegan, head of social work services. "We've got a range of fantastic projects on the go, ranging from decoration and furniture building, to providing vegetable gardens and pavilions for schools.

"Statistics show that three out of five people on schemes like these don't reoffend. These orders in turn bring environmental benefits to local areas, local businesses benefit from placements and ex-offenders feel they are making amends for crimes."

Robert Lees, from North Lanarkshire, told how he carried out his community service in a local workshop. With over 20 years' of joinery experience, Robert was given a range of projects to work on.

He said: "I'm a qualified joiner and was able to use my skills in the workshop. I also worked closely with other young people and taught them basic joinery skills. I helped make sandpits for nurseries, a school pavilion and benches for memorial gardens.

"I really enjoyed the work and the experience. It was good to give something back."

[Source: http://www.dailyrecord.co.uk/news/local-news/community-benefits-offenders-payback-scheme-2571764/]

GO! **Activity**

Discuss
Discuss with your shoulder partner the cases of Cheryl Ferguson and North Lanarkshire Council. Discuss why some people may argue that CPOs work, and why others may argue they don't. Come to an overall **conclusion** as to whether CPOs have been successful or not. You should then produce a written report for your teacher that has two structured paragraphs which use the 'Point, Explain, Example' structure (see page 240). They should provide **explanations of your decision** on CPOs. You should then produce a final paragraph as a conclusion.

Figure 7.19: *An electronic tag to be worn by an offender*

Restriction of Liberty Order (electronic tagging)

A Restriction of Liberty Order requires an offender to be restricted to a specific place for a maximum period of 12 hours per day for up to a maximum of 12 months, for example their own home or a temporary residence. The offender may also be restricted from a specified place or places for up to 24 hours a day for up to 12 months. There are three main situations when the court tends to use this sentence:

1. For offenders whose behaviour outside their home is dangerous to themselves or others.

2. As an alternative for offenders who could otherwise have been imprisoned; a tag may be used as an effective part-time home imprisonment.

3. To restrict the offender from going to a certain area, for example to reduce the risk of the offender either carrying out or being the victim of an assault.

A person wearing an electronic tag is expected to:

• stay at the restriction place during the times specified, and not arrive there late

• not attempt to remove the tag

• not move address without permission

Drug Treatment and Testing Order (DTTO)

DTTOs are aimed at breaking the link between drug use and crime. Courts can make an order requiring offenders to undergo treatments either as part of another community order or as a sentence in its own right. It is a high-level, demanding treatment that can last from six months to three years. Offenders are forced to confront their addictions and also take part in therapy to encourage them to confront the issues that made them drug users in the first place. Although DTTOs do work for some offenders, those given a DTTO have the highest reconviction frequency rate, with around 70% of those given DTTOs reoffending within a year.

The number of non-custodial sentences imposed (excluding fines) increased during 2011–12 to 19,700. Nearly 70% of DTTOS, CPOs and tagging orders that finished in 2011–12 resulted in successful completion, the highest number in eight years. During this period there has been a decline in the one-year reconviction rate (the number of offenders who receive another conviction within a year of the end of their previous sentence). Some say that this proves that non-custodial sentences are more effective, however others would still argue that non-custodial sentences are not harsh enough and do not provide an effective deterrent to committing crime.

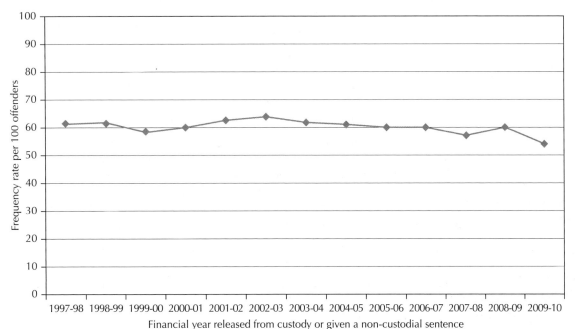

Figure 7.20: *Offenders released from custody or given a non-custodial sentence, 1997–98 to 2009–10 One year reconviction frenquency rate*

Questions

1. What is the difference between custodial and non-custodial sentences?
2. Why have some people criticised prisons as a method of punishment?
3. Choose the three strongest arguments that support the use of prison sentences. **Explain** why you consider them to be the best arguments.
4. What are the main non-custodial sentences available to Scottish courts?
5. Kenny MacAskill, the Cabinet Secretary for Justice in Scotland in 2014, says 'community sentences are proven to be more effective than prison at reducing reoffending'.

   Give one reason to **support** his statement.
6. Using Figure 7.14, make **conclusions, with evidence**, about:
   • the crime that received the longest sentences
   • the crime where most people received custodial sentences
7. 'Reoffending rates have been falling since 2000.'

   Using Figure 7.20, give one piece of **evidence to support** this statement.

SOCIAL ISSUES IN THE UNITED KINGDOM

Summary

In this chapter you have learned:

- What the role of the police is
- How the court system in Scotland works
- What sentencing each court can hand out
- About the unique youth justice system in Scotland

Learning Summary

Now that you have finished the **Convicting criminals** chapter, complete a self-evaluation of your knowledge and skills to assess what you have understood. Use the checklist below and its traffic lights to draw up a revision plan to help you improve in the areas you identified as red or amber.

- I can identify when Police Scotland was formed and what geographical areas it covers, both nationally and in its divisions. ○ ○ ○

- I can outline the duties and powers laid out by the Police (Scotland) Act 1967. ○ ○ ○

- I can list the ways police approach crime fighting and what resources they have to help combat crime. ○ ○ ○

- I can outline the three different levels of criminal courts in Scotland. ○ ○ ○

- I can describe summary and solemn procedure and the role of the Procurator Fiscal. ○ ○ ○

- I can describe the Children's Hearing system, what it allows young people to experience and what decisions it can take. ○ ○ ○

- I can give examples of non-custodial punishments that courts can give out and argue why they are thought of as both effective and not effective. ○ ○ ○

- I can give examples of the advantages and disadvantages of custodial sentences. ○ ○ ○

Examples

In Modern Studies it is essential that you are able to back up any point you make with relevant evidence. When you are considering the statements above try to think of relevant examples for each response. You may wish to note these examples under each statement in your revision notes.

Terrorism

In Unit 3 there is a choice of topic; you can study **either** a major world power **or** a significant world issue. In this book we will be looking at the significant world issue of **terrorism.**

Level 3 and 4 experiences and outcomes relevant to this topic

The International Issues Unit naturally builds upon the knowledge already secured in the third and fourth level experiences and outcomes, and in particular:

❖ By examining the role and actions of selected international organisations, I can evaluate how effective they are in meeting their aims. **SOC 4-19b**

❖ I can contribute to a discussion on the actions and motives of a group or organisation that seeks to achieve its aims by non-democratic means. **SOC 4-18c**

❖ I can present an informed view on how the expansion of power and influence of countries or organisations may impact on the cultures, attitudes and experiences of those involved. **SOC 4-19a**

❖ I can use my knowledge of current social, political or economic issues to interpret evidence and present an informed view. **SOC 3-15a**

❖ I can explain why a group I have identified might experience inequality and can suggest ways in which this inequality might be addressed. **SOC 3-16a**

❖ I have compared the rights and responsibilities of citizens in Scotland with a contrasting society and can describe and begin to understand reasons for differences. **SOC 3-17a**

Outcome and Assessment Standards

National 4 *(International Issues)*	National 5 *(International Issues)*
Outcome 1	**Outcome 1**
1 Use a limited range of sources of information to draw and support conclusions about international issues, focusing on either a major world power or a significant world issue by:	**1 Use a range of sources of information to draw and support conclusions about international issues, focusing on either a major world power or a significant world issue by:**
1.1 Drawing a conclusion using up to two sources of information.	1.1 Drawing a conclusion using between two and four sources of information.
1.2 Briefly supporting a conclusion using evidence from up to two sources of information.	1.1 Supporting, in detail, a conclusion using evidence from between two and four sources of information.
Outcome 2	**Outcome 2**
2 Draw on a straightforward knowledge and understanding of international issues, focusing on either a major world power or a significant world issue by:	**2 Draw on a detailed knowledge and understanding of international issues, focusing on either a major world power or a significant world issue by:**
2.1 Giving straightforward descriptions of the main features of an international issue that draws on a factual knowledge of either a major world power or a significant world issue.	2.1 Giving detailed descriptions of an international issue that draws on a factual and theoretical knowledge of either a major world power or significant world issue.
2.2 Giving straightforward explanations relating to an international issue.	2.2 Giving detailed explanations relating to an international issue.

International Issues

8 Terrorism as an international issue

What you will learn in this chapter

- Understand and identify terrorist behaviour.
- Understand why terrorist organisations exist.
- Explain the differences between domestic and international terrorism.
- Understand how terrorism has affected Scotland.

The origins of terrorism

International terrorism has arguably become the biggest threat to global security in recent years. In fact, according to the 2012 Global Terrorism Index, the number of terrorist incidents has quadrupled since the start of the Iraq War in 2003.

Make the Link

In History you may learn that the French Revolution was also known as the 'reign of terror'.

Figure 8.1: *More than 50 people were killed in the 2013 Reyhanll car bombings in Turkey*

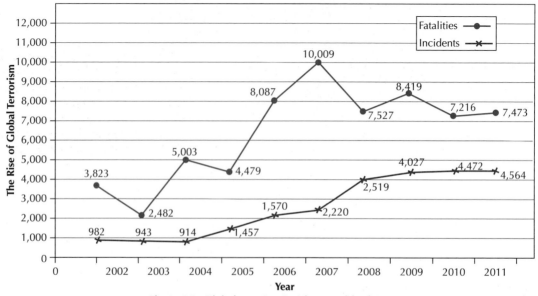

Figure 8.2: *Global terrorism incidents and fatalities over a recent 10-year period*

The word 'terrorism' itself originally comes from the French word 'terrorisme' and dates from the time of the French Revolution. Causing 'terror' or 'fear' hasn't changed much in the intervening years. Terrorist organisations and individuals sympathetic to their actions continue to exist today.

What is 'terrorism'?

Terrorism is the use of violence to achieve a stated political goal. Organisations and individuals who are members of terrorist organisations want to achieve a political aim; this might be a greater say in how their country is run, or they might disagree with a foreign government's ideology.

It is important to remember when studying this global issue that some members of terrorist groups would not consider themselves to be so; they might consider themselves to be members of a pressure group and might even consider action taken in defence of their beliefs as justifiable.

Both pressure groups and terrorist organisations seek to make political gains through their actions. The difference between them, however, is that terrorist organisations use violence and other illegal actions to further their cause. This could be in the form of a mass killing, for example as was the case in London in 2005 when a group of Islamic fundamentalists killed 52 people and injured over 700 others in what became known as the 7/7 attacks (they happened on the 7th of July that year). Terrorism can be identified, therefore, by the way in which violence is used to try to achieve stated aims.

Figure 8.3: *The French Revolution was characterised by the use of the guillotine*

📖 Word bank

- **Justifiable**
Able to be shown to be right, reasonable or defensible.

- **Fundamentalist**
A person who believes in the strict and literal interpretation of their religion's holy texts.

Figure 8.4: *The wreck of the double-decker bus blown apart in the London 2005 bombings*

⚫ Make the Link

In History you may have studied groups such as the suffragettes and the Bolsheviks; do you think that these groups were 'terrorists'?

📖 Word bank

• **Domestic**
Within your own country.

❓ Questions

1. **Describe** what you understand by the term 'political goal'.

2. **Explain** the type of behaviour that terrorist organisations and supporters use in order to achieve their goals.

3. Outline the differences between terrorist organisations and pressure groups.

✹ Make the Link

You will have learned in Unit 1 how pressure groups can work legitimately to affect government and make change happen.

Domestic terrorism

Historically, terrorist organisations have focused on domestic struggles. You may already know of groups such as the Irish Republican Army (IRA) and the Spanish group Euskadi Ta Askatasuna (ETA). These organisations have tried to achieve their political goals by carrying out terrorist attacks.

Figure 8.5: *Northern Ireland was formed in 1921, following the end of British rule in the Republic of Ireland*

📖 Word bank

• **Ceasefire**
A truce; a temporary stopping of fighting.

The IRA

The IRA's historical goal was to create a united Ireland. Members of this terrorist group believed that the only way to achieve this goal was to carry out terrorist attacks in order to make their position heard. While the IRA has split into various different groups since its beginnings, those sympathetic and supportive of the cause remain active. In 1998 one of these groups, 'The Real IRA', was responsible for the Omagh bombing in which 29 people were killed and another 220 people injured.

ETA

Similarly in Spain, ETA have existed since the 1950s, and were founded with the stated aim of creating a 'homeland' for the Basque regions of Spain. Whilst ETA, like the IRA, have declared many ceasefires over the years, the group are responsible for the deaths of 829 people in total since their emergence. Both ETA and the IRA operated at a relatively local level and their attacks were rarely carried out outside the country they operated in. This is what is meant by *domestic terrorism*.

Figure 8.6: *Memorial to the victims of the IRA's bombing in Omagh*

Figure 8.7: *ETA regularly tried to negotiate with the Spanish government via anonymous video broadcasts like the one shown*

September the 11th

Modern-day terrorism has changed significantly since the events of September 11th 2001. On that day four planes were hijacked by Islamic terrorists. Two of the planes were flown into the World Trade Center towers in New York. The towers collapsed killing thousands of people. Another plane was crashed into the Pentagon, the centre of America's military headquarters in Washington D.C. and a fourth plane crashed nearby in the state of Pennsylvania. It is thought that this fourth plane was bound for the White House and that the passengers on board managed to overpower the terrorists.

Al-Qaeda, a terrorist organisation headed by an individual named Osama bin Laden, was quickly linked by American intelligence to the attacks.

In total, almost 3,000 people died in the attacks, including 227 civilians and the 19 hijackers aboard the four planes; 67 British people were also killed that day.

Global terrorism

Today, the modern face of terrorism is global and terrorist organisations are no longer limited in terms of how they can cause terror, fear and intimidation in the actions that they carry out. Global terrorism affects us all – from travelling on a plane to entering a public building, and even using the internet, security measures across the world are now much stricter than they were before 2001. The Global Terrorism Index study shows how the threat of terrorism to global security has increased in recent years.

 Hint

You might be part of your school council and try to bring about change in school through having meetings with your teachers, for example.

📖 **Word bank**

• **Intelligence**
Information gathered by national security organisations.

Figure 8.8: *The World Trade Center shortly after the first hijacked plane hit*

Year	Terrorism incidents	Terrorism deaths
2002	982	3,823
2012	4,564	7,473

[Source: The Global Terrorism Index http://www.reuters.com/article/2012/12/04/us-security-attacks-idUSBRE8B306M20121204]

Defining terrorism

In November 2004, a United Nations Secretary General report described terrorism as any act 'intended to cause death or serious bodily harm to civilians or non-combatants with the purpose of intimidating a population or compelling a government or an international organisation to do or abstain from doing any act.'

Today the term 'terrorism' remains a hotly debated concept. Those in terrorist organisations, such as the IRA or Al-Qaeda, often would not consider themselves to be 'terrorists'. Equally, there are many people who sympathise with the beliefs of terrorist organisations but who do not support the way they try to gain political support. In 2002, for example, the then UK Prime Minister's wife, Cherie Blair, commented that many young Palestinians felt they had 'no hope' but to resort to blowing themselves up. Mrs Blair was referring to suicide bombings that had taken place hours before in Jerusalem, killing 19 Israelis and injuring 40 others. Whilst Mrs Blair was forced to apologise for her comments, it nevertheless shows that people can be sympathetic to terrorist organisations' aims without necessarily supporting their behaviour.

Word bank

• United Nations

An organisation of independent states formed in 1945 to promote international peace and security. There is more information about the UN on page 196.

Figure 8.9: *Aftermath of a Palestinian suicide bomb attack in Dimona, 2008*

❓ Questions

1. **Explain** where the word 'terrorism' originates from.
2. **Describe, in detail,** what has changed about the focus of terrorist attacks in recent years. In your answer you should refer to the IRA and to ETA.
3. Outline the events of September 11th 2001.
4. 'Terrorism isn't a global threat today. After September the 11th the number of incidents decreased. More people were dying because of terrorism in 2002, but that isn't the case anymore.' Helen McLean.

   Using only the information in the above table, give two reasons to **oppose** the view of Helen McLean.

The Scottish connection

Scotland has its own experience of the effects of international terrorism. In 1988 a bomb exploded on Pan Am 103, a flight from London Heathrow destined for New York. The bomb killed all 243 passengers on board and 11 people on the ground as the aircraft crashed into the town of Lockerbie in the Scottish Borders.

Figure 8.10: *Aftermath of the Lockerbie bombing*

Activity

Discuss

Discuss the UN definition of terrorism with your shoulder partner and decide upon your own definition. Try to limit your definition to 140 characters (the length of a tweet) so that it may be shared and discussed with your classmates.

Figure 8.11: *Protests at Prestwick airport over 'torture flights'*

📖 Word bank

- **Rendition flights**

Those used to transport suspected terrorists to a country where torture is not illegal before interrogation.

- **Waterboarding**

A form of torture that simulates drowning by pouring water over a cloth covering the face and mouth of a prisoner.

The use of Scotland as a 'refuelling' centre for rendition flights has also received media attention. It has been claimed that during the 'War on Terror' (see chapter 3 of this Unit) the United States used locations in Scotland to refuel planes that were travelling to other destinations where suspects would then be tortured as an interrogation tactic. A study by researchers at the universities of Kent and Kingston published in 2013 claimed that flights had landed regularly in Prestwick, Aberdeen and Inverness. The team of researchers noted a plane that had landed at Wick in 2004 had been 'logged flying to secret prison and torture destinations'.

Former American President George W. Bush allowed the use of torture methods such as hypothermia, stress positions and waterboarding as part of interrogation. The American Central Intelligence Agency (CIA) and the Department of Defense (DoD) used these methods in 'black sites' (secret prisons), the Guantanamo Bay detention camp, and in Abu Ghraib – a US prison in Iraq. Waterboarding can cause extreme pain and damage to the lungs as well as brain damage from oxygen loss. Barack Obama, the current US President in 2014, has criticised the use of waterboarding, stating in 2011, 'if we want to lead around the world part of our leadership is setting a good example. And anybody who has actually read about and understands the practice of waterboarding would say that that is torture and that's not something we do. Period.'

Figure 8.12: *The gas chamber at Abu Ghraib prison*

The Glasgow airport attack

In June 2007, on the first Saturday of the school summer holidays, Glasgow airport was attacked by two Islamic extremists. Bilal Abdullah was born in England and was a qualified doctor working in the Royal Alexandria Hospital in Paisley. His accomplice in the attack was Kafeel Ahmed, born in India, a qualified engineer who was studying for a PhD.

At approximately 3pm on the 30th of June, a green Jeep Cherokee that was loaded with propane was driven into the front doors of Glasgow International Airport and set on fire. Security bollards outside the airport prevented the car from actually entering the airport itself where it could have caused serious destruction. Ahmed, the driver, was badly burnt in the incident and five members of the public were also injured.

Figure 8.13: *Partial view of the damaged Jeep used in the Glasgow airport attack*

The suspects were both arrested, but Ahmed later died of his injuries in hospital. Abdullah was found guilty of conspiracy to commit murder and was sentenced to 32 years in prison. Police later linked the attack to a foiled car bomb explosion in London.

Asked of his motivations for the attacks whilst on trial, Dr Bilal said the destruction of Iraq was the main driving force behind his actions.

❓ Questions

1. **Explain** what you understand by the term 'rendition flight'.
2. **Describe** what 'waterboarding' is.
3. Make notes on the Glasgow airport attack of 2007. In your notes you must detail the names of the individuals responsible, the cause of the attack and any damage that occurred as a result.

🔵 Activity

Research
With your shoulder partner, research the use of torture as an interrogation technique for terrorist suspects. Present your findings to the class in PowerPoint format.

🔵 Activity

Use your skills
The Global Terrorism Index considers the impact of terrorism in the last decade on countries across the world. The statistics below are documented from the period 2002–2011.

Rank	Country	GTI Score
1	Iraq	9.56
2	Pakistan	9.05
3	Afghanistan	8.67
4	India	8.15
5	Yemen	7.30
6	Somalia	7.24
7	Nigeria	7.24
8	Thailand	7.09
9	Russia	7.07
10	Philippines	6.80

Figure 8.14: *Source 1: Ten countries most affected by terrorism, 2011*

(continued)

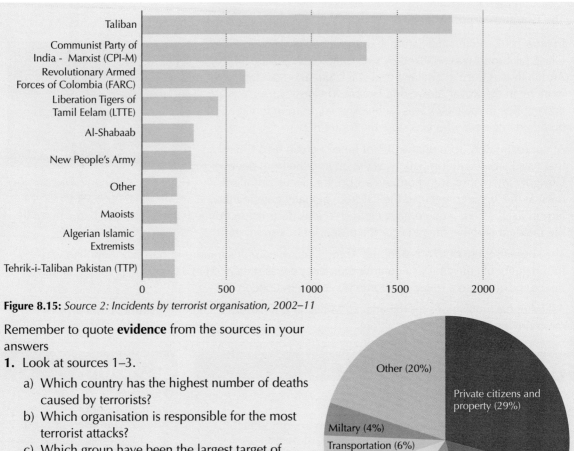

Figure 8.15: *Source 2: Incidents by terrorist organisation, 2002–11*

Remember to quote **evidence** from the sources in your answers

1. Look at sources 1–3.

   a) Which country has the highest number of deaths caused by terrorists?

   b) Which organisation is responsible for the most terrorist attacks?

   c) Which group have been the largest target of terrorist attacks?

2. 'The Taliban are the only real terrorist threat globally. It's always the military which are the biggest target for terrorists to attack. Afghanistan is still the country most affected by terrorism today.' View of political journalist.

   • You should give information that the political journalist has **not selected** as it does not **support** her view.

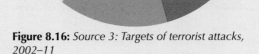

Figure 8.16: *Source 3: Targets of terrorist attacks, 2002–11*

   • You should give information that the political journalist has **selected** as it **supports** her view.

   • Your answer must be based on all three sources.

Summary

In this chapter you have learned:

- how to identify terrorist behaviour

- why terrorist organisations exist

- the differences between domestic and international terrorism

- how terrorism has affected Scotland

Learning Summary

Now that you have finished the **Terrorism as an international issue** chapter, complete a self-evaluation of your knowledge and skills to assess what you have understood. Use the checklist below and its traffic lights to draw up a revision plan to help you improve in the areas you identified as red or amber.

- I can describe what is meant by a 'political goal'.
- I can identify how terrorists try to achieve their aims.
- I can explain what 'domestic terrorism' is.
- I can explain what 'global terrorism' is.
- I understand why terrorism has become a 'global issue'.
- I can describe the types of behaviour that terrorist organisations/supporters use.
- I can outline the difference between a terrorist organisation and a pressure group.
- I can explain what has changed about the focus of terrorist attacks in recent years.
- I can outline what happened on September 11th 2001.
- I understand how the events of September 11th have changed the role of terrorism.
- I can describe what a 'rendition flight' is.
- I understand why 'rendition flights' have been used by governments.
- I can explain what 'waterboarding' is.
- I understand why 'waterboarding' has been used by governments.
- I can explain what happened in the Glasgow airport attack in 2007.
- I understand how the global issue of terrorism is relevant to me as a student in Scotland.

Examples

In Modern Studies it is essential that you are able to back up any point you make with relevant evidence. When you are considering the statements above try to think of relevant examples for each response. You may wish to note these examples under each statement in your revision notes.

9 The causes of terrorism

What you will learn in this chapter

- How to identify the factors that make individuals become involved in terrorism.
- How to identify the factors that make terrorist groups most likely to attack.
- How to explain the different tactics used by terrorists.

GO! Activity

Discuss
Discuss with your shoulder partner the reasons why you believe people become involved in terrorist organisations or terrorist behaviour.

Hint

Peer pressure is often used in school to make people do things they might not ordinarily be inclined to do.

📖 **Word bank**

- **Radicalisation**

When a person or a group become extreme in their belief system.

- **Ambush**

A surprise attack.

- **Sabotage**

Deliberately damage or destroy something for political advantage.

 Make the Link

You may learn about radicalisation in RMPS.

The causes of terrorism

The actions individuals and groups take are very rarely without reason or cause. Whilst many people might disagree with that reason entirely, others believe that they have no option but to engage in terrorist activity in order to achieve their aims. Even when unsuccessful, terrorists may consider the activity worthwhile as it draws attention to their cause.

There are many different factors that can drive someone to become a terrorist. Sometimes people can become radicalised because of their beliefs or because of their distrust in others. For others, political decisions can mean that they feel so disempowered that they view violent terrorist activities as a last resort.

The Elves

CASE STUDY

The Earth Liberation Front (ELF), also known as The Elves, use guerrilla warfare to prevent or protest environmental destruction. Guerrilla warfare is usually small scale in nature, and might include tactics such as ambush or sabotage. The Elves have been responsible for the highest number of attacks in America in the last decade (see Figure 9.1 below).

Rank	Organisation	Number of attacks	Number of fatalities
1	Earth Liberation Front (ELF)	50	0
2	Animal Liberation Front (ALF)	34	0
3	Al-Qaeda	4	2,996
4	Coalition to Save the Preserves (CSP)	2	0
4	Revolutionary Cells-Animal Liberation Brigade	2	0
5	Al-Qaeda in the Arabian Peninsula (AQAP)	1	0
5	Ku Klux Klan	1	0
5	Minutemen American Defense	1	2
5	Tehrik-i-Taliban Pakistan (TTP)	1	0
5	The Justice Department	1	0

For example, in 2008 The Elves set fire to four multi-million dollar homes in Washington, causing $7 million worth of damage. Police authorities commenting on the act described it as 'domestic terrorism'. Graffiti found at the homes mocked claims that the homes were built to be environmentally friendly: 'Built Green? Nope black! McMansions in RCDs [a rural cluster development] r not green. ELF.'

Figure 9.2: *A development of new homes in California, burnt by the ELF*

? Questions

1. **Describe** what 'radicalisation' means.
2. **Identify, with evidence,** the top three organisations responsible for the most terrorist attacks in the United States.
3. **Explain** whether or not you believe the actions of the group ELF represents terrorist behaviour. **Justify** your response with **evidence** from the case study.

Why do people become involved in terrorist behaviour?

There are a number of factors that can motivate individuals to become involved in terrorist activity and support.

Identity

Some people feel that they have no identity or belonging. This means that they may feel frustrated with the government of their country or another, and they might view violence as the only way to express this. When people feel cut off from society they may also become less engaged with democratic participation, for example through protest.

In July 2011, the Norwegian Anders Behring Breivik was responsible the deaths of 77 people after he planted a car bomb in Oslo and then opened fire at a youth camp outside the city. Breivik, an anti-Islamic

Figure 9.3: *Flowers laid around Oslo cathedral following the attacks of July 2011*

extremist, claimed that the attacks were justified in order to stop the 'Islamisation of Norway'.

Beliefs

Some individuals feel that their beliefs are not properly represented by the country in which they live. As such, they feel that making a political statement through terrorist activity is the only way to have their beliefs heard.

In 2009 a judge in England branded seven animal rights extremists 'urban terrorists' and jailed them for a total of 50 years. The group worked to intimidate workers at Huntingdon Life Sciences, which carries out animal testing for medical research. They sent hoax bombs allegedly contaminated with the AIDS virus to employees' homes, poured paint stripper on cars and wrote things like 'murderer' or 'puppy killer' on the walls of employees' houses.

Figure 9.4: *A sign for Huntingdon Life Sciences outside the facility*

📖 Word bank

- **Militant**

Using aggressive or violent methods to support their cause.

- **Late-term abortion**

Termination of a pregnancy once it has gone past a certain number of weeks.

Pressure

Other individuals are pressurised into becoming involved in terrorist groups or activities. It has been claimed that the Lord's Resistance Army, which is a militant Christian movement, has been responsible for the abduction, abuse and recruitment of thousands of children across Africa since the 1980s. The group's controversial leader, Joseph Kony, claims to be the spokesman of God and was brought to public prominence through the film *Kony* in 2012.

Radicalised

Some people become radicalised because of their beliefs. Pro-life groups (groups who are against abortion) have often resorted to terrorist tactics in America in response to laws they do not agree with. On 31st May 2009 George Tiller, a doctor from Kansas who was nationally known for being one of the few doctors in the United States to perform late-term abortions, was shot and killed by an anti-abortion activist.

Retaliation

Others may retaliate against what they see as the unjust actions of individuals or groups. In May 2013 Palestinian resistance fighters in the Gaza Strip sent a mortar shell into southern Israel, a day after an air strike by Israeli forces.

The conflict in the Middle East continues and focuses on the recognition of borders. Estimates claim that since the year 2000 at least 1,104 Israelis and 6,829 Palestinians have been killed in the conflict.

❓ Question

Using the headings below, summarise the individual factors which can make a person become involved in terrorist activity:

- identity
- beliefs
- pressurised
- radicalised
- retaliation

Figure 9.5: *The disputed Gaza Strip highlighted by the arrow.*

GO! Activity

Research
Working individually, use the internet to research a recent example of a terrorist attack. Provide a written one-page report to your teacher. In your report you may wish to consider:

- when the attack happened
- where the attack happened
- a description of what happened
- who accepted responsibility for the attack
- how many people were injured/killed as a result of the attack
- the reason the attack happened (try to link your report to one of the individual factors identified)

Terrorist ideology

As we have seen, not all terrorist organisations exist for the same reasons. The ideology which informs a terrorist organisation is therefore very important when analysing the causes of terrorism.

An ideology is a body of ideas or beliefs that determine the aims of an organisation. It can be social, economic or political in nature. The Global Terrorism Index has broadly identified three different types of terrorist ideology, based on the number of incidents that have occurred. These are:

- religious
- political
- national/separatist

Word bank

• **Evangelical**

Belonging to a Christian group that stresses the authority of the Bible.

Religious ideology

Religious extremism continues to be the most likely cause of a terrorist attack. Whilst organisations such as Al-Qaeda and the Taliban often dominate the news headlines, it is important to understand that extremism happens in many different religions. In April 2013 the American government listed evangelical Christianity as the highest terrorist threat to their national security.

The Christian Patriot movement believes that the American government is involved in a conspiracy to deny its citizens their 'constitutional rights.' Their ideology is associated with White Supremacy – the belief that white people are superior to all other racial backgrounds.

Hutaree

CASE STUDY

Hutaree is an extremist Christian group that follows the ideology of the Christian Patriot movement and is based in Michigan in America. The name 'Hutaree' means 'Christian warriors'. The Hutaree claim 'we see the end of the age coming quickly, and with it some very rough times ahead, as foretold by God's word'.

In March 2010, nine people thought to be Hutaree members were arrested in police raids in Ohio and Indiana for their apparent involvement in a plot to kill police officers. The group was allegedly preparing for what they believed would be the end of the world.

? Questions

1. **Describe** what is meant by 'religious extremism'.
2. **Explain** what the group Hutaree stand for and how they try to achieve their aims.

Political motivations

The type of political system used by a country can make terrorist behaviour and attacks more likely; in countries which are not democratic, people feel they do not have a say in how their country is run and terrorism is more likely to occur (see Figure 9.6 below).

Country	Government type
Afghanistan	Authoritarian regime
India	Flawed democracy
Iraq	Hybrid regime
Nigeria	Authoritarian regime
Pakistan	Hybrid regime
Philippines	Flawed democracy
Russia	Hybrid regime
Somalia	Unclassified
Thailand	Flawed democracy
Yemen	Authoritatian regime

Figure 9.6: *Top 10 countries affected by terrorism and their governments*

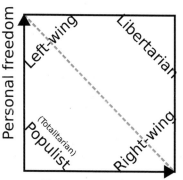

Figure 9.7: *The Nolan chart of political viewpoints*

Political extremism is usually characterised by which side of the political spectrum it sits on. In politics, parties are sometimes referred to as being 'left wing' or 'right wing' (see page 61). Left wing politics has traditionally been linked to high levels of tax (especially for the rich), and welfare programmes, such as the NHS for example. Right wing politics have traditionally been associated by low tax levels (especially for the rich), and individual responsibility for welfare.

Any political party or movement can become extreme in its beliefs if it moves too far on either side of the political spectrum. For example the British National Party, who are against immigration and are often accused of racism, are an example of an extremist right wing organisation. They have been accused of having terrorist links in the past, but in recent years they have actively tried to become more appealing to mainstream voters. In 2009 the party leader Nick Griffin was controversially given airtime on the BBC *Question Time* programme.

❓ Questions

1. **Explain** what you understand by the terms 'left wing' and 'right wing'.
2. Consider your own political beliefs. Would you describe yourself as 'left wing' or 'right wing'? You may wish to use an online 'political spectrum' tool to help you decide.

UKIP (The United Kingdom Independence Party) is often cited as an example of an extremist right wing party in UK politics. Whilst the party has no elected representatives in Scotland, it has nine MEPs representing English constituencies, three members in the House of Lords and one member in the Northern Ireland Assembly.

🔵 GO! Activity

Discuss
Discuss with your shoulder partner the reasons why not having a democratic government might make terrorism more likely.

🔵 GO! Activity

Discuss
Read the newspaper article on the next page. Discuss with your shoulder partner whether the leader of UKIP, Nigel Farage, experienced racism at the hands of Scottish protestors or whether you think those protesting were simply demonstrating their dislike of UKIP's policies.

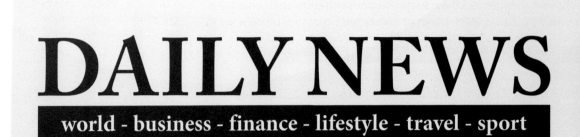

DAILY NEWS

world - business - finance - lifestyle - travel - sport

UKIP leader Nigel Farage hits back at 'fascist' hecklers in Edinburgh pub

Nigel Farage hit back today at demonstrators in Scotland who branded him "racist, Nazi scum" by describing them as "fascist, deeply racist" and "anti-English".

Figure 9.8: *Nigel Farage*

Mr Farage, whose party has no elected representatives in Scotland, ventured north of the border on Thursday but was besieged in an Edinburgh pub when supporters of Scottish independence mounted a protest.

Yesterday he described the demonstrators as "deeply racist with a total hatred of the English and a desire for Scotland to be independent from Westminster". He added: "The fact that 50 yobbo, fascist scum turn up and aren't prepared to listen to debate, I absolutely refuse to believe is representative of Scottish public opinion."

He hung up the phone in the middle of his radio interview after being quizzed about Ukip's knowledge of Scottish politics and its level of support in the country. He said: "We could have had this interview in England a couple of years ago, although I wouldn't have met with such hatred that I'm getting from your questions, and frankly I've had enough of this interview. Goodbye."

A Scottish National Party spokesman said: "Anyone who heard the interview with Nigel Farage would have thought he has completely lost the plot. He accused the BBC of hatred when under pressure and panicked during an interview. Nothing he says can be treated with a shred of credibility."

Liam O'Hare, a spokesman for the Radical Independence group, said: "Farage's attempts to paint our protest as anti-English is pathetic. Our vision is for a Scotland that welcomes people from across the world, including England. This is the exact opposite of Farage and Ukip's vision for Scotland, which is a parochial, bigoted British nationalism. We're against his racist ideas, not where he comes from."

[Source: http://www.independent.co.uk/news/uk/politics/ukip-leader-nigel-farage-hits-back-at-fascist-hecklers-in-edinburgh-pub-8619819.html]

Nationalism

Those who support a nationalist cause are also sometimes drawn into a terrorist organisation. Nationalism, like left and right wing politics, can become extremist in nature if it begins to use violence to achieve its stated goals. In the UK context the most obvious example of nationalist terrorism would be the IRA and the many affiliated organisations which support its goal of a united Ireland.

Russia

In 2011 Moscow's busiest airport was attacked by a 20 year old suicide bomber, Magomed Yevloyev. Yevloyev was from Ingushetia, which is a federal subject of Russia and borders the country of Chechnya. In the attack 37 people lost their lives and 173 were injured.

Figure 9.9: *A Russian TV channel shows a paramedic treating one of the many injured at Domodedovo International Airport.*

A group known as the 'Caucasus Emirate' claimed responsibility for the attack and threatened to carry out more in the future. The group have asked for American support in the past against what it calls 'Russian aggression'.

After the attack, Russian Prime Minister Vladimir Putin, commenting on the bombing, stated that 'retribution is inevitable'.

Russia has a historically uneasy relationship with many of the countries who were once part of the Union of Soviet Socialist Republics (USSR). Chechnya is another federal subject of Russia which is rich in oil reserves; the second Chechen War in the late 1990s led to the death of more than 25,000 people and Russian airstrikes at the time forced over 100,000 Chechens to leave their homes.

The USSR dissolved in 1991. Prior to that time the greatest threat to international security was arguably that of Communism and Russian expansionism.

📖 Word bank

- **Nationalism**
  A devotion to the interests and culture of your home nation.

- **Federal subject**
  A geographical area, province, territory etc. that depends on the main country for some powers but also has its own authority.

- **Expansionism**
  A nation's policy of expanding into new territories.

Make the Link

In History you may have studied the USSR.

? Questions

1. Consider the case study about Russia. Outline:
    - the name of the individual responsible for the Moscow airport bombing
    - the reasons why the attack happened
    - the Russian government's response to the attacks

2. Summarise the individual causes of terrorism and the ideological factors in two mind maps.

Tactics of terror

Terrorist organisations use a variety of different tactics to achieve their aims. One of their most important tactics is often the element of surprise; this means that terrorist tactics are often unpredictable. However, many terrorist organisations use similar tactics in order to achieve their goals.

Tactic	Explanation	Example
Bombing	This is when terrorists use bombs to cause mass destruction and loss of life in order to highlight their cause.	
Hijacking	This is when terrorists take control of something, such as a plane, in order to draw attention to their cause.	For example, on September 11th 2001 Al-Qaeda terrorists hijacked four planes.
Arson	This is when terrorists deliberately burn buildings or targets of importance to their cause.	
Assault		
Kidnapping		For example, in 2010 Scottish aid worker Linda Norgrove was kidnapped and killed by the Taliban in Afghanistan.
Hostage taking		

? Questions

1. Copy and complete the table above. You may wish to use the internet to find relevant, up-to-date **examples** of the different terrorist tactics used across the world. Some of the examples and explanations have been filled in for you to get your started.

2. Terrorists use a variety of different tactics in order to achieve their goals. **Describe** these tactics. In your answer you must:
    - refer to at least two different tactics used by terrorists
    - provide relevant **examples** that explain your response

🔘 Activity

Use your skills

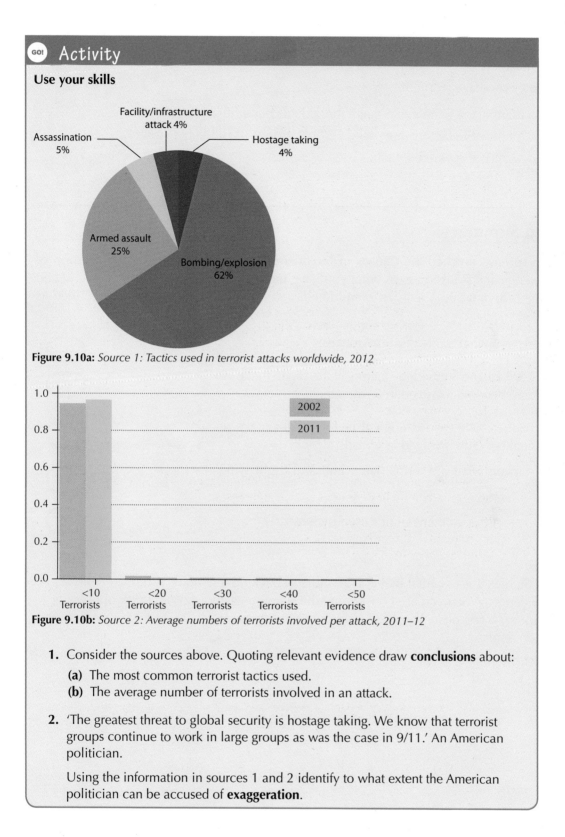

Figure 9.10a: *Source 1: Tactics used in terrorist attacks worldwide, 2012*

Figure 9.10b: *Source 2: Average numbers of terrorists involved per attack, 2011–12*

1. Consider the sources above. Quoting relevant evidence draw **conclusions** about:
   (a) The most common terrorist tactics used.
   (b) The average number of terrorists involved in an attack.

2. 'The greatest threat to global security is hostage taking. We know that terrorist groups continue to work in large groups as was the case in 9/11.' An American politician.

   Using the information in sources 1 and 2 identify to what extent the American politician can be accused of **exaggeration**.

Summary

In this chapter you have learned:

- how to identify the factors that make individuals become involved in terrorism
- how to identify the factors that make terrorist groups most likely to attack
- how to explain the different tactics used by terrorists

Learning Summary

Now that you have finished the **Causes of terrorism** chapter, complete a self-evaluation of your knowledge and skills to assess what you have understood. Use the checklist below and its traffic lights to draw up a revision plan to help you improve in the areas you identified as red or amber.

- I can explain what 'radicalisation' means.

- I can explain the individual factors that might make an individual become involved in terrorism.

- I can explain why the ideological factors might make an individual become involved in terrorism.

- I can explain what the terms 'left wing' and 'right wing' mean.

- I can explain the different tactics used by terrorists.

Examples

In Modern Studies it is essential that you are able to back up any point you make with relevant evidence. When you are considering the statements above try to think of relevant examples for each response. You may wish to note these examples under each statement in your revision notes.

10 The War on Terror

The War on Terror

The term 'War on Terror' was first used by former American President George W. Bush in response to the terrorist attacks of September 11th 2001. The phrase characterises the international military campaign that began in response to those attacks. One of the biggest supporters of America's War on Terror was the then UK Prime Minister, Tony Blair.

On 20th September 2001 President Bush made a speech in which he directly linked the terrorist organisation Al-Qaeda to the attacks.

Who are Al-Qaeda?

Al-Qaeda is an extremist Sunni Muslim movement founded by Osama bin Laden. Al-Qaeda is a global terrorist organisation and has a network of supporters and active members across the world. The group are in favour of global jihad – which translates as 'to struggle' – and are often interpreted as justifying a 'holy war'. Al-Qaeda also supports sharia law, which is a very strict form of religious law laid down by Islam.

Sharia law

In 2009, UN journalist Lubna Ahmed al-Hussein was arrested in the Sudan for the crime of wearing trousers (article 152 of Sudanese criminal law bans dressing 'indecently' in public). Sharia law is enforced in Sudan and permits corporal punishment for those who disobey. Lubna's punishment should have been a fine and 40 lashes but because of her status as a UN journalist Lubna was spared this punishment. Those that she was with that day were not.

Figure 10.1: *Tony Blair and George W. Bush*

Figure 10.2: *Sudan is located in North Africa*

Figure 10.3: *Sudanese journalist Lubna Ahmed al-Hussein*

? Questions

1. **Explain** the role of George W. Bush and Tony Blair in the War on Terror.
2. **Explain** who the organisation Al-Qaeda are and why they exist.
3. Outline what you understand by 'sharia law' and **explain, with a relevant example,** what sharia law means for many women.

Invading Afghanistan

The first military target of the War on Terror was the country of Afghanistan. Afghanistan is a war-torn nation where 42% of the population live below the poverty line. Until 2001 the country was governed by the Taliban, an Islamic fundamentalist political movement which had spread into Afghanistan from Pakistan and had managed to form a government. American intelligence suggested that Afghanistan and the Taliban were harbouring key members of Al-Qaeda, including Osama bin Laden. President Bush issued an ultimatum to the Taliban regime in Afghanistan to hand over bin Laden and the leaders of Al-Qaeda.

Figure 10.4: *George W. Bush: 'By aiding and abetting murder, the Taliban regime is committing murder'*

While recommending to bin Laden that he leave the country, the Taliban would not hand him over without direct evidence to link him to the attacks. The United States refused to negotiate and for the first time in its history NATO invoked Article 5 of its constitution – that an attack on one member country is an attack on all (for more information on NATO's role in combating terrorism, see page 199). America decided to act with its own coalition – including the United Kingdom, France and Spain. In October 2001 allied forces invaded Afghanistan under the umbrella 'Operation Enduring Freedom'. Their aim was to remove the Taliban regime, find Osama bin Laden, and destroy

Al-Qaeda's networks. Members of Al-Qaeda and the Taliban quickly went into hiding in Afghanistan's mountains.

The Taliban were removed from formal political power relatively quickly. However, the Taliban have not disappeared and have been proactively engaged in a series of insurgency attacks since 2001. Their guerrilla war tactics and knowledge of the mountains of Afghanistan means they have been able to hide and build support easily.

The position of women in the country, one of the main criticisms of the regime, has not improved in the intervening years. Whilst the number of girls attending school has increased by over 30 percent since 2002, approximately 1.5 million school-age girls are still not enrolled in school today.

In 2006 NATO's International Security Assistance Force (ISAF) took control of military operations in the country (see page 199 for information on the role of NATO in combating terrorism). When this book was published in 2014 the war in Afghanistan was ongoing. To date approximately 3,500 members of the coalition forces have been killed in action and it is estimated that at least 17,000 Afghan civilians have been killed as a direct result of the war (with many estimates being far higher). In 2010, NATO announced it would withdraw all international troops from Afghanistan in 2014 and control would pass to the new Afghan army and police force.

Osama bin Laden managed to escape capture for many years until he was discovered in Abbottabad in Pakistan in 2011. In May that year, intelligence led US Navy SEALs to a building where bin Laden was shot and killed. Al-Qaeda have promised to avenge bin Laden's death. A statement posted at the time on an Al-Qaeda-supporting website read 'we will remain, God willing, a curse chasing the Americans and their agents, following them outside and inside their countries'.

Hint

You should remember the word coalition from Unit 1, it means an alliance.

Figure 10.5: *Taliban fighters display their weapons*

Word bank

- **Insurgency attacks**
Attacks against the government or authority by rebel forces.

- **Guerrilla war**
Small independent groups fighting against powerful forces, using tactics such as ambush and sabotage.

- **Navy SEALs**
Members of a US naval special warfare unit.

- **Avenge**
Inflict harm in return for wrongdoing.

Figure 10.6: *Map of Pakistan showing location of Abbottabad where Osama bin Laden was killed*

📖 Word bank

• **Coalition of the willing**

A group of nations prepared to engage in military operations outside of the United Nations peacekeeping operations.

• **Weapons of mass destruction**

Nuclear, biological, or chemical weapons able to cause widespread devastation and loss of life.

❓ Questions

1. **Describe** who the Taliban are.
2. **Explain** why Afghanistan was invaded in 2001.
3. **Explain** what 'Operation Enduring Freedom' was.
4. Outline what 'ISAF' stands for.
5. Has the role of women improved in Afghanistan since the invasion? **Explain** your answer with relevant **evidence** from the text.
6. **Describe** the tactics used by the Taliban.
7. 'The Invasion of Afghanistan was extremely successful.' **Identify and explain** three pieces of **evidence** from the text above to **oppose** this statement.

Figure 10.7: *Dick Cheney*

The invasion of Iraq

In 2003 America led a 'coalition of the willing' in the invasion of Iraq. The purpose of this mission was to find weapons of mass destruction which it was alleged that the Iraqi leader, Saddam Hussein, had been developing. Newspaper reports at the time claimed that these weapons could be deployed to reach the UK within 45 minutes of launching. In 2002, the then US Vice President Dick Cheney commented 'simply stated, there is no doubt that Saddam Hussein now has weapons of mass destruction'.

George W. Bush's administration directly linked Iraq to the War on Terror. The President used the term the 'axis of evil' in early 2002 to describe 'rogue' nations, such as Iraq, he believed were harbouring terrorists and building up weapons of mass destruction. Later evidence would prove that Iraq had no weapons of mass destruction. Saddam's government additionally had no proven links to Al-Qaeda.

International support

Unlike the invasion of Afghanistan in 2001, military action in Iraq was not well supported. In the UK millions of people took to the streets to protest; in February 2003 nearly 100,000 people marched in Glasgow against the UK government's support for American intervention in Iraq.

At the United Nations (UN), America's foreign policy ambitions didn't fare much better. America and the UK withdrew a draft resolution when it became clear that they did not have international support for an invasion. The UN had taken many different actions in Iraq over the years and had supported attempts in the past to allow their weapons inspectors to find out whether or not Iraq had the capability to develop weapons of mass destruction. As George W. Bush gave Saddam Hussein an ultimatum to leave power, the UN removed all weapons inspectors from Iraq. Days later the invasion began.

Following the invasion in April 2003 the capital city of Baghdad fell to allied control and Saddam Hussein's government quickly dissolved. However, as in Afghanistan, an insurgency quickly arose against the

Figure 10.8: *Iraqis pass by a mosaic of their President, Saddam Hussein, in 1999*

US-led coalition. The insurgency, which included groups supportive of Al-Qaeda, led to far more coalition deaths than the invasion.

Iraq's former president, Saddam Hussein, was executed in 2006 after being sentenced to death in an Iraqi court. By the time the last US forces left in 2011 at least 116,903 Iraqi 'non combatants', 4,487 Americans and 179 British troops had lost their lives.

Since the start of the Iraq invasion the number of global terrorist incidents has quadrupled.

❓ Questions

1. Outline the key events which led to the Iraq invasion in 2003.
2. Outline why **you think** the invasion was unpopular.

🔵GO! Activity

Class debate: 'The invasion of Iraq has helped in combating the threat posed by international terrorism'
Your teacher will now divide your class into two groups. Your challenge is to research either the Proposition (supporting the motion) or the Opposition (opposing the motion). Even if you do not agree with the viewpoint that you have been given, a good debater should be able to argue from any perspective.

You should try to find evidence from the internet on life in Iraq before the 2003 invasion and life in Iraq today. You may wish to focus on:

*   life expectancy
*   infant mortality
*   morbidity
*   literacy levels
*   incidents of domestic terrorist attacks

Once you have gathered your evidence, use it to make a valid point. Produce a structured paragraph which uses the 'Point, Explain, Example' structure (see page 240).

You will now all be able to make a contribution to the debate. After everyone has made a point your teacher will invite you to participate in debating the issues that have been raised. Your teacher will explain how the debate is to be structured to allow everyone the opportunity to contribute to the discussion.

Reflect on your learning
Following the debate your teacher may take a vote and may ask the class which side of the debate they now agree with.

Underneath your paragraph reflect upon your class debate:

*   has the debate altered your opinion of what you believed previously?
*   did you feel that you were able to contribute in a confident manner?
*   what might you change if you were to debate in the future?

The end of the War on Terror?

Perhaps the two strongest supporters of the War on Terror were the UK Prime Minister Tony Blair, and American President George W. Bush. While neither of these individuals are in power today the, legacy of the War on Terror remains. In May 2013, UK Prime Minister David Cameron commented 'we will defeat violent extremism by standing together, backing our police and security services, and, above all, by challenging the poisonous narrative of extremism on which this violence feeds'.

Figure 10.9: *US President Barack Obama*

The phrase 'War on Terror' is no longer used by the American government. Indeed, in May 2013, President Barack Obama declared that the 'global war on terror is over.' President Obama used this speech to focus on the 'networks' of terrorists and ways in which the international community can stop them gaining support.

The War on Terror has cost America substantially: in total it has cost more than a trillion dollars and more than 7,000 lives have been lost. Of the term 'War on Terror' some people would say that a war against terrorism was unwinnable. These people would argue that terrorism has always existed in some form and there will always be individuals who will use violence in order to make a political statement.

? Questions

1. Has the threat posed by international terrorism worsened since 2001? **Justify** your response with **evidence** from this chapter.
2. **Describe** America's new approach towards tackling international terrorism.
3. **Explain** why some people have been critical of the term 'War on Terror'.

Summary

In this chapter you have learned:

- why the war in Afghanistan happened
- why the war in Iraq happened
- the ways in which the War on Terror has affected global security today

Learning Summary

Now that you have finished **The War on Terror** chapter, complete a self-evaluation of your knowledge and skills to assess what you have understood. Use the checklist below and its traffic lights to draw up a revision plan to help you improve in the areas you identified as red or amber.

- I can explain where the term 'War on Terror' comes from.

- I can explain who Al-Qaeda are.

- I can understand why Al-Qaeda exist.

- I can explain who the Taliban are.

- I can describe the tactics used by the Taliban.

- I understand who Osama bin Laden was.

- I can describe what is meant by 'sharia law'.

- I can understand how sharia law affects the role of women.

- I can outline why Afghanistan was invaded in 2001.

- I can outline what 'ISAF' stands for.

- I can explain why some people think invading Afghanistan was unsuccessful.

- I can outline why Iraq was invaded in 2003.

- I can explain who Saddam Hussein was.

- I can explain why some people were opposed to the Iraq invasion.

- I can describe how the threat of global terrorism has changed since 2001.

- I can outline America's approach toward tackling global terrorism.

- I can explain why some people have been critical of the term 'War on Terror'.

Examples

In Modern Studies it is essential that you are able to back up any point you make with relevant evidence. When you are considering the statements above try to think of relevant examples for each response. You may wish to note these examples under each statement in your revision notes.

11 Terrorism, rights and responsibilities

What you will learn in this chapter

- To understand how rights are affected by terrorism.
- To understand how responsibilities are affected by terrorism.

Make the Link

You learned about rights and responsibilities in Unit 1 of this book.

Figure 11.1: *Human rights are guarded in democratic countries like ours*

Activity

Discuss

With your shoulder partner, take two minutes to discuss:

1. Examples of times when you might have felt that your opinion was not listened to.
2. Examples of ways in which you dealt with that situation.

Make the Link

In History you may have studied the Second World War of 1939–1945.

Rights and responsibilities

Rights and responsibilities are something that we often take for granted living in a democratic country. For example, in a democracy we can vote for a variety of different parties or individuals in regular elections. This means that the government of the day regularly changes and as a result we feel our views are being heard.

In many countries where terrorist attacks occur, however, people are often denied even the most basic of rights.

When people have their rights and responsibilities denied they can feel that they have no other option left than to join an extremist group or take part in terrorist activity. They may feel frustrated that the country they live in does not reflect their beliefs and opinions. This most often happens in poorer, 'developing' countries and these countries are more often victim to terrorist attacks and terrorist organisations taking root. In these types of countries organisations such as the Taliban can take advantage of people's dislike of the government or feelings of political frustration.

Questions

1. State the rights you have as a citizen living in Scotland.
2. **Explain** the responsibilities you have as a citizen living in Scotland.

Human rights

Human rights are something that every human being is entitled to. It is important to remember, however, that the idea that all individuals should have certain rights protected by law only became popular after the end of the Second World War in 1945.

World leaders of the time wanted to make sure that international law would stop countries from carrying out genocide and mass killing ever again.

In 1948 the Universal Declaration of Human Rights (UDHR) was adopted by 56 members of the United Nations. For the first time in history the way in which a government treats its citizens became an international matter. Article 1 of the UDHR states 'all human beings are born free and equal in dignity and rights. They are endowed with reason and conscience and should act towards one another in a spirit of brotherhood'.

> **📖 Word bank**
>
> • **Genocide**
> The deliberate killing of a large group of people, especially those of a particular nation or ethnic group.

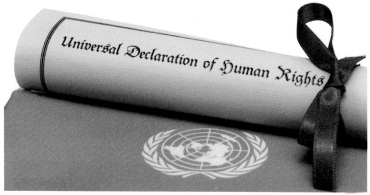

Figure 11.2: *The Universal Declaration of Human Rights*

The Universal Declaration of Human Rights

> **GO! Activity**
>
> **Discuss**
> With your shoulder partner take two minutes to discuss what do you think Article 1 means?

1. **We Are All Born Free and Equal.** We are all born free. We all have our own thoughts and ideas. We should all be treated in the same way.

2. **Don't Discriminate.** These rights belong to everybody, whatever our differences.

3. **The Right to Life.** We all have the right to life, and to live in freedom and safety.

4. **No Slavery.** Nobody has any right to make us a slave. We cannot make anyone our slave.

5. **No Torture**. Nobody has any right to hurt us or to torture us.

6. **You Have Rights No Matter Where You Go.** I am a person just like you!

7. **We're All Equal Before the Law.** The law is the same for everyone. It must treat us all fairly.

8. **Your Human Rights Are Protected by Law.** We can all ask for the law to help us when we are not treated fairly.

9. **No Unfair Detainment.** Nobody has the right to put us in prison without good reason and keep us there, or to send us away from our country.

10. **The Right to Trial.** If we are put on trial this should be in public. The people who try us should not let anyone tell them what to do.

11. **We're Always Innocent Till Proven Guilty.** Nobody should be blamed for doing something until it is proven. When people say we did a bad thing we have the right to show it is not true.

12. **The Right to Privacy.** Nobody should try to harm our good name. Nobody has the right to come into our home, open our letters, or bother us or our family without a good reason.

13. **Freedom to Move.** We all have the right to go where we want in our own country and to travel as we wish.

14. **The Right to Seek a Safe Place to Live.** If we are frightened of being badly treated in our own country, we all have the right to run away to another country to be safe.

15. **Right to a Nationality.** We all have the right to belong to a country.

16. **Marriage and Family.** Every grown-up has the right to marry and have a family if they want to. Men and women have the same rights when they are married, and when they are separated.

17. **The Right to Your Own Things.** Everyone has the right to own things or share them. Nobody should take our things from us without a good reason.

18. **Freedom of Thought.** We all have the right to believe in what we want to believe, to have a religion, or to change it if we want.

19. **Freedom of Expression.** We all have the right to make up our own minds, to think what we like, to say what we think, and to share our ideas with other people.

20. **The Right to Public Assembly.** We all have the right to meet our friends and to work together in peace to defend our rights. Nobody can make us join a group if we don't want to.

21. **The Right to Democracy.** We all have the right to take part in the government of our country. Every grown-up should be allowed to choose their own leaders.

22. **Social Security.** We all have the right to affordable housing, medicine, education, and childcare, enough money to live on and medical help if we are ill or old.

23. **Workers' Rights.** Every grown-up has the right to do a job, to a fair wage for their work, and to join a trade union.

24. **The Right to Play.** We all have the right to rest from work and to relax.

25. **Food and Shelter for All.** We all have the right to a good life. Mothers and children, people who are old, unemployed or disabled, and all people have the right to be cared for.

26. **The Right to Education.** Education is a right. Primary school should be free. We should learn about the United Nations and how to get on with others. Our parents can choose what we learn.

27. **Copyright.** Copyright is a special law that protects one's own artistic creations and writings; others cannot make copies without permission. We all have the right to our own way of life and to enjoy the good things that art, science and learning bring.

28. **A Fair and Free World.** There must be proper order so we can all enjoy rights and freedoms in our own country and all over the world.

29. **Responsibility.** We have a duty to other people, and we should protect their rights and freedoms.

30. **No One Can Take Away Your Human Rights.**

This simplified version of the 30 Articles of the UDHR has been created especially for young people by Youth for Human Rights (www.youthforhumanrights.org).

Rights in Scotland

Scotland is a developed country. As such, all children (under 18) should have their rights recognised within school, at home and by society. With these rights, however, come associated responsibilities. This means that individuals cannot abuse the rights they have been given. In Scotland, for example, individuals have the right to drive a moped at the age of 16; the responsibility that comes with that right is that individuals obey the speed limit and road traffic laws accordingly.

> **⚫⚫ Make the Link**
>
> You learned about road traffic laws in Unit 2.

❓ Questions

1. **Explain** why terrorists often find support in developing countries.
2. Make a table with 'Rights in School' and 'Responsibilities in School'. Show how three of the UNCRC rights are met in your school.
3. **Explain** why the UDHR was written in 1948.
4. Choose three of the human rights documented above. Note down these rights and try to think of a corresponding responsibility for each one.

Children's rights

In 1989 governments from across the world again came together to approve the United Nations Convention on the Rights of the Child (UNCRC). The UN recognised that as children are a vulnerable group their rights are often more open to exploitation than those of other groups. If children do not have parents or guardians to look after them then they have very little way of stopping these rights from being taken away. The UNCRC therefore acknowledged the rights of children, those under 18, in international law. Some examples of children's rights from the convention are shown below:

> **📖 Word bank**
>
> • **Exploitation**
> Treating someone unfairly in order to benefit from their work.

- the right to life
- the right to name and identity
- the right to be protected from abuse or exploitation
- the right to an education
- the right to have privacy protected
- to be raised by, or have a relationship with, their parents
- the right to express their opinions and have these listened to and, where appropriate, acted upon
- the right to play

Figure 11.3: *Child labour would go against the children's right 'to be protected from abuse or exploitation'*

❓ Questions

1. **Explain** why the UN produced a separate document to acknowledge the rights of children.
2. Choose three rights from the summary above.
   - Outline how these rights are met within your school community.
   - Outline the corresponding responsibilities that match with these rights.

Universal rights?

> ### 📖 Word bank
>
> • **Social scientists**
>
> Experts in the study of human society and its personal relationships.

Despite international law protecting both human and children's rights, there are still countries that exploit and discriminate against their own people. Figure 11.4, shown below, shows the percentage of women who were married when under the age of 18 in selected countries in South Asia and Sub-Saharan Africa. The position of women in society is one way which social scientists can measure a country's human rights record. Figure 11.4 uses this information and compares it to literacy levels.

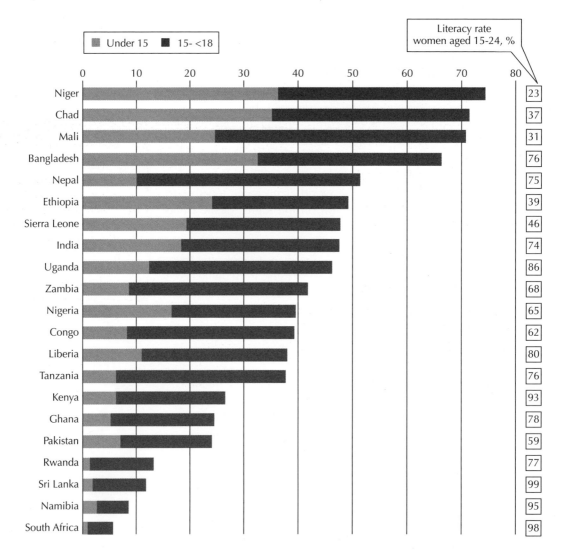

Source: UNICEF: World Bank *Based on surveys conducted in 2008 or latest available data

Figure 11.4: *Percentage of women married <18 and literacy rate of women aged 15–24*

N5 **?Questions**

1. Consider the information in Figure 11.4. Using relevant statistics draw **conclusions** on:
    *   the country with the highest % of child brides aged under 15
    *   the country with the highest % of child brides aged between 15 and 18
    *   the country with the lowest literacy rate for women aged between 15 and 24
2. Having considered the **evidence**, what is the overall **conclusion** that can be reached regarding the percentage of child brides in a country and the literacy rate of women in that country?

Malala Yousafzai & women's rights

CASE STUDY

In October 2012 Malala Yousafzai was shot in the head by the Taliban in Pakistan while returning home on the school bus. Fifteen year old Malala was well-known to the Taliban for her work in promoting girls' education. She had even written a blog for the BBC in 2009 about abuses against women in Pakistan. The Taliban regime have become infamous for their sexist treatment of women: forcing them to wear the burqa in public, not allowing them to work at all, or to receive any level of education past the age of eight.

Figure 11.5: *Malala Yousafzai*

In the days immediately following the attack she remained unconscious and in critical condition, but later her condition improved enough for her to be sent to the Queen Elizabeth Hospital in Birmingham for intensive rehabilitation.

Later that month a group of 50 Islamic clerics in Pakistan issued a fatwā (a ruling in Islamic law) against those who tried to kill her. The Taliban ignored this and restated their intent to kill Malala and her father. Malala's father is an educational activist and runs a chain of schools in Pakistan.

Addressing the UN on her 16th birthday Malala said she was fighting for the rights of women as 'they are the ones who suffer the most'. Only 38% of public schools in Pakistan are for girls. Malala said 'let us pick up our books and our pens. They are our most powerful weapons. One child, one teacher, one book, and one pen can change the world. Education is the only solution. Education first'.

📖 Word bank

*   **Burqa**
A long, loose garment covering the whole body from head to feet, worn in public by women in many Muslim countries.

*   **Cleric**
A religious leader.

GO! **Activity**

Discuss
With your shoulder partner, consider the list of human rights from the UNDHR above. Which human rights were violated by the Taliban in the case of Malala?

? Questions

1. Outline what happened to Malala Yousafzai in October 2012.
2. **Explain** why you think that Malala was targeted by the Taliban.
3. Malala stated that 'Education is the only solution'. **Do you agree** with this statement? Give **reasons** for your answers.

GO! **Activity**

Group work
Working in pairs you are now going to prepare a news report focused on the role of women in Pakistan. This report will be delivered to your classmates in the style of a news broadcast, with an anchor (presenter) and a reporter(s). Here are some factors you may wish to consider:

- educational opportunities for women
- marriage
- the role of religion
- crimes against women
- employment opportunities for women

Consider the role of the Pakistani government and the role of the Taliban. Explain how these organisations help or do not help to promote the role of women. Your news report should also include relevant statistics.

Human rights ignored?

The Human Rights Risk Atlas measures 197 countries based on human rights violations. In the 2013 results it found 32 countries which have an 'extreme' risk of human rights violations – this is a 60% increase in the past six years.

Focus on South Sudan: human rights and terrorism

Overview

South Sudan became an independent country from the former country of the Sudan in July 2011. It has a population of approximately nine million people and the capital city is Juba. South Sudan's main export is oil. Salva Kiir Mayardit is the current President (2014).

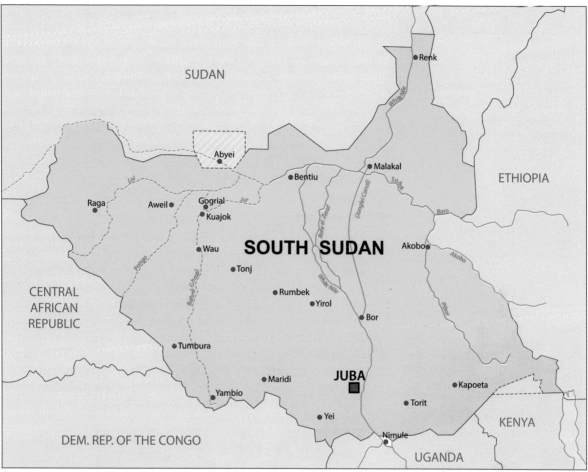

Figure 11.6: *South Sudan marked on this political map*

Human rights issues in South Sudan

1. **Right to a free trial/freedom of press**

    In 2013 the UN warned that the country's weak legal system had led to serious human rights violations such as poor conditions for those awaiting trial. On 2nd May 2013 South Sudanese Police arrested Michael Koma, the managing editor of South Sudan's daily newspaper the *Juba Monitor* and held him for four days. This followed the publication of an article that criticised the deputy security minister of the country.

2. **Child marriage**

    Approximately 48% of girls aged between 14 and 19 are married in South Sudan; some girls as young as 12 have been forced into arranged marriages. Dowries are still in place and can be paid for in cattle; like livestock the girl is considered to be the 'property' of the family and can be bought and sold accordingly. The girl has no choice in this transaction. She may be beaten, assaulted or even arrested if she refuses to marry the man who has provided the dowry. South Sudanese women and children face the highest levels of maternal mortality in the world. Girls are not encouraged to go to school or attend further study.

> 📖 **Word bank**
>
> ● **Dowry**
> An amount of money paid by the husband's family to secure his bride.
>
> ● **Maternal mortality**
> A woman's death while pregnant, during childbirth or within a few days of the birth.

3. Freedom of expression

Lesbian, gay, bisexual, and transgender (LGBT) individuals in South Sudan are subject to legal challenges. Male same-sex sexual activity is illegal and carries a penalty of up to 10 years' imprisonment. Before South Sudan's independence in 2011, the Sudan was governed by sharia law and individuals found to be engaging in LGBT relationships could be punished by death. In July 2010 the South Sudanese President commented that homosexuality was not in the 'character' of Southern Sudanese people. The US Department of State's *2011 Human Rights Report* found 'widespread' discrimination against those from the LGBT community.

4. Terrorist activity

The Lord's Resistance Army (LRA) is the main terrorist threat to South Sudan. The LRA is a military movement. Its leader, Joseph Kony, began his rebellion 20 years ago in Uganda. Mr Kony says he wishes to install a Bible-based theocracy in the country. The LRA has been accused of widespread human rights violations including murder, abduction, mutilation, child sex slavery, and forcing children to fight in armed conflict. In 2010 it was reported that more than 25,000 South Sudanese people had been forced from their homes by the LRA; some had their homes burned to the ground. Joseph Kony is wanted by the International Criminal Court.

Figure 11.8: *Joseph Kony*

Figure 11.7: *Child soldiers in South Sudan*

❓ Questions

1. **Explain, in detail,** the human rights violations that South Sudan has been guilty of in recent years. In your answer you must mention:
    *   right to a free trial/freedom of press
    *   child marriage
    *   freedom of expression
2. **Describe** the threat posed by terrorists in South Sudan.

GO! Activity

Group work

The Human Rights Risk Atlas ranked South Sudan in the top 10 human rights offenders in 2013. The full list was as follows: Yemen, Syria, Iraq, Mynamar, Pakistan, Afghanistan, Somalia, The Democratic Republic of Congo, The Sudan.

Select a country from the above list. Produce a poster presentation on your country. Your poster must contain:

- background information about the population, government and geography of the country
- at least three pieces of different information regarding human rights in that country

Factors you may wish to consider:

- the role of women
- the type of government (e.g. is it a dictatorship?)
- access to food/clean water
- the availability of housing
- freedom of movement

You may also wish to refer to your notes from the UNDHR for suggestions of areas to consider, such as:

- information on the terrorist threat in that country
- at least one conclusion on whether there is a link between human rights and terrorism/terrorist activity in that country

You may also wish to take your own notes for revision purposes.

Ensure that all members of your group have been given a role for this task. Make sure you can all give evidence of your individual input as this will be recorded by your teacher. For example, a classmate may be able to film your presentation.

Counter-terrorism – compromising rights?

Because of the threat of international Terrorism, countries across the world have had to develop ways of dealing with Terrorism before it even has a chance to happen. The threat posed by international terrorism in recent years has meant that countries across the world have had to develop ways of dealing with terrorism before it has a chance to happen. These strategies – often known as 'counter-terrorism' – can be controversial if they mean that individuals have to give up some of their human rights for the sake of 'security'.

In 2005, the Prime Minister Tony Blair was defeated in the UK Parliament when he tried to increase the amount of time that terrorist suspects could be held without charge to 90 days. This would have meant that potentially innocent people could have spent up to three months in prison without being charged. The Prime Minister claimed that the London bombings in July of that year had shown the need for stronger security laws on terrorism.

Hint

Counter-terrorism strategies are discussed in more detail in chapter 7 of this Unit.

❓ Questions

1.   **Explain** what is meant by 'counter-terrorism'.
2.   **Describe** why some people are critical of counter-terrorism strategies.

N5 GO! Activity

Discuss

Some civil liberties groups have criticised the UK government's policies on dealing with terrorism. Read the extract from the *Liberty* website below and discuss with your shoulder partner whether or not you believe that people should be made to give up certain rights in order to have greater security from the threat of terrorism. Feedback your answers to the whole class.

Human rights law requires the State to take steps to protect the right to life - which includes measures to prevent terrorism. However, any measures taken to counter terrorism must be proportionate and not undermine our democratic values. In particular, laws designed to protect people from the threat of terrorism and the enforcement of these laws must be compatible with people's rights and freedoms. Yet, all too often the risk of terrorism has been used as the basis for eroding our human rights and civil liberties:

* *After the tragic events of September 11th 2001, emergency laws were passed which allowed for the indefinite detention of foreign nationals who were suspected of being terrorists. Under this law individuals could be detained for an unlimited period at a maximum security prison despite never being charged, let alone convicted of any offence.*

* *Before it was repealed, section 44 of the Terrorism Act 2000 allowed people to be stopped and searched without suspicion. This overly broad power was used against peaceful protesters and disproportionately against ethnic minority groups.*

* *Broad new speech offences impact on free speech rights and non-violent groups have been outlawed.*

📖 Word bank

* **The State**

A nation or territory considered as an organised political community under one government.

* **Proportionate**

Corresponding in size to something else.

* **Foreign national**

A person who is not a citizen of the host country in which they are staying.

* **Repeal**

To officially cancel a law.

* **Disproportionately**

Out of proportion; not corresponding in size.

* **Speech offences**

Speaking to a group in order to incite violence or hate.

Summary

In this chapter you have learned:

* how rights are affected by terrorism
* how responsibilities are affected by terrorism

Learning Summary

Now that you have finished the **Terrorism, rights & responsibilities** chapter, complete a self-evaluation of your knowledge and skills to assess what you have understood. Use the checklist below and its traffic lights to draw up a revision plan to help you improve in the areas you identified as red or amber.

- I can explain what is meant by 'human rights'.

- I can describe examples of human rights and their matching responsibilities.

- I can explain what is meant by 'children's rights'.

- I can describe examples of children's rights and their matching responsibilities.

- I can explain different examples of human rights violations.

- I can describe how women's rights have been affected by terrorist regimes.

- I can explain how free speech has been affected by terrorist regimes.

- I can describe the ways in which terrorists/terrorist organisations can present a threat to a country's security.

- I understand how human rights relate to global terrorism.

- I can explain what is meant by 'counter-terrorism'.

- I can describe why some people are critical of counter-terrorism strategies.

Examples

In Modern Studies it is essential that you are able to back up any point you make with relevant evidence. When you are considering the statements above try to think of relevant examples for each response. You may wish to note these examples under each statement in your revision notes.

12 The consequences of terrorism

What you will learn in this chapter

- How to identify the social consequences of terrorism.
- How to identify the economic consequences of terrorism.
- How to identify the political consequences of terrorism.

The consequences of terrorism

The most serious consequence of terrorism is loss of life. The US government reported that in 2012 a total of 6,771 terrorist attacks happened worldwide resulting in more than 11,000 deaths.

The social consequences of terrorism

Fear

Terrorism causes fear and panic, which can make individuals' lives very stressful. Governments across the world have responded to the threat posed by international terrorism by stepping up security measures (more information on responses to terrorism can be found in chapters 14 and 15).

> ## 📖 Word bank
>
> ### • Sensationalise
> To present news in a way that is intended to provoke interest and excitement, at the expense of accuracy.

Figure 12.1: *Social consequences of terrorism*

Panic and social unrest can make individuals feel unsafe in their own homes and suspicious of people they may have previously trusted. However, the threat posed by terrorism has arguably been sensationalised by the media and governments.

For example, more than 227,000 people died in the 2004 tsunami compared to less than 3,000 people on September 11th 2001, yet those attacks spawned a global sense of terror. The media provide 24-hour reporting and, in an attempt to attract a large audience, may present information in a biased manner and make a big story out of something that might statistically be rather unlikely to happen. This makes people believe that the issue – terrorism – is far more likely to happen than might be the case.

Figure 12.2: *Tsunami devastation in Thailand*

The Politics of Fear

The Politics of Fear is when those in power use fear to help achieve policy changes, for example by pressurising people to vote in a certain way or agree with foreign policy decisions.

In the UK the government and security services monitor the terrorist threat on a scale (see Figure 12.3). Critics of these types of measurements say that they keep populations under a constant 'threat' of terrorist attacks and that they therefore help to keep the population living in fear.

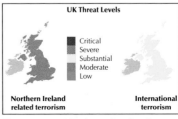

Figure 12.3: *UK threat level colours*

> ### ⚙ Hint
>
> The UK government has been accused of using the politics of fear to support controversial changes to the benefits system such as the 'bedroom tax'.

> ## GO! Activity
>
> ### Use your skills
>
>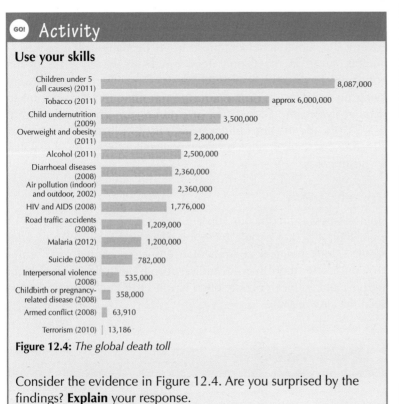
>
> **Figure 12.4:** *The global death toll*
>
> Consider the evidence in Figure 12.4. Are you surprised by the findings? **Explain** your response.

> ### ⠿ Make the Link
>
> In History you may have studied periods in the past where the politics of fear was used to control populations and individuals; for example in Nazi Germany, or during the civil rights era in the United States.

Islamophobia

Islamophobia is prejudice against those of the Muslim faith. The Runnymede Trust (who promote a multi-ethnic Britain) have defined Islamophobia as the 'dread or hatred of Islam and therefore, [the] fear and dislike of all Muslims'.

After the killing of British soldier Lee Rigby in May 2013 Britain experienced a rise in Islamophobic attacks. A total of 11 mosques were targeted and the *Guardian* reported that women wearing the hijab (Muslim head-dress) complained about being spat at, or having their hijab pulled off. However, religious extremism also exists in many other religions, including Christianity. Some critics argue that the media have sensationalised Islam and portrayed it, unfairly, as a violent religion.

> ### ⠿ Make the Link
>
> In History or RMPS you may have learned about the Second World War and the ideologies of Hitler, including that of anti-Semitism.

> ### 📖 Word bank
>
> • **Anti-Semitism**
>
> When individuals have a distrust or irrational hatred of those from the Jewish faith.

Figure 12.5: *Anti-Muslim graffiti defaces a mosque in the USA*

Breakdown in social cohesion

Social cohesion is the glue that binds a community together. People feel connected to a place if they feel their opinion matters – for example, if they are able to vote in regular elections. While terrorist attacks cause damage to property and loss of life it has been argued that this is not their primary aim. Indeed, a UN report stated in 2002 that 'the purpose [of terrorism] is not to take lives or destroy property. That is the mechanism, not the goal. The goal is to weaken the sense of cohesion that binds communities together, to reduce its social capital and to sow distrust, fear and insecurity.'

Poverty

Poverty is a consequence of terrorism. In Nigeria, which is ranked at number seven in the Global Terrorism Index, nearly 61% of the population are in poverty; in 2012 almost 100 million Nigerians were living on less than a $1 (£0.63) a day. Similarly in Yemen, ranked number five in the Global Terrorism Index, poverty levels stand at nearly 70% and the unemployment rate is more than 40%. It is clear therefore that there is a link between poverty levels and the threat that terrorism poses.

Homelessness

Homelessness is an obvious consequence of terrorism. In April 2013 more than 430,000 people were forced to flee Mali in Africa after Islamists took political control. Mali has also suffered from major drought, leaving more than 4.5 million people affected by malnutrition. Terrorist attacks mean people often have to flee their homes – as has been the case in Mali.

 Think point

You will learn about state-sponsored terrorism in the next chapter. Do you think the events in Mali could be described as state sponsored terrorism?

Figure 12.6: *Archbishop Desmond Tutu, South African social rights activist*

? Questions

1. Summarise the social consequences of terrorism. In your answer you should refer to:
    *   fear
    *   Islamophobia
    *   social cohesion
    *   poverty
    *   homeslessness

2. Archbishop Desmond Tutu has stated 'you can never win a war against terror as long as there are conditions in the world that make people desperate – poverty, disease, ignorance'. Do you agree with the Archbishop's opinion? **Explain** your answer with relevant **evidence** from this chapter.

The economic consequences of terrorism

In 2011 American experts calculated that the War on Terror had cost the United States over $4.4 trillion. The costs associated with terrorism include increased budgets for defence, personal security and the impact of terrorism on tourism within the countries it has affected.

Figure 12.7: *Economic consequences of terrorism*

Direct economic impact of terrorist attack

Terrorism is costly for governments across the world. Estimates have put the direct cost to America of the September 11th attacks at over $2 trillion.

Item	Cost
The loss of four civilian aircraft.	$385 million
The destruction of major buildings in the World Trade Center and replacement cost.	$3–$4.5 billion
Damage to a portion of the Pentagon.	$1 billion
Clean-up costs.	$1.3 billion
Property and infrastructure damage.	$10–$13 billion
Federal emergency funds (heightened airport security, sky marshals, government takeover of airport security, retrofitting aircraft with anti-terrorist devices, cost of operations in Afghanistan).	$40 billion
Direct job losses amounted to 83,000.	$17 billion wages lost
The amount of damaged or unrecoverable property.	$21.8 billion
Losses to the city of New York (lost jobs, lost taxes, damage to infrastructure, cleaning).	$96 billion
Losses to the insurance industry.	$40 billion
Loss of air traffic revenue.	$10 billion

Source: http://www.iags.org/costof911.html

GO! Activity

Research
Sometimes the media may report on terrorism in a way that deliberately causes fear in order to support their political point of view. Research different case studies of terrorist attacks and how they have been presented by the mainstream media. Focus on the use of **exaggeration and/or bias**. Present your findings to your class.

Hint

The media have their own agenda, one that is often biased. Think about the political stance of newspapers in Scotland and the UK. How do you think this affects people's political beliefs?

Word bank

• **Bias**
Prejudice for or against one thing over another.

Similarly, in the UK, the inquest into the 7/7 London bombings in 2005 was estimated to have cost more than £4.6 million. We can see, therefore, that the price-tag associated with even one terrorist attack such as the 7/7 bombings or the September 11th attacks can be great.

Insurance against terrorism

Figure 12.8: *Most travel insurance includes a terrorism clause*

Companies have recently begun offering insurance against terrorism. This protects owners against any losses they might have due to a terrorist attack. The odds of a terrorist attack happening remain unlikely – but if a terrorist attack did happen the insurance company might have to pay out a lot of money – making it very difficult to insure against terrorism. Most travel insurance now protects people against being stranded as the result of a terrorist attack (60% of all travel insurance now includes cover against situations arising due to terrorist attacks) and the cost of travel insurance has increased as a result.

Businesses and tourism

Terrorism is more likely to affect poorer developing countries where the effects of the loss of income to their businesses and tourism industry as a result of terrorism can be devastating.

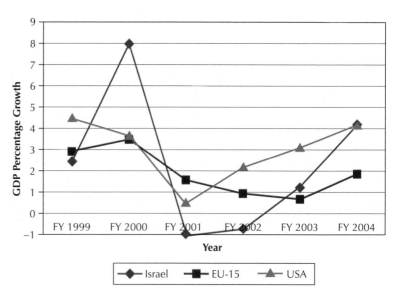

Figure 12.9: *Gross Domestic Product growth for various countries*
[Source: http://www.mafhoum.com/press9/289E19.htm]

? Questions

1. Using Figure 12.9, identify in which year GDP fell for Israel, the EU and the USA.
2. Account for why **you think** this might be the case.

Tourism is an example of an industry directly affected by terrorism; indeed, research in Spain has shown that a typical terrorist act scares away over 140,000 tourists. Since September the 11th 2001 it is now much more expensive to fly due to security fees which are added on to ticket costs by airports and airlines.

Terrorism is most likely to directly affect poorer developing countries. For such countries, tourism is usually a very valuable source of income. When terrorist attacks occur and tourists are put off from visiting it can have a negative impact on that country's income.

In 2002 the island of Bali suffered at the hands of Islamic extremists when a bomb killed 202 people and injured 240 others. The bomb was deliberately set off in a local nightclub which many tourists and young backpackers frequented. The main impact of the Bali bombings on the tourism industry was loss of income: the beach vendors on the islands reported a drop of nearly two-thirds in their income. Businesses in the tourism sector therefore suffered due to the consequences of terrorism.

Figure 12.10: *Smoke rising from the debris of the buildings bombed in Bali in 2002*

Business can also be impacted upon globally. In the wake of the September 11th attacks, New York's financial markets did not open for a week and stock markets around the world fell sharply. There was damage to the communications and other transaction processing systems that had been located in the World Trade Center.

Defence costs

In 2010–11 the total cost of anti-terrorist initiatives stood at £3.5 billion, more than three times what it was at the start of the decade in the UK. The US alone now spends about $500 billion annually – 20% of the US federal budget – on departments directly engaged in preventing terrorism. Terrorism costs governments across the world as they are required to have effective counter-terrorism strategies to try to protect their populations from the effects of a terrorist attack. More information can be found on counter-terrorism in chapter 14.

> ### 📖 Word bank
>
> • **Federal budget**
> The total amount of money the US government has available to spend in one year.

? Questions

Using the headings below, summarise the economic consequences of terrorism:

- direct economic impact of terrorist attack
- insurance against terrorism
- businesses and tourism
- defence costs

> **GO! Activity**
>
> **Research**
> Carry out a mini-investigation with your peers, family and/or teachers about holiday destinations.
>
> - For this task you will need to design a questionnaire. Information on how to conduct a questionnaire can be found on page 223.
> - Design no more than 10 questions to help you find out about how the issue of international terrorism affects tourism.
> - Present your information in the form of a blog entry. You should have at least two different sources that show your results, such as a bar graph or a bullet point list.
> - The blog page should also contain at least two conclusions from your research.

The political consequences of terrorism

Global instability

The world has become increasingly unstable in recent years; some political analysts would argue that this is directly due to the threat of international terrorism.

Figure 12.11: *Political consequences of terrorism*

Figure 12.12: *Protests in Egypt during the Arab Spring*

> 📖 **Word bank**
>
> - **Diplomatic staff**
> Officials representing their country abroad, e.g. in their country's embassy.

Arab Spring

In late 2010, 26 year old Tunisian street vendor Mohamed Bouazizi set himself on fire. Local police had prevented him from selling fruit which was his main source of income. Protests against the corrupt authorities in Tunisia began and over the next 12 months the revolution spread, affecting Tunisia, Egypt, Libya, Bahrain, Yemen and Syria, as people stood up to their countries' long established regimes. The 'Arab Spring', as it has become known, has created substantial global instability. Whilst it was not caused by terrorism, the consequences of changes in political leadership have led to opportunities extremists. In Yemen, for example, the group AQAP (Al-Qaeda in the Arabian Peninsula) is currently creating global uncertainty for governments in the West and in August 2013 the UK and the US withdrew all diplomatic staff from the country. Extremists have used the Arab Spring, and the instability it has created, to gain political power and support for their cause.

Figure 12.13: *Word cloud for the Arab Spring uprising in the Middle East*

Increased security

Security has increased as a result of international terrorism. Today when travelling on an plane, for example, travellers can expect the following restrictions:

- specific ID required; ID name must match name on ticket
- shoes must be removed at checkpoints
- all baggage, both carry-on and checked, must be screened
- no liquids (above 100ml) allowed through checkpoints
- special items must be pulled from luggage (laptops)
- jackets/outerwear must be removed
- body scan machine screening
- enhanced pat-downs
- no more non-ticketed visitors allowed at airline gates

Figure 12.14: *Airport security scanners*

Figure 12.15: *President Bashar al-Assad*

Terrorism has also affected security in public buildings; for example, in 2010 the Scottish Parliament had security bollards built outside the perimeter of the building to prevent an attack similar to the Glasgow airport bombing of 2007.

UK and Scottish government responses to terrorism

War

War is often a direct consequence of terrorism. When Terrorist attacks happen they can often create instability - If terrorists are able to use this to their advantage, it can lead to war. For example, the Arab Spring that began in 2010 has created instability in many countries – in Syria it has directly led to civil war. The conflict is being fought between the forces of the Syrian government and those opposed to it. Protesters have demanded the resignation of President Bashar al-Assad, whose family has held the presidency in Syria since 1971. In April 2014 estimates put the death total in Syria at over 150,000.

? Questions

1. Using the headings below, summarise the political consequences of terrorism:
   - global instability
   - increased security
   - war
2. 'There are many different social and economic consequences of international terrorism'. **Explain, in detail**, the different social and economic consequences of international terrorism. In your answer you must include at least two **examples** and also refer to the Point, Explain, Example structure (see page 240).

Summary

In this chapter you have learned:

- identify the social consequences of terrorism
- identify the economic consequences of terrorism
- identify the political consequences of terrorism

Learning Summary

Now that you have finished **The consequences of terrorism** chapter, complete a self-evaluation of your knowledge and skills to assess what you have understood. Use the checklist below and its traffic lights to draw up a revision plan to help you improve in the areas you identified as red or amber.

- I can describe the main social consequences of terrorism.
- I can describe the main economic consequences of terrorism.
- I can describe the main political consequences of terrorism.

Examples

In Modern Studies it is essential that you are able to back up any point you make with relevant evidence. When you are considering the statements above try to think of relevant examples for each response. You may wish to note these examples under each statement in your revision notes.

13 Theories of terrorism

What you will learn in this chapter

- Be able to identify and explain theories surrounding terrorist behaviour, specifically:
  - lone wolves
  - terrorist cells
  - home-grown terrorism
  - state-sponsored terrorism

Theories of terrorism

📖 Word bank

- **Hypothesis**

A proposed explanation for something that can be tested and therefore proved or disproved.

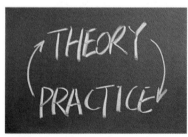

Figure 13.1: *Theories have to be put into practice to prove them*

Figure 13.2: *Lee Rigby*

Theories in social science are usually based upon a hypothesis (a statement) which can be proved or disproved. A theory is a statement that tries to explain things. In Modern Studies, theories might be used to explain why things happen within a society.

In order to understand terrorist motivations and behaviours you need to think about the theories that exist. Terrorists have a variety of different reasons that they might use to justify their actions. Just as there is not one universal motivation for terrorist acts, there is no one theory that can explain why terrorism continues to exist.

'Lone wolves' or organised terrorists?

Some terrorists are working from within a terrorist organisation. However, recently changes in the UK and America have suggested that an increasing number are becoming 'lone wolf' terrorists. These individuals may say that they support the beliefs of a terrorist group, such as Al-Qaeda, but act completely independently.

In May 2013, British soldier Lee Rigby was attacked with knives and a meat cleaver in the street. The two men responsible claimed that they were acting to avenge the killing of Muslims by the British Army. Similarly, a month earlier in America, two individuals acted independently by planting pressure cooker bombs on the route of the Boston marathon. Three people were killed in the attacks and 264 were injured. One of the two brothers responsible for the Boston attacks claimed later that they were acting to avenge the wars in Afghanistan and Iraq.

Cells

'Terrorist cells' are organised groups of terrorists. It is thought that due to the global spread of support for its cause Al-Qaeda has many terrorist cells operating in a number of different countries.

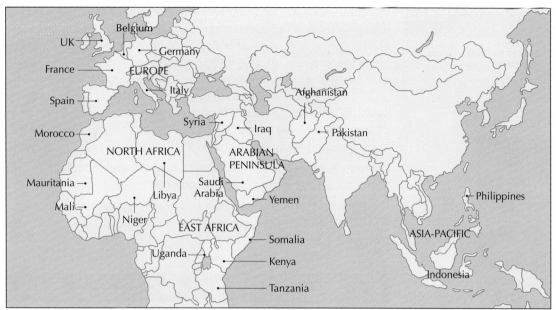

Figure 13.3: *The named countries in this map are those in which Al-Qaeda is believed to operate*

? Questions

1. **Explain** what a 'theory' is in social science.
2. Outline, with **examples**, what the expression 'lone wolf terrorist' means.
3. **Describe**, with **examples**, what terrorist 'cells' are.

Home-grown terrorism

Home-grown terrorism is carried out by individuals who live in the country that they have attacked or plan to attack. It is perhaps the greatest security risk to developed countries, such as Scotland, because it means that there are individuals living lawfully in the country who feel so frustrated that they see terrorist activity as the only way to have their opinions heard. In 2010 The Centre for Social Cohesion considered 124 individuals convicted of Islamic terrorism since 1999 in the UK. Their findings showed that 69% of offences were carried out by individuals of British nationality.

Figure 13.4: *British nationality is no guarantee that a person will not commit an act of terrorism*

> ## 🧠 Hint
>
> You can find information on how to carry out your own social research for the Added Value Unit or Assignment on page 218.

Figure 13.5: *Boston Marathon bombing*

Make the Link

You may learn more about social theories in other subjects such as History.

Figure 13.6: *Nidal Hasan*

Activity

Discuss
Discuss Sir David Omand's statement with your shoulder partner. **Do you agree** with Sir David Omand? **Explain your view** to your partner.

Word bank

- **Jihad**
An Islamic term often used to refer to a war or struggle against non-believers.

- **Paramilitary**
An organisation whose structure is similar to the military, but is not considered part of a state's official armed forces.

We know that terrorist sympathy exists in developed countries such as the United States and the United Kingdom. In 2009 Major Nidal Malik Hasan carried out a mass shooting at an army base in Texas known as 'Fort Hood'. Nidal, an army psychiatrist, killed 13 people and injured over 30 others during the shooting spree. As he opened fire he shouted 'Allahu Akbar' which means 'God is great'. Nidal had been born and raised in America and had chosen to join the army and fight for his country when he left school. He had become radicalised in his beliefs, however, completely unbeknown to his family and his colleagues.

Former UK security coordinator, Sir David Omand, commented: 'the most effective weapon of the contemporary terrorist is their ideology'.

Nidal's actions were in response to the wars in Iraq and Afghanistan – but as Sir David notes, the ideology of committing jihad is far more difficult to tackle than one lone gunman.

? Questions

1. Outline what the expression 'home-grown terrorist', means.
2. **Describe** why home-grown terrorists exist in developed countries.

State-sponsored terrorism

State-sponsored terrorism is government support of organisations engaged in terrorism. For example, in the United Kingdom the government has been accused of supporting loyalist paramilitaries during the troubles in Northern Ireland (loyalists are people loyal to the British monarchy and the preservation of Northern Ireland as opposed to a united Ireland). In 2003 the Stevens Inquiry claimed that British Army officers gave intelligence to loyalist paramilitaries, provided them with firearms and even training in some instances.

Figure 13.7: *A mural of a loyalist paramilitant in Belfast*

Patrick Finucane

CASE STUDY

Patrick Finucane was a lawyer in Belfast in Northern Ireland who was killed by loyalist paramilitaries in 1989. Patrick was well known to the authorities after successfully challenging the British government in human rights cases in the 1980s. Patrick was shot fourteen times as he sat eating a meal with his wife and three children. In September 2004 loyalist paramilitary informer Ken Barrett pleaded guilty to Patrick's murder.

Public investigations later found that British security forces had colluded in Patrick's murder. In 2011 the Prime Minister David Cameron said that there had been 'state collusion' in Patrick's murder and apologised to his family. In December 2012 the De Silva review found that the case had witnessed 'a wilful and abject failure by successive governments'.

Patrick Finucane's family have called the De Silva report 'a sham'.

📖 Word bank

- **Collude**
  Conspire to come to a secret understanding.
- **Mujahedeen**
  Guerrilla fighters in Islamic countries, especially those who are fighting against non-Muslim forces.

America also has a history of sponsoring terrorist activity when it suits a certain political goal. In the 1980s America supported the Afghan Mujahedeen against the Soviet Union. It is thought that this group developed to become Al-Qaeda and provided Osama bin Laden with essential training in paramilitary activities.

More recently, America's use of drone strikes has been questioned. Drones are unmanned aircraft that attack a certain target. When President George W. Bush left office in January 2009 the US had been responsible for approximately 45 drone strikes. Under President Obama the US reportedly carried out more than 292 strikes between 2009 and 2012. Due in part to this, American academic Noam Chomsky has called the United States 'a leading terrorist state'.

Figure 13.8: *Protest against USA drone attacks in Pakistan*

❓ Questions

1. **Explain** what 'state-sponsored terrorism' means.
2. Summarise the case study of Patrick Finucane.
3. **Explain** why Noam Chomsky has called America 'a leading terrorist state'.
4. Consider Figure 13.9 below. **Identify**:
   - The percentage of US nationals who believe the US government should launch airstrikes in other countries against suspected terrorists.
   - The percentage of US nationals who believe the US government should launch airstrikes in the US against suspected terrorists living there.

   What **conclusions** can be drawn from the **evidence** you have identified?

Do you think the US government should or should not use drones to:	% Yes, Should	%No, should not	%No opinion
Launch airstrikes in other countries against suspected terrorists*	65	28	8
Launch airstrikes in other countries against US citizens living abroad who are suspected terrorists*	41	52	7
Launch airstrikes in the US against suspected terrorists living here**	25	66	9
Launch airstrikes in the US against US citizens living here who are suspected terrorists**	13	79	7

*Based on Sample A of 502 national adults
** Based on Sample B of 518 national adults

Figure 13.9: *Survey of US citizens, 20–21 March 2013*

Summary

In this chapter you have learned:

- to identify and explain theories surrounding terrorist behaviour
- to identify and explain lone wolf terrorists
- to identify and explain terrorist cells
- to identify and explain home-grown terrorism
- to identify and explain state-sponsored terrorism

Learning Summary

Now that you have finished the **Theories of terrorism** chapter, complete a self-evaluation of your knowledge and skills to assess what you have understood. Use the checklist below and its traffic lights to draw up a revision plan to help you improve in the areas you identified as red or amber.

- I can understand what a 'theory' is in social science.
- I can explain what is meant by a 'lone wolf terrorist'.
- I can describe what terrorist 'cells' are.
- I can outline what is meant by 'home-grown' terrorism.
- I can explain why support for terrorism exists in developed countries.
- I can explain what 'state-sponsored terrorism' is.

Examples

In Modern Studies it is essential that you are able to back up any point you make with relevant evidence. When you are considering the statements above try to think of relevant examples for each response. You may wish to note these examples under each statement in your revision notes.

14 Governments: responding to and resolving terrorism

What you will learn in this chapter

- To understand how the UK and Scottish governments have responded to terrorism.
- To explain the problems that they have faced in responding to terrorism.

Government response to terrorism

Terrorism is, in the main, a reserved power as it is related to defence. This means that it is the UK government's responsibility to ensure that Scotland is protected against the threat posed by international terrorism.

The ways in which governments and organisations respond to terrorism directly affects the threat that terrorism will pose in the future. Governments often like to be seen to be 'cracking down', with tough measures on terrorism. They may do this by introducing a 'threat level' (see Figure 14.4 on page 194) or by introducing new laws regarding terrorist suspects.

Figure 14.1: *People may feel vulnerable when governments talk about threats*

However, this can often have a negative effect on a population: increasing the 'threat level' can frighten people, and as a result they feel less protected. Also some critics argue that introducing 'threat levels' and asking people to be vigilant doesn't actually target terrorists and would-be supporters.

The main way in which any government can respond to terrorist activity is through passing relevant laws:

Make the Link

You will have learned about reserved and devolved powers in Unit 1.

Think point

Think about the ways in which you keep safe in school. Consider the following:
- does your school have a security policy?
- are there secure doors?
- do staff wear identity badges?

Make the Link

In Unit 1 you learned about how are laws made.

An overview of UK government counter-terrorism legislation	
The Prevention of Terrorism Act 2005	• Allowed the Home Secretary to impose 'control orders' which restrict an individual's movement in order to 'protect members of the public from a risk of terrorism'. • In April 2006, a High Court judge issued a declaration that section 3 of the act was incompatible with the right to a fair trial under article 6 of the European Convention on Human Rights. • The act was replaced by the Terrorism Prevention and Investigation Measures Act 2011.
The Terrorism Act 2006	• Drafted in the aftermath of the 7th July 2005 London bombings. • Created new offences related to terrorism, and amended existing ones. • As part of this act, Tony Blair, then Prime Minister, tried to push through a law that would allow terror suspects to be held for up to 90 days without trial. Parliament did not agree to include this but did, however, agree to increase the number of days a suspect can be held without charge from 14 to 28 days.
The Counter-Terrorism Act 2008	• Allows the UK government to force the financial sector to take action on suspected money laundering or terrorist financing. • Allows police to enter – by force if necessary – and search the premises of individuals subject to control orders. • Allows police to take fingerprints and DNA samples from individuals subject to control orders. • The number of days someone detained for suspicion of terrorism can be held without charge was increased to 42.
Terrorism Prevention and Investigation Measures Act 2011	• Abolished system of control orders and replaced with new measures – 'Terrorism Prevention and Investigation' (TPIMs) (see page 192). • Some critics have argued that TPIMs are simply a watered down version of control orders.
Protection of Freedoms Act 2012	• Removes the 'stop and search' regulations of the Terrorism Act 2000 and allows the power to search people and vehicles. • Reduced the number of days someone detained for suspicion of terrorism can be held without charge from 28 to 14.

? Questions

1. **Explain** why terrorism is mainly dealt with by the UK government.
2. Using the information in the table above, make a time-line showing the name of each of the acts and the year in which they were passed.
3. **Describe** the setbacks the UK government has faced when trying to make new laws to tackle terrorism. You must mention at least three in your answer.
4. Look at the dates the laws were introduced. Outline what might have led to their introduction.
5. Consider Figure 14.2 below. Draw **conclusions** supported by **evidence** on:
   • the total number of arrests from 2005/06–2007/08
   • the total number of people released without charge

📖 Word Bank

• **Home Secretary**

The minister in the Westminster government responsible for the security of the UK.

• **Money laundering**

A way of hiding the fact that money has been gained in an illegal way.

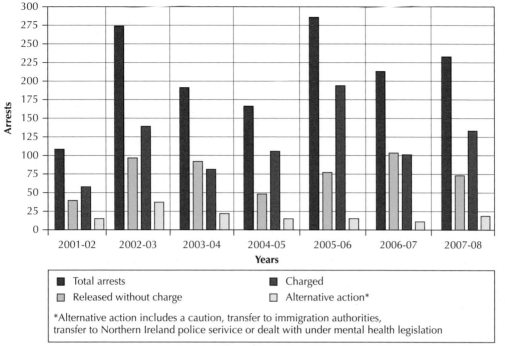

Source: Office of the National Co-ordinator of Terrorists Investigations

Figure 14.2: *Outcome of terrorism arrests 2001–2008.*

Problems with the UK government's response

Both the Labour government of 1997–2010 and the current (in 2014) Conservative-Liberal Democrat coalition experienced much opposition when trying to introduce new laws to tackle terrorism.

In 2005 Prime Minister Tony Blair was defeated in the House of Commons over his plans to hold terrorist suspects for up to 90 days without trial. When the next Prime Minister, Gordon Brown, managed to pass the **Counter-Terrorism Act 2008** he was successful in increasing the number of days suspected terrorists could be held without charge to 42. However, Gordon Brown, much like Tony Blair, faced criticism from his own party and from others for this law.

Since assuming power in 2010, David Cameron's government have introduced two significant pieces of counter-terrorism legislation: the **Terrorism Prevention and Investigation Measures Act 2011** and the **Protection of Freedoms Act 2012**. However, this government has also faced opposition to its attempts to tackle the problems caused by global terrorism.

Figure 14.3: *Former UK Prime Ministers Gordon Brown (left) and Tony Blair (right)*

Terrorism prevention and investigation measures CASE STUDY

Control orders were put in place to be used by the Home Secretary with the aim of restricting the freedom of individuals suspected of involvement in terrorist activities. They were introduced by the **Prevention of Terrorism Act 2005**. In 2011 control orders were replaced in the **Terrorism Prevention and Investigation Measures Act 2011**; the Coalition government argue they are fairer than the old control orders.

Terrorism prevention and investigation measures (TPIMs) are very similar to control orders in that they restrict an individual's freedom and are imposed directly by the Home Secretary. Those subject to a TPIM are not able to:

- leave their house overnight
- go beyond the geographical boundaries decided by the Home Office
- remove their electronic monitoring tag
- talk to or meet with whoever they want
- stop the police or staff from the monitoring company entering and searching their home without a warrant
- have friends or family to their home unless approved by the Home Office, approval of which can be removed at any time
- travel overseas

Liberty's objections to TPIMs 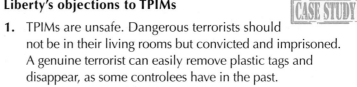 CASE STUDY

1. TPIMs are unsafe. Dangerous terrorists should not be in their living rooms but convicted and imprisoned. A genuine terrorist can easily remove plastic tags and disappear, as some controlees have in the past.

2. TPIMs are unfair. Innocent people should not be subjected to years and years of punishment without trial. TPIMs place dehumanising sanctions on people based on suspicion rather than evidence.

3. TPIMs go against the British traditions of justice and liberty. They undermine the presumption of innocence and the right to a fair trial.

4. There are alternatives to TPIMs that better ensure public safety and respect for civil liberties. Liberty urges the government to use criminal law and the courts to lock up dangerous terrorists, and to allow the use of intercept evidence in court.

[Source: http://www.liberty-human-rights.org.uk/human-rights/countering-terrorism/tpims]

DAILY NEWS

world - business - finance - lifestyle - travel - sport

Terror suspect's disappearance sparks criticism of control-order regime

The government has put the public at greater risk by watering down the previous control-orders regime, a Labour MP has said after a hunt for a terrorist suspect was launched.

Ibrahim Magag, 28, absconded from a terrorism prevention and investigation measures (TPIMs) notice after failing to meet his overnight residence conditions on Boxing Day, police said. He was last seen in Camden, North London, on the same day at 5.20pm.

Pat McFadden told BBC Radio 4's *The World at One* on Tuesday that the Home Secretary had been complacent in introducing a new system for controlling terrorist suspects who had not been charged with crimes.

"I think what they have done is complacent and dangerous and I warned the Home Secretary and the Prime Minister about this when the legislation was going through.

To take these suspects and give them access to mobile phones and the internet, the government chose to disarm itself from the powers to relocate suspects and I believe this gentleman was previously excluded from coming to London", he said.

In 2010 a study by the Centre for Social Cohesion found that under the control-order system introduced by the last Labour government, one in six controlees (16%) had absconded.

The most well-known was Zeeshan Siddiqui, who was believed to have attended a training camp with two of the July 7th bombers and has not been seen since he jumped out the window of a psychiatric unit in 2006.

[Source: http://www.theguardian.com/uk/2013/jan/01/terror-suspects-disappearance-control-order]

❓ Questions

1. **Explain** what a control order is.

2. **Describe** what a terrorism prevention measure is.

3. Make a table with two headings: 'Civil Liberty Criticisms' and 'Government Critics'. Note down the main arguments in the case study and newspaper article above in your table.

4. **Do you think** that more laws need to be introduced to make the UK safer from the threat of terrorism? **Explain** your answer.

📖 Word Bank

- **Abscond**
To leave hurriedly and secretly in order to avoid arrest.

UK counter-terrorism strategy

While governments often choose to make laws in response to a terrorist attack, the main way in which governments can tackle terrorism is through effective counter-terrorism strategies. These are the tactics used by governments to stop terrorism from happening. In the UK the policy is called 'CONTEST' and it is carried out by the Office for Security and Counter-Terrorism in Westminster.

There are four aims of the strategy:

- pursue: to stop terrorist attacks
- prevent: to stop people becoming terrorists or supporting terrorism
- protect: to strengthen our protection against a terrorist attack
- prepare: to mitigate the impact of a terrorist attack

The UK government also monitors the 'threat level'. The threat level shows the likelihood of a terrorist attack happening the UK and is calculated in response to any known 'terrorist activity'.

There are five levels of threat:

- low – an attack is unlikely
- moderate – an attack is possible but not likely
- substantial – an attack is a strong possibility
- severe – an attack is highly likely
- critical – an attack is expected imminently

The threat level is currently set separately for Northern Ireland and Great Britain.

The Scottish government

While counter-terrorism policy is reserved to the Westminster government, many aspects of preventing and dealing with a potential terrorist act in Scotland are managed by the Scottish government. The Specialist Crime Division has responsibility for counter-terrorism in Scotland.

 Make the Link

You learned about the Westminster government departments in Unit 1.

Word bank

- **Mitigate**
  To make the effects of something less severe.

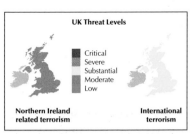

UK Threat Levels

Critical
Severe
Substantial
Moderate
Low

Northern Ireland related terrorism

International terrorism

Figure 14.4: *The UK was placed on 'critical' alert after the Glasgow airport bombing (see page 141)*

Hint

You can find more information about internet research on page 226.

Think point

Whilst Defence is currently a reserved issue, the Scottish government has a role in dealing with the problems and issues associated with terrorist behaviour. Can you think why this might be the case?

? Questions

1. Outline the four aims of the UK's counter-terrorism strategy.
2. Visit the UK's security service website: https://www.mi5.gov.uk (QR code below) and find out what the current threat levels are for:
   - International terrorism
   - Northern Ireland-related terrorism

   Explain why you think the two terror threat levels might be different.

3. Using a suitable search engine, try to find two recent **examples** of counter-terrorism in action in:
   - The UK
   - Scotland

   Describe whether or not you think the examples you selected have been successful in decreasing the threat posed by terrorism. You may wish to present your findings using a PowerPoint presentation to illustrate your answer.

Summary

In this chapter you have learned:

- to understand how the UK and Scottish governments have responded to terrorism
- to explain the problems that they have faced in responding to terrorism

Learning Summary

Now that you have finished the **Governments: responding to and resolving terrorism** chapter, complete a self-evaluation of your knowledge and skills to assess what you have understood. Use the checklist below and its traffic lights to draw up a revision plan to help you improve in the areas you identified as red or amber.

- I can explain why the UK government is responsible for dealing with terrorism.

- I can describe relevant laws which have been passed by the UK government, to try to stop terrorism.

- I can outline the criticisms of the laws the UK government has passed in order to deal with terrorism

- I can describe the UK government's counter-terrorism strategy.

- I can explain which organisation is responsible for counter-terrorism strategies in Scotland.

- I can explain what a control order is.

- I can explain what a terrorism prevention measure is.

Examples

In Modern Studies it is essential that you are able to back up any point you make with relevant evidence. When you are considering the statements above try to think of relevant examples for each response. You may wish to note these examples under each statement in your revision notes.

15 Multilateral organisations: responding to and resolving terrorism

What you will learn in this chapter

- To understand how multilateral organisations have responded to terrorism.
- To explain the problems these organisations have faced in responding to terrorism.

Multilateral organisations

> ### ✶ Make the Link
>
> In History you may learn about the League of Nations, the multilateral organisation that preceded the United Nations.

Multilateral organisations are groups of countries, working together for a stated goal.

The opposite of multilateralism would therefore be unilateralism, where countries work completely independently of each other in their own self-interest.

International organisations such as the European Union (EU), the United Nations (UN) and NATO (the North Atlantic Treaty Organization) are multilateral organisations of which the UK has membership. Each organisation has a role to play in international relations and therefore a role to play in responding to the threat of international terrorism.

The United Nations

Figure 15.1: *Flag of the United Nations*

The UN is an international alliance formed in 1945 following the end of the Second World War. It is organised through six main bodies: the General Assembly, the Security Council, the Economic and Social Council, the Trusteeship Council, the International Court of Justice and the Secretariat.

Today the UN has a total of 193 member countries. The most recognisable figure in the UN is the Secretary General who acts as the leader and spokesperson for the organisation.

Figure 15.2: *Ban Ki-Moon, Secretary General since 2007*

In 2006 all member countries of the UN adopted its Global Counter-Terrorism Strategy with the stated aim to co-ordinate counter-terrorism strategies across the world. Specifically the strategy aims to:

- tackle the conditions that support the spread of terrorism
- prevent and combat terrorism
- build countries' capacity to prevent and combat terrorism and to strengthen the role of the UN system
- ensure respect for human rights for all and the rule of law while countering terrorism

The UN's Counter-Terrorism Implementation Task Force helps member states with implementing the strategy. The Task Force is organised into a number of 'working groups'. These groups look at different aspects of counter-terrorism such as addressing radicalisation, protecting human rights, and tackling the financing of terrorism.

❓ Questions

1. **Explain** why the UN was first formed.
2. Outline the UN Global Counter-Terrorism Strategy.

The UN against terrorism

The UN is a diplomatic organisation; this means that it provides a place for countries to discuss and debate international issues of global importance. However, the UN can take action and has done so in recent years in response to the threat of international terrorism.

Resolutions

A resolution is a commitment to take action. This might be to raise awareness, to warn a country or an organisation, or it could be to initiate military action. Following the events of September 11th 2001, the UN acted by passing Resolution 1373 (2001) which called upon Member States to implement a number of measures intended to counter terrorist activities including denying financial support for terrorist groups.

Figure 15.3: *Denying financial support, or money freezing*

Peacekeeping

UN peacekeepers monitor the peace process in countries all over the world. UN peacekeepers (often known as Blue Berets because they wear blue helmets) can include soldiers, police officers, and civilian personnel.

UN peacekeepers are currently positioned in the Middle East where the UN has been working since 1948. As of June 2013 the United Nations Truth Supervision Organization (UNTSO – focused on peacekeeping in the Middle East) had in place:

- 152 military observers
- 92 international civilian personnel
- 136 local civilian staff

Figure 15.4: *A UN peacekeeper at work*

Military observers come from a variety of different countries including America, China and Nepal. UN peacekeepers are therefore directly involved in the peace process in the Middle East.

Military action

Perhaps the strongest action that the UN can take is military intervention. In 2011 the UN passed a resolution that authorised air strikes against tank columns and naval ships in Libya. The UN wanted

Figure 15.5: *Colonel Gaddafi*

to support the 'rebels' who had staged an uprising against the Libyan government, led by Colonel Muammar Gaddafi. Gaddafi ruled the country of Libya for 42 years in total. It has been claimed that his time in power was characterised by torture and human rights abuses and that he was a supporter of international terrorism.

No-fly zones

No-fly zones are areas over which aircraft are not allowed to fly. This stops the military from gaining information by flying overhead, or from dropping bombs for example. The UN has used such zones in Libya, Bosnia and Herzegovina, and in Iraq.

? Question

Using the headings below, summarise the main ways in which the UN has taken action in the global fight against international terrorism in recent years:

- resolutions
- peacekeeping
- military action
- no-fly zones

Criticisms of the UN's counter-terrorism strategy

Critics of the UN say that the organisation has failed as an international peacekeeper. Wars continue today and global threats such as terrorism remain. Other criticisms include the fact that the UN is seen as an elitist institution governed by the most powerful countries in the world and only works in their self-interests.

GO! Activity

Research

- Visit the UN website and look at the list of its 193 members:
  http://www.un.org/en/members

- Then visit the Freedom House members list, which lists those countries deemed to be 'free' (based on the political and civil rights of its citizens):
  http://www.freedomhouse.org/report-types/freedom-world

- Note down the countries which are not classed as free and yet are part of the UN.

Discuss

If countries are not classed as free how **do you think** that might affect dealing with the issue of international terrorism?

Elitism

The Security Council is the key place in which decisions surrounding international security are made. According to the 'post Second World War' political make-up, there are five permanent members of the UN Security Council: China, France, Russia, the UK and the USA.

The Security Council deals with maintaining peace, issuing sanctions, and authorising military action. Critics contend that the permanent members, who all have nuclear capabilities, are able to act in any way they wish without question because of their permanent status. Others argue that permanent membership is an outdated idea, with currently powerful countries such as Germany excluded from the top table. The Security Council has also been criticised in the past for responding slowly to international disputes.

The veto

A final criticism of the power of the Security Council is the power of veto held by the five permanent members. The veto means that even if just one of the five vote against a resolution, such as military action or imposing sanctions for example, the vote will be unsuccessful. Since 1982 the USA has vetoed 32 Security Council resolutions against Israel, which is more than the total number of vetoes cast by all the other Security Council members put together. Critics argue that the American government's 'pro-Israeli' view has led to human rights violations that the international community, through the Security Council, could have stopped from happening.

? Question

Using the headings below, summarise the main criticisms of the UN's counter-terrorism strategy:

- undemocratic membership
- elitism
- the veto

NATO

The North Atlantic Treaty Organization (NATO) is a military alliance created in 1949 following the end of the Second World War. NATO is based on the idea of collective defence – Article 5 of the NATO treaty states that an attack on one member country is an attack on all. Following the events of September 11th 2001, NATO invoked Article 5.

NATO and terrorism

When NATO was formed in 1949 the main threat to global security was communism.

Communism no longer presents as much of a threat today, but international terrorism has increased in recent history; in response to this NATO has had to adapt and develop new ways to protect

Hint

Think about the ways in which support for terrorism develops.

📖 Word bank

- **Sanction**

A threatened penalty for disobeying a law.

- **Invoke**

To activate something, or state that it is now in effect.

Think point

Think about the ways in which the USA conducts herself as a global power. Has this impacted upon the ways in which international organisations have been able to respond to terrorism?

Figure 15.6: *The NATO flag*

Make the Link

You may have learned about the principles of communism in History.

international security. Russia is still not a member of NATO but the NATO-Russia Council (established in 2002) handles security issues and joint projects. Today NATO has 28 member countries in total.

NATO's counter-terrorism strategy

NATO's counter-terrorism strategy is based on:

- awareness of the threat of terrorism
- the shared capabilities of member countries
- engagement with partner countries

NATO now conducts a number of operations that support the fight against terrorism; three examples are shown in the figure below.

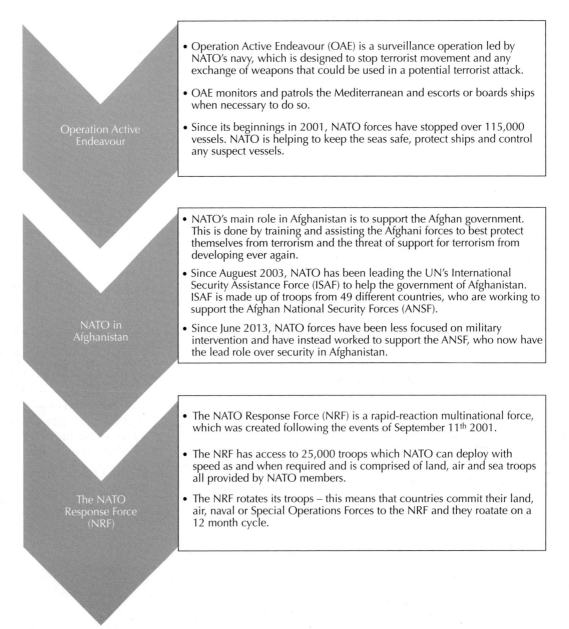

Operation Active Endeavour

- Operation Active Endeavour (OAE) is a surveillance operation led by NATO's navy, which is designed to stop terrorist movement and any exchange of weapons that could be used in a potential terrorist attack.
- OAE monitors and patrols the Mediterranean and escorts or boards ships when necessary to do so.
- Since its beginnings in 2001, NATO forces have stopped over 115,000 vessels. NATO is helping to keep the seas safe, protect ships and control any suspect vessels.

NATO in Afghanistan

- NATO's main role in Afghanistan is to support the Afghan government. This is done by training and assisting the Afghani forces to best protect themselves from terrorism and the threat of support for terrorism from developing ever again.
- Since August 2003, NATO has been leading the UN's International Security Assistance Force (ISAF) to help the government of Afghanistan. ISAF is made up of troops from 49 different countries, who are working to support the Afghan National Security Forces (ANSF).
- Since June 2013, NATO forces have been less focused on military intervention and have instead worked to support the ANSF, who now have the lead role over security in Afghanistan.

The NATO Response Force (NRF)

- The NATO Response Force (NRF) is a rapid-reaction multinational force, which was created following the events of September 11th 2001.
- The NRF has access to 25,000 troops which NATO can deploy with speed as and when required and is comprised of land, air and sea troops all provided by NATO members.
- The NRF rotates its troops – this means that countries commit their land, air, naval or Special Operations Forces to the NRF and they roatate on a 12 month cycle.

Figure 15.7: *NATO's counter-terrorism strategy*

? Questions

1. **Explain** why NATO was first formed.
2. Outline NATO's counter-terrorism strategy.
3. Summarise the three missions in which NATO is currently involved in countering the threat of international terrorism.

Criticisms of NATO

Communism

Critics argue that NATO was formed to protect against a threat which doesn't exist anymore. As terrorism is a global threat the nature of the alliance – which only represents 'North Atlantic' countries – is not helpful in tackling this problem. Therefore it can be argued that more representative organisations, such as the UN, are better at dealing with the threat of terrorism.

Figure 15.8: *This map shows the NATO member countries: far from a global spread*

Cost

Member countries pay money to NATO for the provision of military training and for their protection as part of the alliance. Countries pay an amount of money based on their Gross National Income – in 2013 Albania paid the least and America the most. Critics say that countries who pay more into NATO may expect to get more out of it and therefore smaller countries who pay less, such as Albania, will feel that they have a smaller say in the way in which the organisation is run. This may mean that when it comes to dealing with international threats such as terrorism countries will not be treated equally.

Word bank

• **Gross National Income**
The sum of a nation's Gross Domestic Product (money made within the country) plus Net Income received from overseas.

Illegal wars

NATO is often drawn into conflicts which it did not start. In recent history this has been the case with the wars in Iraq and Afghanistan. As of 2014 NATO troops are still in Afghanistan helping to prevent the threat of terrorism in the country. It was an international coalition led by America, however, which initially began the invasion in 2001 (see page 156).

In the 1990s NATO undertook a bombing campaign against the former Yugoslavia during the Kosovo War; this was criticised by some as a

Figure 15.9: *The flag of the European Union*

Think point

Why do you think we entered into a political and economic union with our EU neighbours?

Word bank

• **Export tariffs**

Taxes on goods going out of the country.

Make the Link

In Unit 1 we looked at different parliaments.

Figure 15.10: *Belgian EU Counter-Terrorism Co-ordinator Gilles de Kerchove*

'humanitarian disaster'. The bombing campaign included targeting electricity and water supplies.

? Questions

Using the headings below, summarise the main criticisms of NATO's counter-terrorism strategy:

• communism

• cost

• illegal wars

The European Union

The European Union (EU) is an economic and political alliance and is made up of 28 member countries in total. The origins of the EU can be traced back to the 1950s when it was then known as the European Coal and Steel Company. The organisation was formed on the basis of trade and a common market in which European nations could trade with limited sanctions and export tariffs.

The EU internal market (sometimes known as 'the single market') tries to guarantee the free movement of goods, capital, services, and people (the EU's 'four freedoms') within the EU's 28 member states.

Figure 15.11: *Map of Europe showing the EU member states*

Citizens across Europe elect MEPs (Members of the European Parliament) every five years to sit in the European Parliament and make decisions on their behalves. The UK has 72 MEPs in total; Scotland is currently designated as a 'region' of this total and is allocated six MEPs.

? Question

Explain why the European Union as we know it today was first founded.

The EU and terrorism

After the terrorist attacks in London in 2005 it was decided that the EU needed to take a more planned approach to managing terrorism (see the table below). The EU also appointed a Counter-Terrorism Co-ordinator to help member states in the fight against terrorism.

In 2006 the EU introduced a law (known as the 'Data Retention Directive') to allow governments to hold on to all telephone records for one year – this makes it possible to trace calls by terrorist suspects. Basic information, such as the caller's number, name and address, now have to be kept for at least six months by telephone service and internet service providers.

The EU has also issued a directive 'on the prevention of the use of the financial system for the purpose of money laundering and terrorist financing'. This directive tries to stop crime by making banks and companies investigate and report any cash transactions in excess of €15,000.

> **GO! Activity**
>
> **Research**
> Find out the names and political parties of Scotland's six MEPs.

> **📖 Word bank**
>
> • **Directive**
> An official instruction.

EU counter-terrorism strategy

Prevent people from turning to terrorism and stop future generations of terrorists from emerging.	The EU is keen to 'prevent' individuals from engaging in terrorism in the first instance. The organisation is keen to 'lead by example' in promoting good governance, promoting prosperity elsewhere and by challenging recruitment.
Protect citizens and critical infrastructure by reducing vulnerabilities against attacks.	The EU is keen to upgrade measures that protect people and infrastructure from attack, including border security. One of the key aims is to make passports issued by member states more secure through the use of biometrics (i.e. by recording unique facial characteristics, iris patterns and fingerprints). Biometrics passports are now issued as standard in the UK.
Pursue and investigate terrorists, impede planning, travel and communications, cut off access to funding and materials and bring terrorists to justice.	The EU aims to investigate and pursue terrorists across its borders. Measures to bring terrorists to justice, to cut off their funds and to disrupt their networks are part of this agenda.
Respond in a co-ordinated way by preparing for the management and minimisation of the consequences of a terrorist attack, improving capacities to deal with the aftermath and taking into account the needs of victims.	This strand allows EU member states to support one another in the aftermath of major terrorist atrocities.

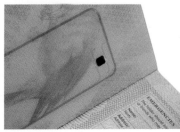

Figure 15.12: *A biometric chip in a British passport*

The European Council reviews progress on the above strategy every six months.

? Questions

1. Using the headings below, summarise the main ways in which the EU has taken action in the global fight against international terrorism in recent years:
   - Counter-Terrorism Co-ordinator
   - Data Retention Directive
   - Financial System Directive

2. Outline the EU terrorism strategy.

Criticisms of the EU

The EU is made up of 28 member states and therefore passing laws or attempting to jointly 'solve' any issue can be difficult as there are 28 countries with 28 different governments of their own. Criticisms of the EU's policy on terrorism often relate to civil liberties.

Proposals on data retention
Proposals on data retention have been criticised both in the European Parliament and in member states.

The Passenger Name Record (PNR) is a database that includes a passenger's name, address, phone number and credit card details. It is used in the airline and transport industry. In April 2013 a EU proposal to allow the use of PNR data for investigating serious crime and terrorist offences was rejected.

Figure 15.13: *Millions of files would be made available via the PNR database*

Biometric security standards for ID cards and passports
Critics argue that whilst the EU can suggest all countries use a form of biometric security for their passports and ID cards, they can't actually 'enforce' a European Policy. Article 18 of the EC Treaty allows for freedom of movement meaning European citizens can live and work in any European country they want to.

Human rights
Others believe that the EU is interfering in countries' domestic affairs by creating laws in country-specific cases of terrorism. The newspaper article below considers this argument in more detail.

📖 Word bank

• EC Treaty

A document that lays out how the union of member states operates; EC being European Community, a former name.

DAILY NEWS

world - business - finance - lifestyle - travel - sport

Al-Qaeda terrorists launch human rights bid

Two Al-Qaeda terrorists, one of whom plotted to kill thousands of people in a bomb attack on a British shopping centre, have launched an attempt to have their convictions quashed on human rights grounds.

The pair have applied to the European Court of Human Rights after claiming MI5 was complicit in their torture by Pakistani security services, a claim that has already been rejected by British courts.

Officials at the European Court have allowed their application to go ahead rather than declaring it inadmissible, as they do with thousands of cases a year.

The government must now respond to the claims, and if its explanation does not satisfy the court it will order a full hearing which, if successful, would almost certainly lead to the British courts being forced to quash the convictions.

The new development raises further questions about the influence of Strasbourg over British sovereignty, and the way human rights legislation is being exploited by defence lawyers.

[Source: http://www.telegraph.co.uk/news/uknews/terrorism-in-the-uk/9499541/Al-Qaeda-terrorists-launch-human-rights-bid.html]

? Question

Using the headings below, summarise the main criticisms of the EU's counter-terrorism strategy:

- data retention
- biometric security standards, ID cards and passports
- human rights

GO! Activity

Show your knowledge
To support your learning and to help you revise, make a mind map which shows the major problems each organisation has faced. You should detail:

- key dates in which the organisation has faced opposition

- the counter-terrorism strategy of each organisation

- a summary under each explaining whether or not you believe the organisation has been successful in countering the threat posed by terrorism

Summary

In this chapter you have learned:

- to understand how multilateral organisations have responded to terrorism
- to explain the problems these organisations have faced in responding to terrorism

Learning Summary

Now that you have finished the **Multilateral organisations: responding to and resolving terrorism** chapter, complete a self-evaluation of your knowledge and skills to assess what you have understood. Use the checklist below and its traffic lights to draw up a revision plan to help you improve in the areas you identified as red or amber.

- I can explain why the UN was first formed.

- I can outline the UN counter-terrorism strategy.

- I can describe the ways in which the UN has acted to prevent terrorism.

- I can explain the main criticisms of the UN's counter-terrorism strategy.

- I can explain how NATO was first formed.

- I can outline NATO's counter-terrorism strategy.

- I can describe the ways in which NATO has acted to prevent terrorism.

- I can explain the main criticisms of NATO's counter-terrorism strategy.

- I can explain why the EU was first founded.

- I can outline the EU's counter-terrorism strategy.

- I can describe the ways in which the EU has acted to prevent terrorism.

- I can explain the main criticisms of the EU's counter-terrorism strategy.

Examples

In Modern Studies it is essential that you are able to back up any point you make with relevant evidence. When you are considering the statements above try to think of relevant examples for each response. You may wish to note these examples under each statement in your revision notes.

16 Interested organisations

What you will learn in this chapter

- To identify how interested organisations have responded to terrorism.
- To understand how you can contribute to this international issue as a global citizen.

Interested organisations

Alliances such as the EU or organisations such as the UN are formal organisations that use the governments of their members to try to change things. Other interested organisations and individuals, however, can also help by responding to the issues surrounding terrorism.

Figure 16.1: *Freedom of expression is guarded by civil liberties groups*

Civil liberties groups

Civil liberties are rights and freedoms that individuals are entitled to. Examples of civil liberties include freedom from torture and freedom of expression. Civil liberties groups therefore exist to protect these freedoms.

Liberty

CASE STUDY

Liberty is a pressure group that campaigns to protect civil liberties and promotes human rights.

'Human rights law requires the State to take steps to protect the right to life – which includes measures to prevent terrorism. However, any measures taken to counter terrorism must be proportionate and not undermine our democratic values. In particular, laws designed to protect people from the threat of terrorism and the enforcement of these laws must be compatible with people's rights and freedoms. Yet, all too often the risk of terrorism has been used as the basis for eroding our human rights and civil liberties. We believe that terrorism can and must be fought within the rule of law and the human rights framework. Repression and injustice, and the criminalisation of non-violent speech and protest make us less safe, not more.

Figure 16.2: *Liberty logo*

These measures act as a recruiting sergeant to the extremist fringe and marginalise those whose support is vital to effectively fight the terrorist threat.

They also undermine the values that separate us from the terrorist, the very values we should be fighting to protect.'

[Source: http://www.liberty-human-rights.org.uk/human-rights/countering-terrorism]

? Questions

1. Summarise what civil liberties groups do.
2. Consider the above case study. **Explain** the work of Liberty in countering terrorism.

Charities

Charities are organisations that exist in support of a cause. Charities can have a vital role, therefore, in combating issues surrounding international terrorism. The charity Amnesty International is looked at in the below case study.

Amnesty International   CASE STUDY

'The so-called 'war on terror' has led to an erosion of fundamental human rights, highlighted by the increasing use and acceptance of torture and other cruel, inhuman and degrading treatment.

Figure 16.3: *Amnesty International logo*

We have seen and heard testimonies of 'terrorist suspects', held or formerly held in places of detention such as Guantánamo Bay and Bagram. We know that such places of detention exist in several locations globally. We know that this new trend for torture must stop.

We are campaigning to hold governments accountable for their actions and to uphold international law and the absolute prohibition of torture under any circumstances.'

[Source: http://archive.is/tGgl]

? Questions

1. Summarise what charities do to counter terrorism.
2. Consider the above case study. **Explain** the work of Amnesty in countering terrorism.

Make the Link

You can find more information about pressure groups in Unit 1 on page 70.

Pressure groups

Pressure groups are organisations that try to influence government by encouraging them to pass laws or to change laws they do not agree with. They are sometimes referred to as 'lobby groups'.

Scotland Against Criminalising Communities (SACC)

SACC campaigns against Britain's terrorism laws, against torture and detention without trial, against laws that criminalise political and community activity, against the so-called 'War on Terror'. SACC stands up for human rights and civil liberties. SACC's aims are:

Figure 16.4: *SACC logo*

- To campaign against the use of excessive state powers to criminalise political activity which are contained within the Terrorism Act 2000, the Anti-Terrorism, Crime and Security Act 2001, the Prevention of Terrorism Act 2005, the Terrorism Act 2006 and the Counter-Terrorism Act 2008; to campaign for the repeal of these acts; to campaign against any other legislation that has a similar effect; to monitor the use of such legislation and to work in close association with the communities most affected by these acts in order to highlight their discriminatory nature.

- To demand that everyone must be treated as innocent until proven guilty; that habeas corpus (the right of a person to be brought before a judge to determine if their detention is lawful) be fully respected and to demand those imprisoned without trial are released or granted a fair trial.

[Source: http://www.sacc.org.uk/about-sacc]

? Questions

1. Summarise what pressure groups do to counter terrorism.
2. Consider the case study above. **Explain** the work of the SACC in countering terrorism.

📖 Word bank

- **Hustings**

A meeting at which candidates in an election address their voters.

GO! Activity

Research

Under the provisions of the Curriculum for Excellence you need to become aware of how what you learn in class can have an impact on the wider world.

Select one of the three organisations from the case studies provided (or you may wish to choose your own civil liberties group or charity). Contact the charity/organisation via email and ask how you might be able to help effect change in countering international terrorism through their work.

To extend your learning, you may like to invite a speaker from your charity to discuss the issues in this Unit in depth. With your teacher's support you could even broaden this out into a hustings with your local MP, for example, to provide a response to the government's actions (or a critique depending on their party) in dealing with international terrorism.

Summary

In this chapter you have learned:

- to identify how interested organisations have responded to terrorism
- to understand how you can contribute to this international issue as a global citizen

Learning Summary

Now that you have finished the **Interested organisations** chapter, complete a self-evaluation of your knowledge and skills to assess what you have understood. Use the checklist below and its traffic lights to draw up a revision plan to help you improve in the areas you identified as red or amber.

- I can explain the role of charities in combating terrorism.

- I can explain the role of pressure groups in combating terrorism.

- I can explain the role of civil liberties groups in combating terrorism.

- I understand the role that I can play in combating terrorism.

Examples

In Modern Studies it is essential that you are able to back up any point you make with relevant evidence. When you are considering the statements above try to think of relevant examples for each response. You may wish to note these examples under each statement in your revision notes.

17 The future of terrorism

What you will learn in this chapter

- To understand how the future of terrorism might develop.
- To explain how terrorists might be able to use technology to support their ambitions.

The future of terrorism

When governments, NGOs and interested organisations think about the best ways to respond to terrorism, they cannot do so in isolation. This means that they need to think one step ahead of terrorists, or would-be supporters. Terrorism today is international and support for different terrorist organisations can probably be found in every country in the world at some level. Terrorism in the future, however, may look very different. Countries and governments across the world need to think about how they will plan for the development of terrorism and the changing tactics terrorists will use to create fear and panic.

Figure 17.1: *Using tactics to stay one step ahead*

Cyber-terrorism

Cyber-terrorism is the use of the internet to disrupt computer systems, for example by creating an online virus, or through hacking into a network. Through hacking, terrorist supporters and organisations can access government materials online which might help them to destabilise a regime. In 2002, Scottish man Gary McKinnon was accused of the 'biggest military computer hack of all time'. The US government claimed that Mr McKinnon hacked into US Army, Navy, Air Force and Department of Defence computers, as well as 16 NASA computers. They have claimed his hacking caused over $700,000 worth of damage to government systems. Mr McKinnon, who has been diagnosed as suffering from Asperger's Syndrome, has maintained his innocence and claimed he was simply looking for information on UFOs. In October 2012, after a series of court battles in the UK, the British government withdrew an extradition order to the United States. This means that he will not have to stand trial for the alleged offences in America where he could have faced up to 70 years in prison.

📖 Word bank

- **NGO**

A non-governmental organisation; any non-profit, voluntary citizens' group that is organised on a local, national or international level.

- **Network**

A group of two or more computers linked together.

- **Destabilise**

To upset or cause unrest.

- **Extradition**

Handing over someone to the foreign state in which they are suspected of having committed a crime.

Figure 17.2: *An online virus could cause untold damage*

Gary McKinnon said 'I was convinced, and there was good evidence to show, that certain secretive parts of the American government intelligence agencies did have access to crashed extra-terrestrial technology which could, in these days, save us in the form of a free, clean, pollution-free energy'.

? Questions

1. **Explain, in detail,** what the term 'cyber-terrorism' means.
2. Summarise the case of Gary McKinnon. Come to a **conclusion** as to whether or not you believe the British government was correct to refuse to extradite Mr McKinnon. **Justify** your response with **evidence** from this chapter.

Why cyber-terrorism?

The internet is a valuable tool for terrorists because it allows them to share materials and brainwash would-be supporters. Members of terrorist organisations often use internet chat rooms to make contact with those that are weak and vulnerable, especially young people. Terrorists often think that the internet is a 'safe place' because they can remain anonymous; however, in 2008 the youngest person in Britain ever arrested and convicted under the Terrorism Act was sentenced to two years in a young offenders' institution based on his internet activity. Hammaad Munshi was 16 when he was arrested in 2006 when police found a guide to making napalm (used for making bombs) on his computer. Sentencing him, the judge said he had been influenced by 'fanatical extremists'.

Social media

Millions of people across the world use social media to interact with friends, show support for certain causes and to share information.

Websites like Facebook, Twitter and YouTube have all been used by terrorists and terrorist supporters to encourage support for their causes. An American study in 2012 found that nearly 90% of cyber-terrorism is carried out via social media. In 2011, following a series of co-ordinated Christmas bombings in Nigeria, the terror group Boko Haram released a video statement on YouTube defending their actions. The Taliban even have their very own Twitter account. In response to criticism, Twitter have altered their online procedures, allowing viewers to 'flag' offensive content under the category 'promotes terrorism'.

Figure 17.3: *Social media is an effective means of mass communication*

Social media is an extremely useful tool for terrorists to gain support: it is free of charge and it allows them access to a huge pool of individuals they might never have been able to connect with using other techniques, such as holding meetings. The UK government's security services monitor all social media and gather information on who is following who on sites like Twitter.

Nuclear terrorism

If terrorists were ever able to find a way to produce a nuclear device political analysts say it could lead to substantial loss of life and devastation.

> **Make the Link**
>
> You may have learned about the science behind nuclear weaponry in Physics.

Figure 17.4: *A nuclear missile*

In 2011 the *Telegraph* newspaper received leaked documents that said that if Osama bin Laden was ever captured or killed by the West, an Al-Qaeda 'sleeper cell' would set off a 'weapon of mass destruction' in a 'secret location' in Europe which they said would cause 'a nuclear hellstorm'. Whilst that has not happened to date, experts fear that terrorism will become even worse in the future as terrorists try to make a bigger impact by creating greater fear and killing larger numbers of people.

In his first speech to the UN Security Council, American President Barack Obama stated 'just one nuclear weapon exploded in a city, be it New York or Moscow, Tokyo or Beijing, London or Paris, could kill hundreds of thousands of people, destabilize our security, our economies, and our very way of life'.

Terrorist interest

Intelligence evidence has suggested that Al-Qaeda have the capability to produce radiological weapons, but that they would need to find nuclear material and recruit rogue scientists to build 'dirty bombs'. A 'dirty bomb' is made of radioactive material and could kill potentially thousands of individuals and contaminate the area of its detonation for many years after.

Al-Qaeda has tried to find or make its own nuclear weapons for the last two decades. When he was alive, Osama bin Laden claimed that gaining nuclear weapons or other weapons of mass destruction was a 'religious duty'.

? Questions

1. **Explain** why terrorist organisations have been drawn to the use of social media in recent years.
2. **Outline** why leaders such as Barack Obama are so concerned by the threat posed by nuclear terrorism.
3. **Explain** what a 'dirty bomb' is.
4. **Describe** Al-Qaeda's ambitions for nuclear weapons.

Summary

In this chapter you have learned:

• to understand how the future of terrorism might develop

• to explain how terrorists might be able to use technology to support their ambitions

Learning Summary

Now that you have finished **The future of terrorism** chapter, complete a self-evaluation of your knowledge and skills to assess what you have understood. Use the checklist below and its traffic lights to draw up a revision plan to help you improve in the areas you identified as red or amber.

• I can describe what is meant by 'cyber-terrorism'.　　◯ ◯ ⬯

• I can explain the role of social media in the fight against terrorism.　　◯ ◯ ⬯

• I can explain what is meant by 'nuclear terrorism'.　　◯ ◯ ⬯

Examples

In Modern Studies it is essential that you are able to back up any point you make with relevant evidence. When you are considering the statements above try to think of relevant examples for each response. You may wish to note these examples under each statement in your revision notes.

Assessment

18 Added Value Unit/Assignment

Figure 18.1: *Research is essential in proving a theory*

Social research

For the Added Value Unit (AVU) of your National 4 course or your National 5 Assignment, you will be asked to carry out some social research in order to prove or disprove a theory. A theory is an idea you might have that can be proved or disproved through carrying out research; in Modern Studies we sometimes call a theory a hypothesis.

Your research

Stage one: identify your topic

First, you should select the Unit you wish to focus your research on. You need to think about the issues that interest you the most; you can do this by brainstorming your prior knowledge on the Unit, and you can also find a list of suggested ideas for your research topic at the end of this chapter on page 235.

Stage two: formulate your research question

You now need to formulate a research question. When you are deciding on your research question you should focus on two different elements that will help you to form aims for your social research. For example:

- 'Should **Scotland** become an **independent** country?'
- '**Community Payback Orders** are a very **effective punishment**.'
- 'Terrorist attacks have increasingly affected the UK in recent years.'

From your research question you should be able to make a list of aims that will help you in finding out the information you require. For example:

1. To find out what a Community Payback Order is – what crimes it is used as a punishment for, and what does it entail.

2. To find out how many people who are given CPOs go on to reoffend.

3. To find out what other punishments might be used instead.

4. To find out how effective the alternative punishments are.

Stage three: selecting your research methods

You now need to select at least two different research methods to help you find out the information you have listed in your aims. There are many different types of research methods used in social research but they are all are based on gathering, evaluating, and interpreting information. You need to select the methods most suited to your AVU/Assignment topic.

Differences between sources of information

There are different kinds of information you could collect. Quantitative and/or qualitative methods, and primary and/or secondary data – you should gather a few different types of information so that you have lots of things to talk about.

Quantitative methods

- Those that focus on numbers and frequencies.
- Quantitative methods include questionnaires, surveys etc.
- Provide information that is easy to analyse statistically and fairly reliable.
- These methods can be cost- and time-effective as there is a lack of involvement from the researcher – i.e. they do not need to make face-to-face contact with participants.
- However, in order for the results to be reliable they usually involve a high number of people being questioned.

Qualitative methods

- Those that focus on descriptive data, which is usually written.
- Qualitative methods include case studies and interviews.
- May be less reliable than quantitative methods, but the information collected is usually more in-depth and descriptive.
- Qualitative methods usually involve a lot of input from the researcher, e.g. they will need to have more face-to-face contact with participants.
- However, this research usually involves a lower number of people being questioned.

> **Make the Link**
>
> Social research is carried out by social scientists. You might have come across social science in Modern Studies, Geography, History and Business Management. Social scientists use social research to help them investigate different questions they may have about society. Scientists carry out experiments to prove or disprove theories; social scientists carry out social research to do exactly the same thing.

> **Make the Link**
>
> Create a list of the different research methods you may already know of; think of the ways you have researched information in Modern Studies and other subjects.

Figure 18.2: *Take time to research using materials available to you*

Primary data

- The researcher goes out and collects new data.
- Examples include interviews, letters and questions/surveys.

Secondary data

- The researcher uses existing sources of information.
- Examples include webpages, books, newspapers and TV/radio programmes.

Your research topic might be better suited to one type of data over another so you need to think carefully about the best ways to find the most useful and reliable information for your topic. For example, if your topic is about terrorism you might not be able to find anyone who knows a lot about this topic to provide you with an interview and secondary data, such as internet research, might therefore be more appropriate.

Over the next few pages you will find step-by-step guides to using three different research methods: interviews (a primary source), questionnaires (a primary source) and internet research (a secondary source).

Interviews

An interview is a conversation between two or more people where questions are asked by the interviewer to gain information from the interviewee (the person being asked). Carrying out an interview is a great way for you to develop your knowledge and skills in a topic or issue from within any Unit in Modern Studies.

Figure 18.3: *Planning is very important when preparing for an interview*

How to plan and conduct an interview

Step one: research
The best way to construct effective questions is to know as much as you can about your subject. Research your chosen topic/issue using secondary sources of information such as webpages, books, newspapers and TV/radio programmes.

Step two: who to interview?
Make a list of people who might be able to help with your research question, for example your MSP, MP or local councillor perhaps.

Contact the person(s) you wish to interview – ensure you do this in plenty of time. Arrange a time and place that would be appropriate to conduct the interview. If it isn't possible to meet the person face-to-face you may wish to conduct the interview via webcam or phone. If the person(s) agree you may be able to record the conversation so that you can transcribe (make a full written copy) of what was said. You may wish to use the transcription as a source of information for your National 4 AVU or during your National 5 Assignment write-up.

Step three: the questions
Read over your research and create a set of questions. Simple questions can be 'closed', this means they will be answered with a simple 'yes or

> **⚙ Hint**
>
> You may wish to contact one of your representatives to arrange an interview with them (see page 31).

no' response. However, most questions will be 'open' meaning they will produce different responses depending on the interviewee. Many open questions begin with 'how', 'what', 'when', 'where', 'why' etc., or ask for an opinion. Ensure you have your questions written down so you don't forget what you want to ask. Become very familiar with your questions before you go into the interview – you could try out the interview with a classmate beforehand. This is known as a 'pilot' interview and will allow you to 'road test' your questions to see how effective they are at gathering the information you require.

Step four: conducting the interview
Make sure you take the following with you:

- your questions
- a pen/pencil
- a notebook to record your notes
- possibly a recording device (remember that you must always ask permission before recording an interview)

Step five: after the interview
After the interview review your notes alongside your existing research. If you recorded the interview you may wish to type it up.

- What do your findings show?
- Are there any patterns in the views expressed?
- Is there evidence of bias?
- Does your own research support the views of the interviewee?
- Does your own research contradict the views of the interviewee?

Key features of interviews

- Can create qualitative and quantitative data.
- A primary source of data.
- Carried out face-to-face by the researcher.
- Researcher can ask a set of pre-prepared questions about a specific topic. However, there is also the option to ask further questions depending on the interviewee's responses.
- Researcher can use both 'open' and 'closed' questions to gain information
- Interviewee can elaborate on any of the areas covered.

Advantages and disadvantages of interviews

Advantages

- Allows the researcher to explore issues in an in-depth way.
- Researcher can create pre-prepared questions but can also ask supplementary questions.
- It is easy to quantify the results of 'closed' questions (by creating a pie chart of responses, for example).

- Researcher can clarify if there is any confusion about the questions posed.
- Interviewee can explore certain points in more detail.
- Good way of finding out what people think and feel about particular topics.

Disadvantages

- Can be time-consuming for researcher and interviewee as it involves face-to-face contact.
- Interviewee may digress into irrelevant areas.
- Can be difficult to quantify the results as much of the data may be descriptive.
- May be difficult to compare answers given by different individuals.
- People may not answer honestly. This may be because they are too embarrassed to say what they really think, or they may give an answer that they think the researcher wants to hear.

GO! Activity

Use your skills

1. Create a list of the topics and issues from the Democracy in Scotland and the United Kingdom Unit that you are interested in. You can include the examples on page 235 or use them to help you think of others.
2. Decide on one topic or issue that are you are interested in researching and create a research question. Make a list of aims which will help you find out the information you require.
3. Conduct research into your chosen topic or issue using a variety of different sources and methods.
4. Select a relevant representative or representatives and arrange an interview with them; your teacher will be able to help you find out how to get in touch with the person(s) if you are unsure.
5. Prepare questions to be asked at the interview. Ask your teacher, a family member or a friend to read over your questions and provide you with some feedback.
6. Conduct the interview. Remember to be prepared!
7. Write up your research and show how it has helped you to gain a better understanding of your chosen topic or issue.

Checklist

- Pick someone who you would like to interview – how can they help you achieve the aims you have for your AVU/Assignment?
- Arrange an interview with that person either face-to-face, or over the phone or internet – make sure you don't leave it until the last minute to ask them.
- Carry out research on the topic for your interview and, if possible, background research on the person you are interviewing.

- Think carefully about your questions and practise them before the real interview.
- During the interview take lots of notes, or record it if the person you are interviewing is happy for you to do so.
- After the interview look at your notes and draw conclusions based on your research – remember to focus on your aims.

Questionnaires

Questionnaires are a valuable way of collecting a wide range of information from a number of people. This section will help you with conducting a questionnaire for a topic from the Social Issues in the United Kingdom Unit. However, you can apply the techniques to all of the Units within the Modern Studies course.

How to construct a questionnaire

Step one: planning your questionnaire
When constructing a questionnaire it is important to have an idea of what information you want to get from the results. Do you want to find out the public's opinion on a topic? Do you want to find out specific information? You can ask many different questions that may have different aims in order to get a wide range of opinions; by designing your questions carefully you can gain some very useful information for your AVU or Assignment.

Step two: writing your questionnaire
When planning your questionnaire you need to carefully consider how you word the questions as this will affect the replies that you get. People may not understand a question properly, or the wording of a question may encourage them to give one answer rather than another (this is known as a 'leading question'). An example of a leading question is 'do you agree that prisons are really unsuitable for people that have drug addictions?' By using the word 'agree' this question encourages the respondent to think that prison is not suitable for people with drug issues. The questions should be clear, precise and not be full of 'jargon' that people might not understand.

Types of question

An effective questionnaire will have lots of different types of questions.

'Closed' questions are specific and have a set choice of answers. They are therefore more likely to communicate similar meanings to all respondents. Closed questions take less time for the interviewer, the participants and the researcher and so are a less expensive survey method for large-scale surveys. Generally, more people return surveys that use closed questions than those that use open questions as it is quicker and easier to answer multiple-choice questions.

'Open' questions do not give respondents answers to choose from, but are worded so that the respondents are encouraged to explain their answers and reactions to the question with a sentence, a paragraph, or

Figure 18.4: *A questionnaire can be written out by hand or compiled online*

 Make the Link

You may be asked to construct a questionnaire in other subjects while carrying out your Added Value Unit or Assignment.

 Hint

A questionnaire is a form of primary research – the collection of data that does not already exist.

Hint

Your teacher will help you develop a research question before you carry out your questionnaire so that you have a focused topic that you are trying to investigate.

even a page or more, depending on the survey. Open questions allow the respondents to express a wider range of opinions than closed questions; however, they can be more difficult to draw results from as their answers cannot be compared as easily.

When constructing your questionnaire try to include a variety of open and closed questions and at least one of each of the following types of questions:

1. Knowledge questions: used to find out how much people know about a particular subject, for example, 'what do you know about the court system in Scotland?'

2. Factual questions: straightforward questions with 'yes', 'no' or 'don't know' answers. Other factual questions may be answered with a number, for example, 'what age are you?'

3. Opinion questions: used to find out how people feel about a topic, for example, 'do you think there are enough police on the streets?'

4. Motivation questions: ask for people's reasons for doing something. They can also usefully follow an opinion question, for example, 'if you answered 'yes' to the last question, tick the boxes that indicate your reasons why.'

Step three: choosing who to send the questionnaire to

You need to be able to draw conclusions from your results so it is important you survey a range of different people, sometimes called a 'sample'. This means asking people from a range of backgrounds, for example men and women, varying age groups and people of different ethnicities, religions and social classes. Using a questionnaire is the quickest and cheapest way to ask a large sample of the population as it will only cost the price of a stamp for each person, or may even be free if you put it online.

Step four: send out the questionnaire

You could do this by post, or if you have put your questionnaire online you could send the link to your sample via email.

Step five: record the findings of your questionnaire

You could make a pie chart or graph to demonstrate your conclusions.

Key features of questionnaires

- Produces mainly quantitative data, but qualitative data can also be produced.
- A primary source of data.
- Can be carried out face-to-face by a researcher, or sent to the respondent in the post or via email.
- All the respondents answer the same list of questions.
- Closed questions are normally used in questionnaires – respondents choose from a range of possible answers given on the questionnaire; for example, 'yes', 'no' or 'sometimes'.
- Respondents may also be asked to express an opinion or attitude; for example, 'what is your attitude to sentencing criminals to time in prison? – strongly in favour, in favour, neutral, against, strongly against?'

Advantages and disadvantages of questionnaires

Advantages

- Once you have written your questionnaire it can be sent to lots of people which will give you a good idea of what the widespread opinion on a certain issue is. This is an inexpensive way of gathering a lot of data.

- It will mainly produce quantitative data (numerical evidence), which can be used to draw conclusions. Quantitative data is easier for researchers to draw conclusions from than qualitative data (more descriptive and varied information) as you can simply add up the results, display it in graphs and pie charts, and draw conclusions accordingly.

- As all respondents are asked the same list of questions it is easier to compare people's answers.

- Can be less expensive and time-consuming than other primary research methods, such as interviews.

Disadvantages

- Not everyone who you send a questionnaire to will respond.

- Some respondents may not answer all of the questions.

- If the questionnaire is not conducted face-to-face then there is no opportunity for the researcher to clarify if the respondent doesn't understand one of the questions.

- There is often no chance for the respondent to elaborate if they would like to answer a question in more detail.

GO! Activity

Use your skills

Work with a partner and re-word the following questions to make them effective questions using the techniques above. Some of the questions might need to be removed altogether.

- 'Do you agree with the prison system?'
- 'Should all knife crime offenders get a jail sentence?'
- 'Why are people in prison responsible for their own situation?'
- 'Why are young males more likely to go to prison than other people?'
- 'How many people do you know that are in prison?'

Explain why each of the questions is not suitable in their current form.

Checklist

- Express questions clearly, making sure that they can be understood.
- Questions should be brief but specific, avoid using 'ifs' and 'buts'.
- If you ask people to tick categories make sure that they do not overlap.

- Have a mixture of open and closed questions.
- Consider your sample.
- Keep a note of the amount of people you ask.
- Make conclusions based on your research; remember to focus on your aims.

Internet research

Figure 18.5: *The internet puts libraries' worth of information at your fingertips*

The internet gives you a variety of opportunities in social research. With one click of a button you have access to millions of different websites that might be able to offer relevant information for your research question. The trick to carrying out internet research, however, is to be highly selective in what information you are looking for. You also need to be cautious about the type of information you find.

How to use the internet for research

Step one: choosing a search engine
There are many different search engines that can help you in finding the information you require. Common examples include Google, Yahoo and Ask Jeeves. You can also use search engines that combine search results, known as 'metasearch engines'. Common examples include SurfWax, Search.com and Ixquick.

Figure 18.6: *Choose the best search engine for your purposes*

Step two: searching appropriately
Search engines are easy to use – you *could* simply type your research question into the search box and it would no doubt generate thousands of different 'hits'. However, you can narrow your search area and access more high-quality results if you focus on the relevant key words you're interested in. You can do this by simply typing in the words of interest, for example 'terrorism fatalities 2013'. Some search engines, such as Google, have 'keyword search' tools that you may also wish to make use of.

You can also try using a 'search operator' through the advanced search page on your chosen search engine.

What you would like to search for	What to type	For example
Search for an exact word or phrase.	Use double quotes: *"[the word or phrase you are looking for]"*	This can be useful if you are looking for a particular phrase or perhaps information about a certain act of parliament: *"Terrorism Act 2008"* You should only use this if you are looking for the exact phrase as this kind of search can exclude otherwise helpful results.

Exclude a word.	Put a '-' before a word to exclude results that include that word: *-[the word you would like to exclude]*	You might do a search and get lots of information you don't need. For example, if you are researching terrorism but are not interested in attacks that took place on public transport you could search: *terrorism -"public transport"* As with the above, you should be careful when using this as you may exclude useful information.
Search within a site or domain.	Include the address of the site you would like to search within using 'site:': *[search] site:[the site you would like to search within]*	You could use this for example, if you wanted information from the Scottish parliament website about the referendum. *referendum site:scottish.parliament.uk* You can also use this if you just want to search for information from sites that end in a certain 'domain' (the .com, .co.uk, .gov etc.); if you only wanted to search only within.gov sites you could search *referendum site:.gov*
Search for pages that link to a certain other page.	Put 'link:' in your search to find pages that include a certain link: *link:[the link you want to be included on the page]*	If you are investigating drugs laws you might look for sites that link to the Talk to Frank site: *link:talktofrank.com* You can also look for links to specific pages: *link:talktofrank.com/legalhighs*
Search for pages that are similar to another.	Use 'related:' to find sites similar to ones you have found useful: *related:[site you would like to find similar sites to]*	You might have found a useful site and want to see if you can find other similar sites. For example, if you have used the Liberty site for looking at human rights issues you could find other sites like it by entering: *related:liberty-human-rights.org.uk*
If there are gaps in your search term.	Use an asterisk '*' to replace unknown words: *[part 1 of search term]*[part 2 of search term]*	This can be useful if you are not sure of a word in your search term. For example, if you couldn't remember what the 'P' in CPO stands for you could search: *"Community * Orders"*
Search for either word.	Use 'OR' to find pages that only include one of the words you list: *[search term 1] OR [search term 2]*	Use this if you only want to look at a page that has certain information. For example if you wanted pages that only included information on trade unions **or** pressure groups you could search: *"trade union" OR "pressure group"*
Search for a number range.	Use '..' to find pages that include numbers within that range: *[number]..[number]*	You can use this for all kinds of numbers including dates, prices and measurements. For example, if you wanted to find information on terrorism between 2000 and 2002 you could search: *terrorism 2000..2002* You can also just use the one number with the two full stops to search for an upper or lower limit; so to find information on terrorism after 2002 you could search *terrorism 2002..*

An advanced search can be completed by combining words and search terms, choosing to search by date, by country or even by limiting your search to the number of results displayed.

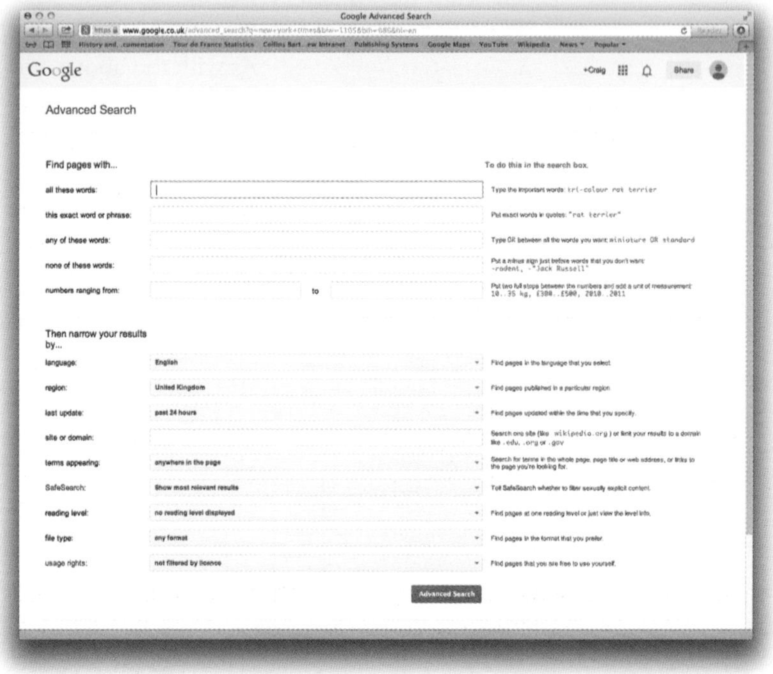

Figure 18.7: *An advanced search*

Using an advanced search is handy if you are considering searching within a website – such as the BBC, for example. Newspapers, such as the *Scotsman*, often have their own search engines that can again help to narrow your results. For example, you might wish to consider the *New York Times* website and use its search engine to find relevant news articles about terrorist attacks in America.

Figure 18.8: *The* New York Times *is one of the most respected news sources in the USA*

You might also want to consider academic results – these could provide you with search results for social research that has already been carried out in your field by social scientists. Academic search engines you could try include Google Scholar, RefSeek and Gooru Learning.

Step three: selecting the information

The information that you use from the internet needs to be treated critically. This means that you should be careful and select information that has come from a reliable source. Websites such as Wikipedia, for example, can contain inaccurate information because anyone who has access to the internet can update or change the content and you therefore have no sure way of knowing if the information is reliable and factual. You might like to consider:

- who is the author of the page?
- is there any reason the page might contain bias?
- is there contact information available to ask further questions of the information presented?

Step four: recording your evidence

When you are carrying out internet research it's important that you keep a record of the different sites you have visited and the dates on which you did so. This will be helpful for your teacher but it will also be helpful for you in deciding which sites you might want to revisit, and which were not as helpful. You may wish to record your research in a log or a table, like this one:

Date visited	URL	Usefulness	Notes
12/05/14	http://www.visionofhumanity.org/sites/default/files/Global_Terrorism_Index_Fact_Sheet.pdf	✓	• From 2002 to 2011 over one-third of all victims killed in terrorist attacks were Iraqi. • Western Europe experiences many more terrorist incidents than the U.S., having also suffered 19 times more fatalities than the U.S.

Step five: using your research

You now need to take the internet research you have gathered and use it to inform your research. It is entirely up to you to decide how your findings can be best presented; you may wish to do so visually in the form of a wall chart with associated explanations. You may wish to write up your findings in a word document. You may even wish to record your findings in a podcast.

Your research needs to link directly to the task in hand, so you need to use what you have found to answer the questions you posed at the beginning of your research. For example, if you were researching

Hint

Your school/college may have an account with academic journals such as JStor that you may wish to access.

Hint

Remember to bookmark the most useful websites you find.

Hint

To shorten URLs you may wish to use the website: https://bitly.com

terrorist attacks in America, you might have found statistics on the number of attacks and fatalities in recent years and could write 'the evidence shows that terrorist attacks in America have reduced substantially since the 1970s, with the exception of September 11th 2001. In 2011 there were no recorded fatal terrorist incidents compared to over 470 attacks in 1970. Therefore, in recent years the number of terrorist attacks have decreased, as has the number of fatalities resulting from terrorist incidents in the US'.

When drawing written conclusions from the evidence you have gathered you should be sure to quote the relevant piece of evidence you would like to cite and to mention the conclusion you wish to draw. For example:

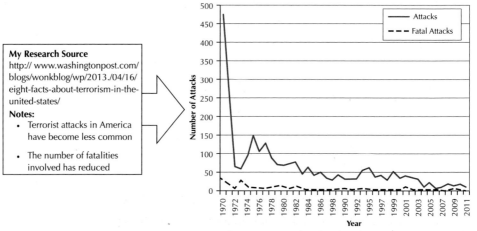

Figure 18.9: *An example of how you could draw a conclusion from your research*

Key features of internet research

- Secondary data.
- You can find both quantitative and qualitative information.
- Can be carried out alone.
- Search engines will be used to find a wide variety of data.

Advantages and disadvantages of internet research

Advantages

- Lots of different kinds of information are available, including official government data, reports from news organisations from around the world, and the results of primary research carried out by other social scientists.
- You can cross-reference information with other websites to check its accuracy.
- You can find out the opinions of people who you probably wouldn't be able to contact for primary research like questionnaires or interviews.
- If you have an internet connection then this method of research will not cost anything.

Disadvantages

- There may be too much information for you to pick out the most relevant pieces.
- It can be difficult to tell which information is reliable.
- You need to have an internet connection.

GO! Activity

Show your skills

With your shoulder partner, come up with a question you would like to find the answer to; for example 'how has the UK responded to the threat posed by international terrorism?'

Use the internet to try and find out the answer.

- Try several different search engines.
- Try typing the full question in, then use just keywords, or an advanced search. Which gives you the most useful response?
- Make a list of the websites you visit; which do you think has the most reliable information and why?

Checklist

- Consider carefully what information you would like to find.
- When carrying out your search think about which search engines and searches might provide the most useful information; should you use key words, or an advanced search?
- Think about which websites will offer reliable sources of information.
- Make a note of all the websites you visit, what information you got from them, and how useful and reliable you found them.
- Make conclusions based on your research; remember to focus on your aims.

Concluding your research

Depending upon the level you are sitting the expectations of how you conclude your research will be different.

National 5 learners will be expected to complete a final write-up, demonstrating evidence of your research and reflecting on this process.

National 4 learners will be required to complete similar social research, however you will not have to produce a write-up to reflect this process. This means that you have a range of options in terms of how you present your final research: from PowerPoint to a poster display to a podcast, for example.

National 5 learners are not prevented from doing likewise; however you should be aware that the final write-up is a requirement at

Figure 18.10: *You have reached the end point of your research*

National 5 because the Assignment is marked externally by the SQA and is worth 25% of your final mark.

The Outcome and Assessment Standards should be used as your success criteria. The information below considers each standard and how you might reflect upon the requirements.

National 4 – Added Value Unit

1.1: Choosing, with support, an appropriate Modern Studies topic or issue for study

You need to be able to explain why you chose the topic or issue you selected for your AVU. Remember, for National 4 this doesn't need to be in written format; it could be in the form of a talk, an interview with your teacher, or in poster format for example.

1.2: Collecting relevant evidence from at least two sources of different types

You should have evidence from two different sources. It's up to you how you show this to your teacher, you might have a graph from a recent opinion poll, or a screen-shot of a web search you carried out; either way you need to be able to show your teacher the evidence you have gathered and make sure this comes from two different sources, for example a questionnaire you carried out, a newspaper cutting, notes taken from a television documentary etc.

1.3: Organising and using the information collected to address the topic or issue

You should organise your research in a logical way. So, if you carried out a questionnaire there might be certain questions where you will focus your attention. In a questionnaire there might be 10 questions – three of these could have been on age, gender and age-group and it might not be appropriate to look at these in detail. Rather, a question later in your questionnaire might be more suitable, because it looks at the topic or issue your AVU is focused on. If your AVU was focused on the issue of youth crime, for example, you may have asked a question about youth crime in that person's area. The answers to that question could be highlighted in a pie chart.

1.4: Drawing on a factual knowledge and understanding to describe and briefly explain some key features of the topic or issue

You will have background knowledge from your work in class about the issue or topic you selected. So, you need to evidence the key areas of your AVU – show your teacher where your starting point was. Explain how carrying out research improved your knowledge by describing this in more depth.

Hint

Use the structure provided by the Outcome and Assessment Standards to help you plan how you present your findings.

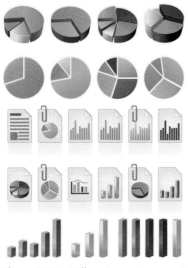

Figure 18.11: *Different ways to present data*

1.5: Apply the skills of either detecting bias and exaggeration, or making decisions, or drawing conclusions

In National 4 you have a choice of which skill-set you would like to address. Remember, these skills are all assessed in every Unit in Modern Studies. So, think about the two different sources you've used. You might wish to consider:

- was there bias or exaggeration present in a website?
- are you able to make a decision?
- can you draw a conclusion from carrying out a questionnaire?

1.6: Presenting findings about the topic or issue

National 4 provides you with the freedom to present your findings in a very flexible way.

Some examples include:

- a PowerPoint presentation
- a poster display
- a talk
- a podcast
- a role play

You can, of course, provide a written write-up of your research for the AVU. However, unlike National 5 this does not need to be completed under timed exam conditions and it will be marked internally by your teacher.

National 5 – The Assignment

Supporting evidence

The requirements for National 5 differ slightly from those of National 4 where Added Value is assessed as a separate Unit. One hour is allocated to carry out the write-up of the N5 assignment. Candidates will produce a research sheet (two A4 sides). It is not permitted to copy any information from these sheets onto the assignment. If information is copied, no marks will be awarded. This evidence will be sent to the SQA along with your final write-up for your assignment, which will be carried out in your school under exam conditions.

Your evidence should not be in the form of a plan. It should show the marker your two different research methods clearly. You may annotate this evidence by highlighting relevant statistics or using an asterisk to draw your attention to certain parts.

Your research may be either primary or secondary. It may include statistics from a recent government survey, for example, or a newspaper article, results from research you have carried out, such as an online survey, notes taken from a recent TV documentary, or any other form of valid information which you have gathered from a reliable source.

Figure 18.12: *Use the MADE acronym to help structure your answer*

A: Choosing, with minimum support, an appropriate Modern Studies topic or issue

You simply need to explain why you chose the issue you selected.

B: Evaluating the effectiveness of two research methods used, commenting on their strengths and weaknesses where appropriate

In this section you need to mention the two research methods that you used – you should directly mention the evidence you brought into the write-up at this stage. Candidates should produce a hypotheses/aims for their research. It might be useful to provide two separate paragraphs on each method and then consider the advantages and disadvantages of each and then come to a conclusion. An acronym to help you structure this answer is shown below:

M Explain the **m**ethod you selected. For example:

'One research method I chose for my Assignment was to carry out a questionnaire.'

A Outline an **a**dvantage of this type of method. For example:

'An advantage of a questionnaire is that it provides you with a large number of responses from which to draw conclusions. For example, I managed to gather questionnaires from 100 people for my topic.'

D Outline a **d**isadvantage of this type of method. For example:

'A disadvantage of questionnaires is that people may not understand the question you have asked. For example, some people didn't understand who Police Scotland were in my questionnaire which meant they struggled to answer the questions in this section of my questionnaire.'

E **E**valuate this research method. For example:

'Therefore, whilst using questionnaires as a research method provided me with lots of data to draw on, some of that data became unreliable because the respondents didn't understand what I was asking.'

C: Drawing on knowledge and understanding to explain and analyse key features of the topic or issue

This part again allows you to directly explain your research and link it to the knowledge you have gained from researching this topic. For example, if your Assignment has focused on the police, describe and explain the key features of policing in Scotland. Link this knowledge to your research. You may wish to use the 'PEE' method (Point, Explain, Example, see page 240) to structure this response. In the 'example' section, make sure to reference your own knowledge AND your research evidence for full credit.

D: Reaching a well-supported conclusion, supported by evidence, about the topic or issue

Using the three assessable skill-sets (see below note), you now need to come to a conclusion based on your evidence.

Make it   What's the conclusion you're drawing? For example:

'One conclusion I can draw from my research is that most people do not think there are enough police officers on the streets.'

Back it   Use your evidence and research to prove your point. For example:

'From my research, 88 respondents out of 100 said that they had not seen a police officer in their community/street in the last year. Furthermore, from Scottish government research in 2011, 56% of those polled did not think the police patrolled regularly enough.'

Link it   Link your evidence to form a valid conclusion. For example:

'Therefore, the conclusion is that the police in my community are not visible enough – this is supported by national research which shows that the government needs to invest more money in community policing.'

Note: This example has focused on the skill-set of drawing conclusions. You can also choose to use making decisions or explaining exaggeration or selectivity in the use of facts in this section, whilst coming to a valid conclusion based on your evidence.

Ideas for your research question

Democracy in Scotland and the United Kingdom

- 'Scotland should become an independent country.'
- 'The voting age should be lowered to 16 in all elections.'
- 'MSPs should work more within their constituency.'
- 'Pressure groups are effective/ineffective in influencing decision making in the Scottish Parliament.'
- 'Trade unions are effective/ineffective in influencing decision making in the Scottish Parliament.'
- 'Political parties are all the same.'
- 'Women and/or ethnic minorities are underrepresented in the Scottish Parliament.'
- 'The work of the Scottish Parliament has helped it achieve its founding principles.'

Crime and the Law

- 'Prisons are not suitable for offenders under 25.'
- 'Poverty is the biggest single factor in influencing criminal behaviour.'

- 'Drug use is a big problem in Scottish society.'
- 'More money should be spent on prisons.'
- 'Community Payback Orders are a very effective punishment.'
- 'Minimum pricing for alcohol will have a positive impact on society.'
- 'CCTV is an effective way to prevent crime.'
- 'The Children's Hearing system effectively deals with young people.'

Terrorism

- 'Religion causes terrorism.'
- 'Terrorism is the greatest threat to global security.'
- 'The UK has dealt effectively with the threat posed by terrorism.'
- 'Counter-terrorism strategies do not infringe on an individual's civil liberties.'
- 'The international community has dealt effectively with the threat posed by terrorism.'
- 'Individuals' rights and responsibilities are weakened because of terrorist activities.'
- 'Terrorism decreases life expectancy in countries where support is widespread.'
- 'Since September 11th 2001 support for terrorist activity has increased.'
- 'Most terrorists are members of terrorist organisations.'
- 'Terrorism attacks are most likely to occur on public transport.'

Learning Summary

Now that you have finished the **Added Value Unit/Assignment** chapter, complete a self-evaluation of your knowledge and skills to assess what you have understood. Use the checklist below and its traffic lights to draw up a revision plan to help you improve in the areas you identified as red or amber.

- I know what I will need to do for my National 4 AVU or National 5 Assignment.

- I can identify a topic I would like to research as part of my National 4 AVU or National 5 Assignment and make a list of aims to help me identify the information I require.

- I can explain the difference between quantitative and qualitative data.

- I can explain the difference between primary and secondary sources of information. ⬭ ⬭ ⬭

- I can explain what an interview is. ⬭ ⬭ ⬭

- I can describe how to construct an interview. ⬭ ⬭ ⬭

- I can describe how to conduct and record an interview. ⬭ ⬭ ⬭

- I can state advantages and disadvantages of using an interview as a method of research. ⬭ ⬭ ⬭

- I can draw conclusions from my interview to help me with my AVU or National 5 Assignment. ⬭ ⬭ ⬭

- I can explain what a questionnaire is. ⬭ ⬭ ⬭

- I can describe how to construct a questionnaire and the different types of questions that might be included and how they might be used: ⬭ ⬭ ⬭

  - Closed questions ⬭ ⬭ ⬭

  - Open questions ⬭ ⬭ ⬭

  - Knowledge questions ⬭ ⬭ ⬭

  - Factual questions ⬭ ⬭ ⬭

  - Opinion questions ⬭ ⬭ ⬭

  - Motivation questions ⬭ ⬭ ⬭

- I can explain what a sample is. ⬭ ⬭ ⬭

- I can draw conclusions from my questionnaire to help me with my AVU or National 5 Assignment. ⬭ ⬭ ⬭

- I can state advantages and disadvantages of using a questionnaire as a method of research. ⬭ ⬭ ⬭

- I can choose a search engine and search appropriately for information on the internet. ⬭ ⬭ ⬭

- I can distinguish which information is useful and reliable from my internet research.

- I can record evidence of my internet research.

- I can draw conclusions from my internet research to help me with my AVU or National 5 Assignment.

- I can state advantages and disadvantages of using internet research as a method of research.

- I understand how to complete my AVU/Assignment.

19 Unit Assessments

What you will learn in this chapter

- How to answer knowledge questions.
- At National 4 to detect and briefly explain bias or exaggeration using evidence from up to two sources of information.
- At National 5 to detect and explain, in detail, exaggeration or selective use of facts using evidence from between two and four sources of information.
- At National 4 to make and justify a decision using evidence from up to three sources of information.
- At National 5 to make and justify, in detail, a decision based on evidence from between two and four sources of information, showing an awareness of alternative views.
- At National 4 to draw and support a conclusion using evidence from up to two sources of information.
- At National 5 to draw and support, in detail, a conclusion using evidence from between two and four sources of information.

In National 4 and 5 Modern Studies you will be assessed according to the knowledge you have gained and the skills you have acquired. It is important that you understand how to apply your knowledge in a written context; however, it will not always be necessary to write your answers – your teacher may, for example, allow you to work in a group. However, even if you are working in pairs, small groups, or larger teams your teacher will still need to be able to show that you have met the requirements for the Outcome and Assessment Standards (you can find the Outcome and Assessment Standards for each Unit on pages 8, 90 and 132).

Make the Link

In all National 4 and 5 social subjects you will be assessed by a mixture of knowledge and skills questions.

Knowledge questions

Knowledge questions assess your understanding of what you have learned. These questions will ask you to 'explain' or 'describe'. For 'describe' questions you should give descriptions of things you have learned about during the course. For 'explain' questions you should clearly show the connections between the different points you make.

Using the correct structure is important when answering knowledge questions. Firstly, make a point in relation to the question. You should try to make your first sentence link back to the question – this will make the point of your paragraph clear. Secondly, you need to go on to explain the point you've made by including relevant information. Remember you need to demonstrate your knowledge but don't waste

Figure 19.1: *The knowledge you have gained will help you answer questions*

time by writing too much. Finally, you should include an up-to-date example such as a person's name, a statistic or a place.

Some people find the '**PEE**' method useful when structuring knowledge questions: for every two marks on offer you should make a **P**oint, **E**xplain that point, and give an **E**xample of that point. A really good PEE paragraph might get three or four marks, but to be safe you should include a PEE paragraph for every two marks (so for a four mark question you should include two PEE paragraphs, for a six mark question you should write three PEE paragraphs etc.). For example you could gain two marks as follows:

> 'The use of the prison system has been criticised in recent years'

Explain, in detail, why the use of the prison system has been criticised in recent years. (8 marks)

Point: Some people believe that a stay in prison will make someone more likely to reoffend.

Explain: Many employers do not want to hire people who have been in prison so ex-prisoners may feel forced to commit more crimes in order to survive.

Example: It has been calculated that three of every four prisoners go on to reoffend.

🔵 Activity

Try writing another three PEE points to get the full eight marks available for this question.

Democracy in Scotland knowledge questions

Here is an example of a knowledge question that could be asked about the Democracy in Scotland and the United Kingdom Unit:

Groups that try to influence the Scottish government		
Pressure groups	Trade unions	The media

1. Choose **one** of the groups above.

   Describe, **in detail**, **two** ways in which the group you have chosen tries to influence the Scottish government. (4 marks)

The first paragraph of your answer could be:

'One way in which pressure groups try to influence the Scottish government is by holding a demonstration. Pressure groups march through the streets holding signs and banners, handing out leaflets etc. Large demonstrations usually attract lots of media attention and this can influence the government. For example, in September 2013

🔵 Activity

Show your knowledge
This question is worth four marks, so try to produce another paragraph that answers the question. You could use the PEE method to help you.

thousands of pro-independence campaigners marched through the streets of Edinburgh in support of their cause.'

Now attempt the following questions. Pay attention to the number of marks available and make sure you make the correct number of points. When you have finished, swap your answers with another pupil and mark each others'.

'The Additional Member System (AMS), used to elect the Scottish Parliament, has both advantages and disadvantages.'

2. Explain, **in detail**, the advantages and disadvantages of the Additional Member System (AMS) that is used to elect the Scottish Parliament. (8 marks)

'Members of the Scottish Parliament (MSPs) represent their constituents in many ways.'

3. Describe , **in detail**, two ways in which MSPs can represent their constituents in **either** the constituency or the Scottish Parliament. (4 marks)

'Local councils in Scotland can raise money in different ways.'

4. Describe, **in detail**, two ways local councils in Scotland can raise money. (4 marks)

Crime and the law knowledge questions

Here is an example of a knowledge question that could be asked about the Social Issues in the United Kingdom Unit:

'The police in Scotland try to reduce crime.'

1. Describe, **in detail**, at least two ways in which the police try to reduce crime levels. (6 marks)

The first paragraph of your answer could be:

'The police try to reduce crime levels by working in the community. They visit schools to talk to pupils and some schools have 'campus' officers who try to get to know pupils and stop them from getting involved in trouble. The Scottish government reported that crimes in schools have gone down because campus officers are good role models.'

Now attempt the following questions. Pay attention to the number of marks available and make sure you make the correct number of points. When you have finished, swap your answers with another pupil and mark each others'.

GO! Activity

Show your knowledge
This question is worth six marks, so try to produce two more paragraphs that answer the question. You could use the PEE method to help you.

'People commit crime for lots of different reasons.'

2. Explain, **in detail**, why some people might commit crime. (6 marks)

'There are types of crime that are often committed by young people.'

3. Describe, **in detail,** the types of crime most commonly committed by young people. (6 marks)

'The criminal courts in Scotland have a range of sentences they can give to those found guilty of crimes.'

4. Describe, **in detail**, the sentences criminal courts in Scotland can give to those found guilty of crimes. (6 marks)

Terrorism knowledge questions

Here is an example of a knowledge question that could be asked about the International Issues Unit:

'In recent years the threat posed by international terrorism has increased.'

1. Describe, **in detail**, the reasons why terrorism has increased in recent years. (4 marks)

The first paragraph of your answer could be:

'One reason the threat posed by terrorism has increased is because of the events of September 11th 2001. This means that the world has become less safe and terrorism has increased. For example, the number of terrorist attacks each year has more than quadrupled in the decade since the 2001 attacks.'

Now attempt the following questions. Pay attention to the number of marks available and make sure you make the correct number of points. When you have finished, swap your answers with another pupil and mark each others'.

'Countries have responded to the threat of international terrorism in different ways.'

2. Describe, **in detail**, the ways in which countries have responded to the threat posed by international terrorism. (6 marks)

GO! Activity

Show your knowledge
This question is worth 4 marks, so try to produce another paragraph that answers the question. You could use the PEE method to help you.

> 'Religion is the only reason individuals become involved in terrorist activity.'

3. Describe, **in detail**, the reasons why some individuals become involved in terrorist activity. (4 marks)

> 'Terrorism has many consequences upon the countries that are affected.'

4. Explain, **in detail**, the consequences of terrorism on the countries that it affects. (8 marks)

Skills questions

For these types of questions you will be given two, three or four sources and asked to do one of the following.

At National 4:

Figure 19.2: *Skills questions give you a chance to show the skills you have built up over the course*

- detect and explain bias and exaggeration
- make and justify a decision
- draw and justify a conclusion

At National 5:

- detect and explain exaggeration and selective use of facts in detail
- make and justify a decision in detail, and show an awareness of alternative views
- draw and justify a conclusion in detail

Bias, exaggeration and selective use of facts

You will usually be given a number of sources on an issue, followed by a statement(s) that has been made by an individual. You will then be asked to give information from the sources to support and oppose the view of the individual. You must include both sides of the explanation.

Example question

Study sources 1, 2 and 3 then answer the question which follows.

Source 1

Total seats won by parties and independents at Scottish Parliament elections

Parties	1999	2003	2007	2011
Conservatives	18	18	17	15
Greens	1	7	2	2
Labour	56	50	46	37
Liberal Democrats	17	17	16	5
SNP	35	27	47	69
Independents	1	3	1	1
Others	1	7	0	0

Note: In the 2011 election the SNP made history by being the first party to ever achieve a majority of MSPs in the Scottish Parliament. The parties in blue are in support of Scotland being an independent nation.

Source 2

Voter turnout in Scotland

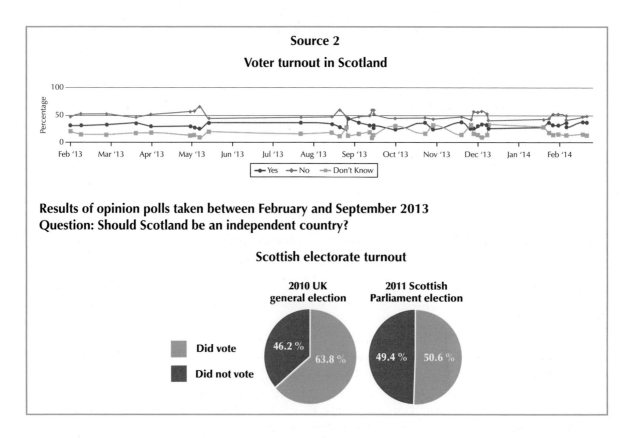

Results of opinion polls taken between February and September 2013
Question: Should Scotland be an independent country?

Scottish electorate turnout

2010 UK general election

2011 Scottish Parliament election

Did vote
Did not vote

46.2 %
63.8 %

49.4 %
50.6 %

Source 3

Results of the 2012 Scottish Social Attitudes Survey

- About six in 10 of those who say they are 'Scottish not British' want the Scottish Parliament to make all decisions for Scotland. That still means, of course, that 40% of them do not, though most of those want devolution max.

- Those who say they are 'more Scottish than British' split evenly between 'independence' and 'devolution-max' (just less than 40% for each). Only one in five of them favour the status quo.

- Those who say they are 'equally Scottish and British' split one-third for devolution max, one-third for the status quo, and just over 20% for independence.

- Those who claim to be 'mainly or only British' (only one in 10 of people living in Scotland) tend to favour the status quo (36%), though 30% support devolution max. Only one in six of them favour independence.

- About 40% of people living in Scotland think of themselves as both 'strongly Scottish' and 'strongly British'. Amongst this group only a quarter support independence. The largest proportion of such people – 35% – favour devolution max, followed by the status quo (30%).

- Those who describe themselves as 'strongly Scottish and weakly British' are much more likely to favour independence (64%).

📖 Word Bank

• Devolution max

The Scottish Parliament would be responsible for most spending in Scotland as it would receive all taxation collected in the country. The parliament would then make payments to the UK government to cover Scotland's share of the cost of providing certain UK-wide services, such as defence.

• Status quo

Existing state of affairs.

Using sources 1, 2 and 3 above explain why the view of Robert Ronan (below) is **selective in the use of facts**.

'Since the 2011 Scottish Parliament election there has been increased support for Scottish independence.'

View of Robert Ronan

In your answer you must:

- give evidence from the sources that support Robert Ronan's view
- give evidence from the sources that opposes Robert Ronan's view

Your answer must be based on all three sources. (8 marks)

How to answer the question

- In order to achieve full marks you must show evidence from the sources that supports Robert Ronan's view, and evidence from the sources that does not support Robert Ronan's view.

- Make sure you show evidence that both supports and opposes the view; an answer that deals with only one side of the explanation will only be awarded a maximum of six marks.

- Make sure you have used all of the sources at least once.
- Your answer should show an understanding of the information and statistics used in the sources – use words and phrases that show you understand, for example 'only half' and 'massive'.

Model Answer

'One reason to support Robert Ronan's view 'since the 2011 Scottish Parliament election there has been increased support for Scottish independence' is because in source 1 it states that the SNP, Green Party and Independent candidates all want Scotland to become an independent country. The election results in source 1 support this by showing that in 2011 the SNP won 69 MSPs, the Greens won two MSPs and there is one Independent candidate. This shows that most (72) MSPs in the Scottish Parliament support independence.

One reason to oppose Robert Ronan's view 'since the 2011 Scottish Parliament election there has been increased support for Scottish independence' is because in source 2 it states that more Scottish voters turned out to vote in the 2010 UK general election (63.8%) than they did the 2011 Scottish Parliament election (50.6%). This can be linked to the fact that in source 3 it states that only one in six of those who claim to be 'mainly or only British' and are living in Scotland favour independence. This shows that amongst this group most people do not support Scottish independence.'

Making and justifying decisions

You will usually be given two options and will have to pick one and explain why it is the best option, using the sources available. At National 4 and 5 levels you need to provide evidence from at least two sources to support the decision that you reach. You need to explain why the evidence supports your decision; this means you must give at least two reasons why you choose your option.

At National 5 level only, you should also identify evidence that supports the alternative decision and state why you chose to reject this option.

Activity

Use your skills
Attempt to answer the rest of this question. Give one other reason to support and one other reason to oppose the view of Robert Ronan.

Hint

Remember that in skills questions you will only get marks for using information that is in the sources.

Example question

| Option 1 Spend more money on prisons | Option 2 Spend more money on alternatives to prison |

Source 1

Facts and viewpoints

The Scottish government spends around £325million a year on the Scottish Prison Service. In February 2011 the Scottish government decided to get rid of almost all sentences below 3 months and has given out many alternative sentences.

- Scotland's prisons are overcrowded. The Scottish Prison Service says the average daily population of Scotland's prisons was 7,853 in 2013; Scotland's prisons are only designed to hold 7,330 prisoners.

- Having a convicted person at home keeps families together and stops innocent family members from being punished by having a loved one taken away.

- Taking away someone's freedom is a good form of punishment; it lets the victims see that something has been done.

- Prisons are very expensive and alternatives to prison are a cheaper option. The cost of keeping someone in prison for 16 weeks is £9,760, compared to the cost of electronic tagging which is £2,718.

- Spending more money on prisons would improve the facilities and increase the number of spaces available.

- Most criminals in Scotland's prisons have previous convictions. Around 70% of the prison population are repeat offenders.

- A recent study by Glasgow University suggests that when criminals work in the community where they have committed a crime they start to realise the impact of their actions and are less likely to reoffend.

- A recent government document suggests reoffending rates have reduced in the last two years, some people think this is because electronic tags are being used more regularly.

- Alternatives to prison do not always work, many people commit crimes whilst on Community Payback Orders and of those that complete the Community Payback Order many go on to reoffend later.

- Over half of criminals reoffend after being released from prison.

Source 2

Statistics

Average daily prison population (Scotland): 1900 to 2011-12

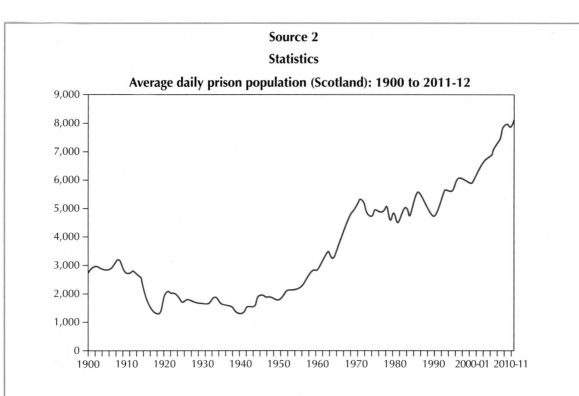

Results of a poll asking Britons opinions on the prison system

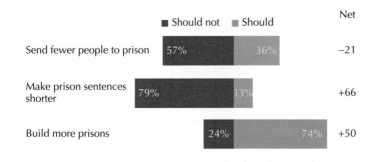

	Net
■ Should not ■ Should	
Send fewer people to prison 57% 36%	−21
Make prison sentences shorter 79% 13%	+66
Build more prisons 24% 74%	+50

Results of a poll asking Britons if community service should be used more as an alternative to prison

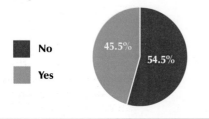

■ No

■ Yes

45.5% 54.5%

Source 3

Viewpoints

'Prison is a deterrent; it prevents some from committing crimes and reoffending. The use of electronic monitoring devices and community service is an easy option for criminals, they can still continue with the other aspects of their lives. The public do not support an increased use of alternatives to prison. The size of the prison population and overcrowding needs to be tackled by providing more money to the prison service. The public all believe that facilities should be improved with more spaces made available.'

David Reynolds

'Alternatives to prison encourage people to consider their actions. Those convicted are forced to confront their criminal behaviour instead of being allowed to block it out whilst mixing with other criminals in prison. Giving more money to alternatives to prison could improve all the programmes available. For example it could make drug rehabilitation programmes stronger and encourage even the most prolific offenders to stop reoffending.'

Laura Kane

You must decide which option to recommend to the Scottish government, either they should spend more money on prisons (**Option 1**) or they should spend more money on alternatives to prison (**Option 2**).

- Using sources 1, 2 and 3, **which option would you choose**?
- Give reasons to **support** your choice.
- **Explain** why you did not make the other choice. (**National 5 only.**)

How to answer the question

- Pick your option.
- Underline or highlight all the evidence that supports your option. Make sure you have used all of the sources at least once. You can draw lines on your question paper between your highlighted bits and the correct information to help you do this.
- Write at least two paragraphs explaining why you choose your option, including quotes from the evidence that supports your option.

N5
- At National 5 level only, you also need to write at least one paragraph explaining why you rejected the other option. Include a piece of evidence from the sources which supports your decision to reject this option.
- In the National 5 level exam this question will be worth 10 marks; in order to achieve full marks you should give three reasons to support your decision and two reasons to reject the other option. You would also need to use all the sources to get full marks.

GO! Activity

Use your skills
Attempt to answer the rest of this question by writing at least one more paragraph in support of option 1. Try writing another answer supporting option 2. This will help you practice the skill of justifying a decision.

Model Answer

Below is an example of a paragraph you might write explaining why you picked option 1:

'Source 1 states that prisons are overcrowded and that money needs to be spent to increase the numbers available. Source 2 backs this up by showing an increase of the number of people in prison to over 8,000 in 2011–12.'

N5 For National 5, below is an example of a paragraph you might write explaining why you rejected option 2:

'Option 2 is not suitable because source 3 says electronic tagging is an easy option for criminals and the public do not support it. This is backed up by source 2 which shows that 54.5% of the public do not agree with a greater use of community service.'

> **Hint**
>
> You will be able to find enough evidence in the sources to support either option so don't worry about picking the 'right' one.

Drawing and supporting conclusions

You will usually be presented with 2–4 sources from which to draw your conclusions; these will be supplemented by bullet points in the question itself that you can use as a guide to frame your answer.

Example question

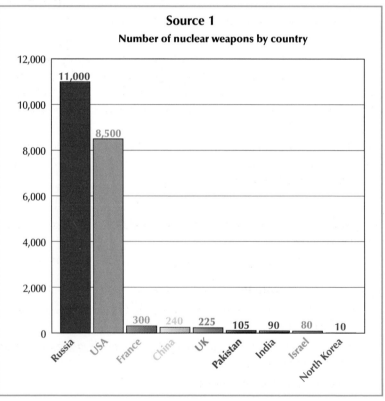

Source 1
Number of nuclear weapons by country

Source 2

In June 2013, American President Barack Obama called for Russia to join the United States in decreasing its number of strategic nuclear warheads. He said, 'we may no longer live in fear of global annihilation, but so long as nuclear weapons exist, we are not truly safe. And I intend to seek negotiated cuts with Russia to move beyond Cold War nuclear postures.'

America is the only country to ever have used nuclear weapons in war, in the Japanese cities of Hiroshima and Nagasaki in 1945. The American Nuclear Threat initiative has predicted that America will spend at least $143 billion over the next eight years on its nuclear arsenal.

Source 3

In April 2013, UK Prime Minister David Cameron claimed that the UK would be 'foolish' to abandon Trident in the face of the potential threat of nuclear attack from North Korea and Iran. He claimed the UK still needs an 'ultimate weapon of defence'. The UK government has recently approved the renewal of Trident.

Trident is the UK's nuclear deterrent programme. It is a sea-based programme containing submarines, missiles and warheads. Trident is based at Faslane near Helensburgh on the river Clyde.

The Scottish government is opposed to nuclear weapons. First Minister Alex Salmond commented, 'nobody seriously believes that Scotland, a country of 5.25 million people, would want to be in possession of nuclear weapons. That would be a bad thing for Scotland. I think that would be a bad thing for nuclear proliferation around the world.'

The UK government has estimated that the bill for replacing Trident will be between £15bn and £20bn. Campaign group Greenpeace has claimed it will run to at least £34bn.

Using sources 1, 2, and 3 above what **conclusions** can be drawn about nuclear weapons?

You should reach conclusions about at least three of the following:

- the countries with the highest number of nuclear weapons
- the difference between America's policy on nuclear weapons and that of the UK
- the difference between the UK's policy on nuclear weapons and that of Scotland
- the cost of nuclear weapons

Your conclusions must be supported by evidence from the sources. You should compare information within and between sources.

> **⚙ Hint**
>
> For your Unit Assessment, to meet the requirements of the Outcome and Assessment Standards, you need only reach **one** conclusion. The bullet points above are similar in terms of layout to that found in the National 5 specimen question paper.

Hint

You will be able to find enough evidence in the sources to support your conclusion. Make sure you link the evidence to your conclusion.

Activity

Use your skills
Attempt to answer the rest of this question by writing at least three more paragraphs using the bullet points to frame your answer.

How to answer the question

- Use the bullet points provided to frame your answer.
- Underline or highlight the evidence that supports your conclusion. Make sure you have used all of the sources at least once. You can draw lines on your question paper between your highlighted bits and the correct information to help you do this.
- Work across the sources to identify relevant evidence that will support the conclusion you are making.
- Complete your paragraph by spelling out what the conclusion that you have reached is.

Model Answer

Each of the points provided will be worth two marks in the final National 5 exam. Below is an example of a paragraph you might write drawing conclusions on the question above:

'One conclusion that can be drawn about countries with the highest number of nuclear weapons comes from source 1. America and Russia have 19,500 nuclear weapons between them – more than the other countries combined. For example, France only has 300 nuclear warheads and India has 10. Therefore, the conclusion is that America and Russia have the highest number of nuclear weapons.'

Learning Summary

Now that you have finished the **Unit Assessment** chapter, complete a self-evaluation of your knowledge and skills to assess what you have understood. Use the checklist below and its traffic lights to draw up a revision plan to help you improve in the areas you identified as red or amber.

- I know how to structure and answer knowledge questions.

- When asked to detect and explain bias, exaggeration and/or selective use of facts I can select information from the sources that both supports and does not support an opinion.

- When asked to detect and explain bias, exaggeration and/or selective use of facts I can show an understanding of the statistics from the sources.

- When asked to make and justify a decision I can give at least two pieces of evidence taken from the sources to support my decision.

- At National 5 level when asked to make and justify a decision I can explain why I rejected the alternative option.

- When asked to make and justify a decision I can link the evidence from the sources to the option I have chosen.

- When asked to draw a conclusion I can select appropriate evidence to support my view.

- When asked to draw a conclusion I can use appropriate evidence and link it to supporting evidence from another source.

- When asked to draw a conclusion I am able to use the evidence selected to support a valid conclusion.